OCEANIA

An Important Part of the Pacific

OCEANIA

An Important Part of the Pacific

Edited by
Dariusz Zdziech

Jagiellonian University Press

REVIEWER
Rev Prof Krzysztof Kościelniak, Jagiellonian University

COVER DESIGN
Sebastian Wojnowski

This publication is funded by the Jagiellonian University from the funds of the Institute of the Middle and Far East

ISBN 978-83-233-4532-9
ISBN 978-83-233-9892-9 (e-book)

JAGIELLONIAN
UNIVERSITY
PRESS

www.wuj.pl

Jagiellonian University Press
Editorial Offices: Michałowskiego 9/2, 31-126 Kraków
Phone: +48 12 663 23 80, Fax: +48 12 663 23 83
Distribution: Phone: +48 12 631 01 97, Fax: +48 12 631 01 98
Cell Phone: +48 506 006 674, e-mail: sprzedaz@wuj.pl
Bank: PEKAO SA, IBAN PL 80 1240 4722 1111 0000 4856 3325

Table of Contents

Preface

Oceania contains the islands located in the Pacific Ocean that are a part of Melanesia, Micronesia and Polynesia. The region located between Asia, Australia and both Americas is worth a special attention not only for cultural but also political and economic reasons. During the first decades of the current century the importance of Pacific in the international relations increased. Politics, economics, history and culture of the states of Melanesia, Micronesia as well as Polynesia are subject that cannot be omitted in the global puzzle of the 21st century. The world system of communicating vessels means that lack of knowledge about one region results in not understanding of the situation in the neighbourhood.

Oceania and Australia form a part of the world that is the furthest from Poland. The knowledge of them is not widely spread in our country. Starting from primary schools and ending with universities the development of science concerning areas located in the Pacific is now in Poland far from perfect. It should not be considered that current state of affairs have always existed. Among Polish researchers of Oceania it is worth mentioning such names as: Paweł Edmund Strzelecki, Sygurd Wiśniowski, Jan Stanisław Kubary, Bronisław Kasper Malinowski and Aleksander Lech Godlewski. At present the Institute of Middle and Far East at Jagiellonian University with cooperation with the Australia, New Zealand and Oceania Research Association decided to create a monograph of several authors containing the articles concerning politics, history, culture, law and the environment of Oceania countries as well as the relations of these countries with Asia, the United States, Australia and Poland.

Extremely valuable for this publication are introductions: first about the relation between Australia and the states of Oceania written by the ambassador of Australia in Poland H.E. Paul Wojciechowski. Second introduction about the relation between New Zealand and the states of Oceania written by the ambassador of New Zealand in Poland H.E. Mary Thurston. The article by Zuzanna Jakubowska-Vorbrich is attempting to give an answer to the question: 'Spanish Expedition to Easter Island, 1770, and Its Interpretation: An Example of Cultural Misunderstanding?'. The next two authors focus definitely on a role that Australia plays in the South Pacific: Jan Lencznarowicz – 'The "Pacific Solution" in Australian Refugee Policy', and Mieczysław Sprengel – 'Howard Government Activist Role in the South Pacific'. Jerzy Grębosz writes about another region in Oceania in the article: 'On the Origin of a Diversity of the Cultural Anthropology of the West Oceania'. Krzysztof Konstanty Vorbrich enriches our knowledge on the topic: 'Bass Strait Discovery and Its Consequences for the British Empire and Oceania: Little Known Aspects of Flinders's and Bas's Journals and Maps'. Cecylia Małgorzata Dziewięcka writes about the role of 'Atenisi Institute in the Tonga Kingdom and Piotr Grzybowski presents 'Selected Problems of Wastes Treatment in Tuvalu'. A few other articles focus on the stability of international relations in Oceania: Joanna Siekiera – 'RIMPAC – International Implications of the World's Largest Maritime Exercise', Pedro Henrique Melchior Nunes da Horta – 'A Worldwide Nuclear Disarmament Case: The Leading Role of the Marshall Islands at the International Court of Justice Against the United Kingdom in Terms of an International Security', Justyna Eska-Mikołajewska – 'Stability and Instability in Oceania: The Case of Papua New Guinea, the Solomon Islands and Fiji' and Jowita Brudnicka – 'Strategies of the Oceania States in the Prognostic Perspective: Scenarios of Development'. The other articles concentrate on law and environment of Oceania: Masum Billah – 'Constitutional Property Clause: A Comment on the Bangladeshi, New Zealand and Polish Approach', Adam Jakuszewicz – 'Endangered Statehood of Sinking Island States: A Legal Challenge to the International Community' and Przemysław Osóbka – 'International Responsibility of States on Climate Change Consequences in the Frame of Public International Law'. The last article written by Dariusz Zdziech deals with the relations of Oceania countries with Poland – 'An Overview of the Polish Relation with Vanuatu'.

Dariusz Zdziech

Dear Readers

The Pacific region remains important for Australia and our engagement there is anchored in common interests such as stability and economic development. Australia is a major economic partner and an enabler of opportunity for our Pacific neighbours. Some countries in the region have the natural resources and many have the tourism potential to benefit from increased trade and investment with Australia, New Zealand and Asian economies. Most countries in the region are, however, facing acute development challenges. Their small economies, distance from major markets, high costs, and rapidly growing populations hamper economic growth. Governance and capacity constraints in some countries also limit their ability to deliver services and improve the living standards of their citizens.

In its latest Foreign Policy White Paper, published in November 2017, Australia recognises that new approaches will be necessary to support the development of the Pacific region. Australia will focus on three main priorities: promoting economic cooperation and greater integration within the Pacific and also with Australia and New Zealand, including through labour mobility; tackling security challenges, with and focus on maritime issues; and strengthening people-to-people links, skills and leadership.

Yours sincerely,

Paul Wojciechowski
Ambassador of Australia to the Republic of Poland

Tēnā koutou katoa, greetings to you all

New Zealand and the Pacific are joined by history, geography, politics, shared interests and demographics. Around a quarter of New Zealand's population traces its origins to Māori or Pacific Islands heritage.

A prosperous, secure and stable Pacific is of fundamental importance to New Zealand. The region faces a growing array of development and security challenges, including the impact of climate change, effective management of resources, and consistent delivery of services to citizens.

In 2018, New Zealand has refreshed its strategic approach to engaging with its regional neighbours. This includes building deeper partnerships with Pacific Island countries, and in doing so, applying the following principles to our work: understanding, friendship, mutual benefit, collective ambition, and sustainability.

This engagement is not undertaken in isolation. New Zealand works closely with Pacific Island governments, institutions, civil society organisations and communities as well as with regional partners including Australia and the Pacific Islands Forum.

We welcome this collection of Pacific perspectives for the part it can play in bringing greater understanding and awareness of the Pacific region to a wider audience.

Ngā mihi, best wishes

Mary Thurston
Ambassador of New Zealand to the Republic of Poland

Zuzanna Jakubowska-Vorbrich

Spanish Expedition to Easter Island, 1770, and Its Interpretation: An Example of Cultural Misunderstanding?

Easter Island (Rapa Nui[1]) is an oceanic island of volcanic origin; it is a Chilean Special Territory situated *ca.* 3700 kilometres (1900 NM) west of the American coast. First visited by Europeans in 1722 – by a Dutch expedition under the command of Admiral Jacob Roggeveen – in the course of its post-contact history the island was subject to studies and descriptions by numerous sailors, explorers, naturalists, missionaries, traders, anthropologists and scientists of all kinds, according to the epoch in question. They were authors of various documents: ships' logbooks, diaries, reports, memories, that since then have been interpreted by interested laymen and by scholars, as well as translated into several languages. We have to keep in mind that the focus of these studies is a place and culture that are very distant from the Western civilisation: a Polynesian island of a complicated history, multi-faceted and full of imponderables. That is why the ensuing analysis are not free from misinterpretations, misunderstandings, or even examples of distortions of the original sense of the written sources (especially in case of translations). Moreover, such confusion reigned from the very beginning of the contacts between the two worlds, so distinct from

---

[1] The local toponym for the island is Rapa Nui, but the derived adjective is Rapanui.

one another: the European one and the far eastern Polynesian, located on the Pacific Rim.

In this present paper I would like to expound a case which – in my opinion – constitutes an example of misunderstanding or misinterpretation, by modern researchers, of what happened during the Spanish expedition to Easter Island that took place in 1770.

In that year the Viceroy of Peru, Manuel de Amat y Junyent, ordered to organise a reconnaissance voyage to Easter Island, under the command of Felipe González de Haedo.[2] The expedition was to be conducted by two ships: the naval ship of the line *San Lorenzo* and the frigate *Santa Rosalía*. The crews of both vessels drew up the first maps of Rapa Nui, described its territory and inhabitants, and annexed the island to the Spanish Crown, giving it a brand new name: San Carlos. The annexation ceremony was witnessed by a crowd of indigenous people who – according to the explorers – participated actively in the events: they gave the Spanish an enthusiastic welcome, were offering them help, food and clothing, as well as were singing and dancing with joy. Then they allegedly 'signed' the annexation act.[3] Below I quote two fragments of the narrative written by the nautical pilot (*piloto práctico*) of the *Santa Rosalía* Francisco Antonio Aguera e Infanzón, who describes the ceremony:

> Me pareze que tienen Ministros ó Sazerdotes para sus Ydolos, por que observe que el dia de la colocazion de las Cruzes en que nuestros Capellanes iban acompañando las Sagradas figuras, revestidos de sotana y Pelliz cantando las Letanías les salían al Camino muchos Yndios, ofreciendoles sus mantas, y las mugeres les portavan gallinas, y pollos, y todos gritavan Máca, Máca, tratándoles con mucha venerazion, hasta adelantarse a quitarles las piedras que embarazavan la senda por donde hivan.[4]

---

[2] The main source of information about this expedition is the edition of source texts written as a result of that voyage: Francisco Mellén Blanco, *Manuscritos y documentos españoles para la historia de la isla de Pascua. La expedición del capitán D. Felipe González de Haedo a la isla de David*, Madrid, CEDEX, 1986.

[3] Most probably the signs they drew on the act are glyphs belonging to the local hieroglyphic script known as *rongo rongo*. The original document is lost, but a copy of it survived. The signs are reproduced by Mellén Blanco, *Manuscritos y documentos*, p. 194.

[4] 'It seems to me that they have Ministers or Priests for their Idols, because on the day when we erected the Crosses, when our Chaplains accompanied the Holy figures [i.e. the crosses – ZJV], wearing cassocks and Surplices and singing Litanies, many Indiands were meeting them on

Asi llegamos, y con el mejor orden desembarcamos en una ensenada [...] destinada para el desembarco, por ser el único playazo que se halla en toda esta rada. Aqui desembarcamos, sin obstáculo, y fuimos recividos de una multitud considerable de Yndios, manifestando estos mucho plazer, y algazara. Formada la Tropa, y gente de Armas emprehendimos la marcha acompañados de los Yndios, quienes ayudaron gustosos a llevar las Cruzes cantando, y baylando a su modo: [...] A la 1 1/2 llegamos al sitio destinado para la colocacion lo que se celebró con todo juvilo, prezediendo la bendición, y adoracion de todo el concurso a las Sagradas Imágenes, con cuio exemplo los Yndios practicaron la misma ceremonia. Plantadas ya las Cruzes en sus respectivos cerros se arboló la Vandera española y puesta la tropa sobre las Armas, el Capitan de Fragata Don Josef Bustillo, con las ceremonias acostumbradas tomó posesion de esta Ysla de San Carlos, en nombre del Rey [...] Carlos Tercero, hoy 20 de Noviembre de 1770, de que se tomó posesion con la acostumbrada formalidad y para mayor corraborazion de este acto tan serio, firmaron, ó signaron algunos de los Yndios concurrentes gravando en el documento testimonial ciertos caracteres según su estilo: Luego saludamos al Rey siete veces a la Voz a que siguió una triple descarga de fusilería de todo el campo; y últimamente saludaron nuestros Navios con 21 cañonazos.[5]

---

their way and offering them capes, and the women were bringing them hens and chickens, and everybody was shouting Máca, Máca, treating the chaplains with much respect. They even quickened the pace to remove the stones from the path that [the chaplains] were following.' Francisco Antonio Aguera Infanzón, 'Relación diaria de lo mas particular, y acaecido en la navegacion echa en la Fragata *Santa Rosalia*, del mando de su Capitan D. Antonio Domonte, que salio del puerto del Callao el 10 de Octubre de 1770 rn conserva del navio *San Lorenzo*, a hacer la descubierta, y el reconocimiento de la Ysla de David, y otras en estos mares del Sur, siendo su primer Piloto el Alferez de Fragata Don Francisco Antonio Aguera Ynfanzon', in Mellén Blanco, *Manuscritos y documentos*, p. 285. As to the 'capes' – the term in the original text is *manta*, which may mean a cloak, a cape or a blanket. All quotations – if not indicated otherwise – translated into English by Z. Jakubowska-Vorbrich. All explanations in square brackets – if not indicated otherwise – also by Z. Jakubowska-Vorbrich.

[5] 'So we got there and, in the best formation, we disembarked in a cove [...] that we have chosen in this purpose, as it was the only beach in the whole bay. So here we disembarked, without any hindrance, and we were welcomed with clamorous joy by quite a big crowd of the Indians. Once the troop of [seamen and] soldiers was assembled, we set off, accompanied by the Indians, who helped us carry the Crosses with pleasure, singing and dancing in their own way. [...] At 1:30 we arrived at the place that we had chosen to erect the Crosses, which was done with utmost jubilation, following the benediction and adoration of the Holy Images, in which all the company took part. Seeing our example, the Indians carried out the same ceremony. After the Crosses were put in place, the Spanish banner was hoisted, the troop stood to attention and the Frigate Captain *Don* Josef Bustillo, with the usual ceremonies, took possession of this Island

The above scene may be interpreted in various ways. On the one hand we may be facing a propaganda campaign: the Spanish emphasised in their documents a positive attitude of the indigenous inhabitants of Rapa Nui to legitimise the incorporation of the island to the Crown. The same methods had already been used during the times of Christopher Columbus, that is, in the very first phase of the New World conquest. On the other hand we cannot exclude the possibility that the islanders were indeed happy to see their daily routine interrupted by so unusual a visit. Especially – what is indicated by one of the authors who study Easter Island history – that the strangers brought a very valuable gift: some pieces of solid wood, while the island was at the time almost treeless.[6] We can also hazard a conjecture that the Rapanui sensed that the Spanish were celebrating some special, solemn event; that is why the local community felt infected by the festive mood, although they had no idea of what was really going on.

Several years ago, however, there surfaced an alternative interpretation of the events, offered by Edmundo Edwards and Alexandra Edwards (further I refer to them as the Edwards). First they developed it in their field notes published online,[7] and then they included their idea in an extensive book dedicated to the ancient Rapanui world.[8] The authors claim that the Spanish arrived at Rapa Nui precisely at the beginning of the most significant local festivity: Matariki.[9] Matariki is the indigenous name for the open star cluster of Pleiades, an asterism (that is what astronomers call a prominent pattern or group of stars that is smaller than a constellation), itself located in Taurus constellation, which has been important for almost all

---

of San Carlos, on behalf of the King […] Charles the Third, today on 20th of November, 1770. The annexation of this island was conducted with due formality and, to confirm this solemn act, some of the Indians signed the protocol, drawing certain characters known to them. Then we cheered the King loudly seven times, three rifle salutes of the whole company followed, and finally our Ships responded with 21 cannon salutes.' Ibid., pp. 287–288.

[6] Beverley Haun, *Inventing 'Easter Island'*, Toronto, Bufallo and London, University of Toronto Press, 2008, p. 119.

[7] Edmundo Edwards and Alexandra Edwards, *Rapanui Archaeoastronomy & Ethnoastronomy: Flag #83 Expedition Report, February–June, 2010*, pp. 18–21, www.pacificislandsresearchinstitute.org/Flag_83_Report.pdf [accessed 6 February 2013].

[8] Edmundo Edwards and Alexandra Edwards, *When the Universe Was an Island: Exploring the Cultural and Spiritual Cosmos of Ancient Rapa Nui*, Hanga Roa, Hangaroa Press, 2013, pp. 444–449.

[9] In various Polynesian languages the festivity bears similar names.

civilisations since Palaeolithic times, including peoples of Polynesia:[10] its rising in the evening sky announces the beginning of the food abundance period, and also initiated a deep-sea fishing season. Starting with this premise, the Edwards justify and explain every element of the encounter between the Spanish and the Rapanui, linking it with a festive atmosphere and rituals proper for the Matariki ceremonies. Therefore such behaviours as joy manifested by the islanders, their singing and dancing, the pigments they used (white, yellow and red, the last one being sacred in Polynesia) to decorate their body and tint their clothes, were interpreted as directly connected with the said festivity. The offering of food and clothes can be interpreted as offering to gods, who – according to what Polynesians believed – during the Matariki descended to the Earth and mixed with humans. Moreover, by offering to the Spanish hens, chickens – symbols of abundance and fertility – and bananas (mentioned in other documents from the expedition), the Rapanui were invoking their god Make-Make. During one of their reconnaissance trips the Spanish saw a peculiar figure on the coast: a kind of a dummy stuffed with straw; it could have been yet another symbol of opulence.

Last but not least, the Edwards claim that the Spanish crew disembarked precisely on the day of the beginning of the Matariki festivity, that is the 16 November. The annexation ceremony took place on the 20th of that month, on the Poike Peninsula: the area that was considered sacred, because it was there where the local priests lived. It was also the best spot on the island from where the observations of the night sky could be conducted, that is why it is considered an astronomical centre of utmost importance. And, by a pure chance, it was there that the Spanish decided to erect the three wooden crosses to commemorate the annexation of the island.

It is worth emphasising that the anthropological investigations known under the name of 'paleoastronomy' have quite a long tradition in Easter Island studies. Among the people who devoted their time (also) to this branch of knowledge were Edwin E. Ferdon and William Mulloy during

---

[10] I am deeply indebted to my husband Krzysztof Vorbrich, a professional astronomer, for helping me with the astronomical aspect of this present paper. For the role of the Pleiades in the history, see also e.g. Will Kyselka, 'On the Rising of the Pleiades', *Hawaiian Journal of History*, vol. 27, 1993, pp. 173–183.

the famous expedition of Thor Heyerdahl to the island in the second half of the 1950s,[11] and – more recently – William Liller, Juan Antonio Belmonte, as well as Edmundo Edwards himself.[12] One of the issues analysed was to verify if certain architectural structures – for example ceremonial platforms known as *ahu* – were or were not oriented in such a way as to facilitate solar observations during the equinox and the solstice,[13] or celestial bodies observations at night. Such observations might have been crucial for establishing the agricultural or fishing calendar.

I must admit that – although I value very highly the book by the Edwards – at the same time I have serious doubts about their interpretation of events related to the Spanish expedition to Easter Island. Let me expound my arguments, starting with the inconsistencies in the description of the Spanish visit; then I will discuss the motifs that the authors used to confirm their point of view. At the end I will mention some more general questions that may argue against it.

To begin with, the review of the Spanish voyage, as presented by the said authors, not always coincides with the reality. For example, describing

---

[11] Cf. Thor Heyerdahl and Edwin Ferdon Jr. (eds.), *Archaeology of Easter Island: Reports of the Norwegian Archaeological Expedition to Easter Island and the East Pacific*, vol. 1, Stockholm, Forum Publishing House, 1961, *passim*.

[12] Cf. William Liller, 'The Ancient Solar Observatories of Rapa Nui', *Rapa Nui Journal*, vol. 1, issue 6, Winter 1987/88, pp. 4–5; Jo Anne Van Tilburg, 'Response to "The Ancient Solar Observatories of Rapa Nui"', *Rapa Nui Journal*, vol. 2, issue 2, Summer 1988, p. 4; William Liller, 'Rebuttal', *Rapa Nui Journal*, vol. 2, issue 2, Summer 1988, p. 5; Malcolm A. Clark, 'Solar Observatory Response', *Rapa Nui Journal*, vol. 2, issue 2, Summer 1988; Juan Antonio Belmonte and Edmundo Edwards, 'Astronomy and Landscape on Easter Island: New Hints at the Light of the Ethnographical Sources', in Emília Pásztor (ed.), *Archaeoastronomy in Archaeology and Ethnography: Papers from the Annual Meeting of SEAC (European Society for Astronomy in Culture), Held in Kecskemét in Hungary in 2004* (BAR International Series, vol. 1647), Oxford, Archaeopress, 2007, pp. 79–85; William Liller, 'Review: "Astronomy and Landscape in Easter Island: New Hints at the Light of the Ethnographical Sources" and "Megalithic Astronomy of Easter Island: A Re-assessment"', by Edmundo Edwards & Juan Antonio Belmonte', *Rapa Nui Journal*, vol. 23, issue 1, May 2009, pp. 76–77. The last paper is a critic of two very similar papers. Of course I have not mentioned all texts related to astronomy that have been published in *Rapa Nui Journal*.

[13] Simply speaking, the equinox is the only time of the year when the Sun rises exactly in the east and sets exactly in the west, and spends the same amount of time below and above the horizon, meaning that the day and the night have the same duration. The phenomenon occurs in March and September. The solstice is the time of the year when the Sun reaches its maximum distance from the celestial equator, either to the north (in June) or to the south (in December); as a result, the longest day and the longest night can be observed, depending on the hemisphere. Both phenomena – the equinox and the solstice – are connected to the seasons changing,

the circumstances of the expedition, the authors write: 'Captain Felipe González de Haedo, commanding the Santa Rosalía with 70 cannons, and the frigate San Lorenzo with 30 more, arrived with a total of 814 men in what would be the second contact between the Rapanui and outsiders.'[14]

The flagship of the expedition was not the *Santa Rosalía*, as the Edwards suggest in both texts, mentioning her in the first place,[15] but the *San Lorenzo*, under Felipe González himself, the commander of the expedition. The other vessel was commanded by Captain Antonio Domonte. The *San Lorenzo* was a naval ship of the line, not a frigate, and it had 70 cannons. *Santa Rosalía* – which was a frigate indeed – had 26[16] (by writing that one ship had 70 cannons and the other had '30 more', the Edwards suggest that the vessel had 100 cannons – *sic*).

As an aside: the authors make some allusions to the first European visit to Rapa Nui, namely the Dutch expedition commanded by Jacob Roggeveen (1722). They state: 'During their landing in Hanga Ho'onu, one of Roggeveen's officers ordered a volley of musketry to be fired at a crowd that had congregated near the ship, killing an undetermined number of locals.'[17] Indeed, this is a highly popular vision of events, so I by no means blame the Edwards for repeating it unchecked; however, very few readers are aware of the fact that it may not be true. In the journal by Cornelis Bouman (one of the captains that took part in the expedition[18]), we can read the following explanation:

Wy quamen sonder eenighe tegenstand aan de wal, exept diegene, die in de vaartuygen beschreven waren om dese te bewaren, want de inwoonders hadden, isn't minst nogh meeste, geen wapenen, maar quamen ons met bloote handen by menighte verwelkommen, huppelende en springende van blijdshap. Niettegenstaande soo wierden der 9 a 10 van deselve door de onse dootgeschoten en verscheyde gequest, 'tgene door mijn ondersturman Cornelis Mens toequam, die sonder

---

[14] Edwards and Edwards, *When the Universe Was an Island*, p. 446.

[15] Cf. Edwards and Edwards, *Rapanui Archaeoastronomy & Ethnoastronomy*, p. 19.

[16] Mellén Blanco, *Manuscritos y documentos*, pp. 23, 44.

[17] Ibid., p. 446.

[18] He was commanding the frigate *Tienhoven*. The flagship – also a frigate – was called *Arend* (under Captain Jan Koster), and there was also the third ship: a *hoeker Afrikaanse Galei* (under Captain Roelof Rosendaal). Here I use the modern spelling of the vessels' names.

ordre op deselve vuur gaf, waardoor verscheyde andere een eonclusie maakte, die daarmede vuur op gaven, 't geen hem ser qualijk afgenomen wiert. Hij bragt eenige bloote redenen in tot zyne verschooninge, dat de inwoonders de tromp van zijn snaphaan hadde willen vatten en met steenen ook gedrijgt hadden te werpen, 'tgeen van de heer Roggeveen, Coster, Roosendaal, luytenant, vaandrigh en van my, nevens alle officiereu en vele gemeene niet gelooft wiert. [...] [H]et wier van alle ofiicieren aangenomen dat hy sulkx gedaan hadde als een groote blooddaard.[19]

The journal, which had been lost, was discovered as late as in 1910 and then published in Dutch, so it is very little known among the international scholars. However, there exists an English translation of some parts of the document, important from the point of view of Easter Island studies, made by Herbart von Saher; please compare:

We came to shore without any resistance, except for those of us who had been instructed to stay in the sloops in order to guard them. The inhabitants had absolutely no weapons at all, they approached us in multitudes with their bare hands in order to welcome us, hopping and jumping for joy. Notwithstanding this, 9 or 10 of them were shot dead and several wounded, which was the responsibility of my under-coxswain, Cornelis Mens, who had fired without instruction. Others had concluded that such an order had been given and also fired. This caused great offense. He tried to excuse himself by presenting some invalid arguments such as [that] the inhabitants had tried to fetch the barrel of his gun and had also threatened to throw stones, which was not believed by Master Roggeveen, Coster, Rosendaal, the lieutenant, the ensign and me, neither by the other officers and many sailors [...]. [A]ll the officers supposed that he had behaved in this way because he was a great coward.[20]

---

[19] Cornelis Bouman, *Sheepsjournaal, gehouden op het schip Tienhoven tijdens de ontdekkingsreis van Mr. Jacob Roggeveen, 1721–1722*, ed. F.E. Mulert (Archief; vroegere en latere mededeelingen voornamelijk in betrekking tot Zeeland), Middelburg, Zeeuwsch Genootschap der Wetenschappen, 1911, pp. 139–140.

[20] 'The Complete Journal of Captain Cornelis Bouman, Master of the Ship *Theinhoven*, Forming Part of the Fleet of Jacob Roggeveen, from 31 March to 13 April 1722 During Their Stay Around Easter Island', transl. Herbert von Saher, *Rapa Nui Journal*, vol. 8, issue 4, December 1994, p. 99.

Moreover, the islanders could not 'congregate near the ship', as the Edwards write; the ships were anchored at a considerable distance from the land (it was the only possibility because of their draught and the nature of the coastal waters and bottom), and the reconnaissance group came to the shore by tender boats – much the same as the members of the González's expedition 48 years later.

Returning to the Spanish; the crew of the *San Lorenzo* consisted of 547 people.[21] However, we do not know how many people there were aboard the *Santa Rosalía*. We only know the number of the crew provided for a vessel similar to this particular frigate, which is 267.[22] I may be considered as meticulous, but in my opinion it is somewhat careless to maintain that on this very expedition there took part 814 people.

The Edwards write that the Spanish circumnavigated the island with their ships on 15 November,[23] before the first landing. Nevertheless they did so later – between 16 and 19 November – and it was a reconnaissance trip realised by two shore boats or launches (*lanchas*), belonging to both vessels. The description of this trip is included in the extant copy of the journal by a nautical pilot of the *San Lorenzo* Juan Hervé, who participated in this circumnavigation, and some information is also given by a nautical pilot Francisco Antonio Aguera Infanzón in his journal and narrative. By the way: we possess also some excerpts of the writings by Commander Felipe González.[24] These are the principal documents of the expedition

---

[21] Mellén Blanco, *Manuscritos y documentos*, p. 23.

[22] Ibid., p. 47.

[23] Edwards and Edwards, *When the Universe Was an Island*, p. 446.

[24] Cf. Juan Hervé [?], 'Derrota del navío de Su Majestad *San Lorenzo* a la isla de David, octubre, 10 de 1770', in Mellén Blanco, *Manuscritos y documentos*, pp. 258–263; Aguera Infanzón, 'Relación diaria', pp. 278–290; idem, 'Diario de Navegacion del Alferez de fragata y Primer Piloto de la Real Armada don Francisco Antonio, Aguera, Ynfanzon', in Mellén Blanco, *Manuscritos y documentos*, pp. 295–347; [Felipe González de Haedo], 'Extracto sucinto que acomapaña a la carta n.º 396', in Mellén Blanco, *Manuscritos y documentos*, pp. 221–222; Felipe González de Haedo, 'Extracto del Diario que ha hecho Don Phelipe Gonzalez de Haedo, Capitan de Fragata y Comandante del Navio de Su Majestad nombrado *San Lorenzo*, que a efectos del Real Servicio mandado por el Excelentísimo Señor Don Manuel Amat y Junient, Cavallero de la Orden de San Juan del Consejo de Su Majestad, Gentil hombre de Camara con entrada, Theniente General de sus Reales Exercitos, su Virrey Governador, y Capitan General de estos Reynos y Provincias del Perú y Chile. Salió del Puerto del Callao de Lima en conserva de la Fragata *Santa Rosalia*, su Comandante Don Antonio Domonte, Capitan de Fragata uno y otro Buque con viveres para Seys

that we have to our disposal. To simplify the matter I do not mention other examples of similar documents, that is, similar copies and one important original manuscript by Aguera that has been found several years ago, but is almost identical with one of the listed documents. The Edwards describe the documents – I presume, those by Hervé and Aguera – as 'private journals'.[25] I have serious doubts if those texts can be named such. The expedition was a military one, if not directly an espionage mission.[26] In other documents concerning the voyage we can read about the maps and the captain's logbook delivered to the superiors.[27] In my opinion these documents were considered rather a property of the authorities (as in the instance, say, of the British Admiralty in the case of voyages by Captain James Cook), and not a private property of the authors; I suppose that after the return of the expedition all the writings should have been handed over to the captain who later gave them to his superiors for further consideration.

Last but not least, the Edwards claim that small boats were launched from the ships on 16 November. The mentioned nautical operation is true, because the task of those boats was to lead the vessels to the best place of anchorage. Nevertheless, the boats had been sent to conduct the soundings earlier, namely the day before: on 15 November. The main, official landing operation took place on 20 November, still the crew of the two launches that were circumnavigating the island in the meantime also made various

meses', in Mellén Blanco, *Manuscritos y documentos*, pp. 222–226; Felipe González de Haedo, 'Descripcion de la Isla de San Carlos (alias David), reconocida, de orden del Virrey del Perú, por el Capitan de Fragata Don Felipe Gonzalez, en el año de 1771 [*sic*]. Expresase su circunferencia, producciones, numero de naturales, y demas particularidades que se observaron; con un Plano demonstrativo de ella', in Mellén Blanco, *Manuscritos y documentos*, pp. 270–273; Felipe González de Haedo, 'Descripcion de la Ysla San Carlos, alias David. Y particularidades que se pudieron observar', in Mellén Blanco, *Manuscritos y documentos*, pp. 273–275.

[25] Edwards and Edwards, *When the Universe Was an Island*, p. 444.

[26] See 'Ynstruccion de lo que han de obserbar las dos embarcaciones de Guerra a saver el Navio nombrado »San Lorenzo«, y la fragata denominada »Santa Rosalia«, en la Campaña que ván á hacer desde el Puerto del Callao, con el fin de rexistrar algunas Yslas y costas de este Mar del Sur, conforme á las ordenes de S.M. y resoluciones de este Superior Govierno del Perú, tomadas por si, y con el dictamen del Real Acuerdo', in: Mellén Blanco, *Manuscritos y documentos*, pp. 213–219.

[27] Cf. e.g. 'Carta del Virrey del Perú al Secretario de Estado para las Indias', in Mellén Blanco, *Manuscritos y documentos*, pp. 219–221; 'Extracto sucinto que acompaña a la carta n.º 396', pp. 221–222.

landings. What the Edwards seem not to know is that the very first, unofficial landing of some crew members took place precisely on 16 November.[28] It is a very little known fact which would, paradoxically, corroborate the Edwards' opinion. I want to emphasise all those circumstances, because the authors indicate the date of 16 November as marking the start of the Matariki festivity. I will come back to this later.

I suppose that this paper may be read by people not familiarised with maritime matters, so I would like to add just two remarks: 1) in the proximity of land, the soundings must have been taken prior to any other serious ships' maneuvre, in order to sail the coastal waters and to anchor safely; 2) we must distinguish between two things: *launching* a boat does not necessarily mean *landing* ashore.

All this discourse that I have presented above may give an impression that it is much ado for nothing; just some trivial details. But I am concerned about one thing. Almost all the correct information that I have provided so far can be found easily especially in the aforementioned work by Mellén Blanco, which is an exhaustive critical edition of the Spanish source texts related to the analysed expedition, accompanied by discussion of all the relevant circumstances. The Edwards cite this publication in their book from 2013, but fail to mention it in their field notes from 2010, where they only quote some second-hand sources. Moreover, when paraphrasing or quoting in their book fragments taken from the narratives of the sailors, the Edwards refer either to the work by Mellén Blanco (one page only!), or to the English rendition of those documents prepared by Corney in 1903.[29] The problem is that this translation leaves a lot to be desired.[30] Why, then, do the Edwards not follow a single version of the documents and of the

---

[28] Pedro Guerrero de Torres *apud* Francisco Mellén Blanco, 'La Isla de Pascua en el centenario de su incorporación a Chile', *Revista de Marina*, Year CIV, vol. 105, issue 785, 1988, p. 395.

[29] Bolton Glanvill Corney (transl. and ed.), *The Voyage of Captain Don Felipe Gonzalez in the Ship of the Line San Lorenzo with the Frigate Santa Rosalia in Company, to Easter Island in 1770–1: Preceded by an Extract from Mynheer Jacon Roggeveen's Official Log of His Discovery of and Visit to Easter Island in 1722*, Cambridge, Hakluyt Society, 1903.

[30] Cf. Zuzanna Jakubowska, 'The Spanish Expedition to Easter Island, 1770: Original Documents and Their Rendition by Bolton Glanvill Corney', in Izabela Handzlik and Łukasz Sorokowski (eds.), *Found in Multiculturalism: Acceptance or Challenge?* (Series: Warsaw Studies in Politics and Society, vol. 1), Frankfurt am Main, Berlin, Bern, Brussels, New York, Oxford and Vienna, Peter Lang – International Academic Publishers, 2014, pp. 107–119

facts, that is, the one presented by Mellén Blanco? Why should they consult Corney, if his work is a secondary – and faulty – source (although it was published earlier than the book by Mellén Blanco)? One may argue that the book by the Edwards is written in English; indeed, but – following this logic – they should have been citing only Corney, which is not the case (fortunately).

Let me now proceed to the argumentation of the Edwards, indicating various elements and aspects of the encounter of the Spanish with the Rapanui in order to confirm their thesis of the coincidence between the arrival of the expedition and the beginning of the Matariki. I have already mentioned those motifs: joy and dances, special clothes and body decorations, food and clothing offered to the sailors, the presence of the dummy figure stuffed with straw. Nevertheless it results that those behaviours and objects were observed also during other European expeditions that took place in different moments of the year. Let us see: Roggeveen arrived at the island in April 1722, Cook – in March 1774, Count La Pérouse – in April 1786. Only the Spanish came in November. Although the Edwards maintain that the Matariki festivity lasted five months,[31] this does not necessarily mean that it should have been celebrated with the same solemnity throughout such a long period (if a considerable part of the community is celebrating, who would work during this season of abundance?).

Meanwhile, the Forsters – the naturalists of Cook's expedition – as well as La Pérouse, mention that the islanders were wearing clothes tinted in yellow and their faces were painted red. Moreover, the French count, as well as Bouman of the Dutch expedition, emphasise that the Rapanui manifested a great joy at the sight of the Europeans. The motif of yellow clothes appears also in the logbooks by Roggeveen and Bouman, and the faces painted red – in the texts by Behrens (a German soldier who took part in the same expedition), and not only in his book of memories, which is quite famous, but also in his poem which was rediscovered several years ago by Roelof van Gelder, Roggeveen's biographer.[32] The last mentioned motif is also present in the anonymous Dutch relations that contain the

---

[31] Edwards and Edwards, *When the Universe Was an Island*, p. 444.

[32] The biographer, during his investigations of Roggeveen's life, came across a publication by Behrens, forgotten by the scholars. Cf. Roelof van Gelder, *Naar het aards paradijs. Het rustelose*

first published information about Easter Island, although we have to be aware that they are full of fantasies and exaggerations. Therefore we can conclude that this kind of attire and decorations did not have to be related to the celebrations of the Matariki. According to authors writing about Rapanui textiles, the clothes tinted in red or yellow were probably used by people of high rank.[33] One of the experts in Easter Island studies, Steven Roger Fischer, even suggests that the Rapanui could have put on their special attire to give a proper welcome to the visitors.[34]

Below the Reader can find some quotations that corroborate my point of view:

A very few of them had a cloak which reached to the knees, made of cloth, resembling that of Taheitee in the texture,[35] and stitched or quilted with thread to make it the more lasting. Most of these cloaks were painted yellow with the turmeric root.[36]

We saw a few people with very bright gold-yellow Cloth, which seemed to be the principal people.[37]

[...] we saw the greater part of the natives naked, hardly with a small bitt [sic] of cloth to cover their Nudity: some had yellow Cloth died [sic] with Turmeric-root.[38]

---

leven van Jacob Roggeveen, ontdekker van Paaseiland. 1659–1729, Amsterdam, Uitgeverij Balans, 2012, pp. 282–283.

[33] Andrea Seelenfreund and Francisca Ramírez, 'El universo textil de Rapa Nui', Ch. II, in: A. Seelenfreund (ed.), Vistiendo Rapa Nui. Textiles vegetales, Santiago de Chile, Pehuén Editores, 2013, p. 26.

[34] Steven Roger Fischer, Island at the End of the World: The Turbulent History of Easter Island, London, Reaktion Books Ltd, 2010, p. 49.

[35] I.e. tapa cloak, a fabric made of paper mulberry bark.

[36] George Forster, A Voyage Round the World, in His Britannic Majesty's Sloop, Resolution, Commanded by Capt. James Cook, during the Years 1772, 3, 4 and 5. By Georg Forster, F.R.S., Member of the Royal Academy of Madrid, and of the Society for Promoting Natural Knowledge at Berlin, vol. 1, London, printed for B. White, J. Robsen and P. Elmsly, 1777, p. 563.

[37] Johann Reinhold Forster, The Resolution Journal of Johann Reinhold Forster 1772–1775, ed. Michael E. Hoare, vol. 3, London, Hakluyt Society, 1982, pp. 465–466.

[38] Ibid., p. 467.

[…] quelques uns couverts de pièces d'étoffes blanches ou jaunes ; mais le plus grand nombre était nu : plusieurs étaient tatoués et avaient le visage peint d'une couleur rouge ; leurs cris et leur physionomie exprimaient la joie ; ils s'avancèrent pour nous donner la main et faciliter notre descente.[39]

[…] de aard van 't land (gelyk wy op verseheyde plaetzen sagen) rood en geelach-tig was, 't welk met water synde vermengt, sy alsdan hare kleeden daerin dompe-len en weder latten droogen, 't welk blykt, omdat hun verfsel afgaet; want behan-deld en betast wordende, soo vind men herselve couleur aen de vingers, niet alleen door 't aenraeken van de nieuwe, maer selfs ook van de oude en versleetene.[40]

Quamen alsoo met onverighte saken aan bort, seggende, dat de landaart gele en witte kleedjes droegen.[41]

Bald kam noch eine Schaar, auf Lieben gantz verpicht, / Die waren roth gemahlt in ihrem Angesicht.[42]

---

[39] La Pérouse, *Voyage de La Pérouse autour du monde*, ed. M.L.A. Milet-Mureau, vol. 2, Paris, Chez Plassan, Imprimeur-Libraire, 1798, p. 91. Cf. 'They were unarmed, and several of them cov-ered with pieces of white and yellow stuff; but the greater number were naked, several were tat-tooed, and their faces painted red. Their cries and their physiognomy equally expressed their joy, as they advanced to give us their hands and assist us in landing.' *The Voyage of La Pérouse Round the World, in the Years 1785, 1786, 1787, and 1788, with the Nautical Tables*, ed. M.L.A. Milet Mureau, vol. 1, [no translator given], London, Printed for John Stockdale, Piccadily, 1798, p. 65.

[40] '[…] the soil of this land was red or yellowish; mixing it with water, [the inhabitants] im-mersed their clothes in it and then they let them dry, so the dye did not hold fast. After handling or touching it the colour would stick to the fingers, in case of new clothes, as well as old and worn ones.' Jacob Roggeveen, *Dagverhaal der ontdekkings-reis van Mr. Jacob Roggeveen, met de schepen Den Arend, Thienhoven en De Afrikaansche Galei, in de jaren 1721 en 1722. Met toestemming van Zijne Excellentie den Minister van Kolonien uitgegeven door het Zeeuwsch Genootschap der Wetenschappen*, Middelburg, Gebroeders Abrahams, 1838, p. 140.

[41] Bouman, *Sheepsjournaal*, p. 137. Cf. 'So they returned without having effected their pur-pose and they informed us that the natives wore yellow and white dresses.' 'The Complete Journal of Captain Cornelis Bouman', pp. 97–98.

[42] 'Soon more women came, quivering with passion, / Faces painted red, after the land's fashion.' Carl Friedrich Behrens, *Reise nach den unbekandten Süd-Ländern und rund um die Welt, Nebst vielen von ihm angemerckten Seltenheiten und zugestossenen wunderlichen Begebenheiten; Anbey eine warhaffte Nachricht von der Insul und Historie des Robinson Crusoe. In einem Send-Schreiben an einen guten Freund mit Poetischer Feder entworffen*, Frankfurt and Leipzig, [s.n.], 1728, p. 14.

Die Weiber waren mehrentheils im Gesicht mit rother Farbe bestrichen, welche weit höher von Coleur, als wir sonsten irgend eine gesehen und gefunden haben, wir wissen aber nicht, wovon sie diese schöne Farbe machen.[43]

De mannen waren onder hun aangezigt en op 't lighaam roof of grauw, en de vrouwen met purpere verwe geschildert.[44]

For me also the alleged 'deification' of the Spanish is a doubtful motif. A British anthropologist who explored the island at the beginning of the 20th century, Katherine Routledge, mentions local legends about certain festivities that were said to be organised on Rapa Nui to commemorate the arrival of 'gods of pink cheeks', who came from afar in their ships. The islanders used to form earth mounds that symbolised the ships, made some models of boats with masts, and acted the parts of captains and the crew. They also composed special music for every such occasion.[45] However, another anthropologist, Father Sebastian Englert, who lived on Easter Island for more than 30 years, is of the opinion that those performances were related to celebrations called *koro ate-atua* that were organised to honour an important person or historical event, and this is the correct context to view them.[46]

---

[43] 'The majority of women had their faces painted red, with a paint that was much brighter that any that we have ever found or seen, however we do not know what they use to produce such a beautiful paint.' Carl Friedrich Behrens, *Carl Friedrich Behrens selbst gethane Reise Und Begebenheiten durch die bekannte und unbekannte Südländer und um die Welt worinnen die Canarische und Saltz Insulen, Brasilien, die Magellanische und Lameerische Strassen, Küste von Chili, die neuentdeckte Insulen, gegen Süden und unterschiedene Plätze in Asia, Africa und America; Wie auch Deren Einwohner Lebens-Art, Policey, Commercien, Gottesdienst und dergleichen beschrieben werden*, Franckfurth, Joachim von Lahnen, 1737, pp. 87–88.

[44] 'Below their faces the men had their body red or grey, the women were painted with a purple dye.' *Kort en nauwkeurig verhaal, van de reize, door drie schepen in't Jaar 1721 gedaan, op ordre van de Ed. Bewindhebberen vande West-Indische Compagnie in Holland, om eenige tot nog toe onbekende Landen, omtrent de Zuid-zee gelegen, op te zoeken. Waar in alles wat haar op de reize, van haar uitgaan tot haar terugkomste toe, is wedervaren, word aangetoont; als mede veele wonderlyke manieren, gewoontens, en zeden der ontdekte volkeren, &c.*, Amsterdam, Johannes van Septeren, 1727, p. 8.

[45] Katherine Routledge, *The Mystery of Easter Island*, Kempton, Adventures Unlimited Press, 1998 [1st ed. 1919], pp. 239–240.

[46] Sebastian Englert, *La Tierra de Hotu Matu'a. Historia, Etnología y Lengua de la Isla de Pascua*, Rapa Nui, Rapanui Press, 2010 [1st ed. Padre Las Casas, 1948], p. 301.

As an aside: what the islanders shouted during the semi-religious ceremony of annexation of Rapa Nui to the Spanish Crown is generally understood as 'Make-Make', which is the name if the principal ancient deity of the island. There is no doubt that this interpretation adds more solemnity to the story. The Spanish, who did not speak the local language, transcribed this term as *Máca Máca*. Aguera in his logbook says that *maca* means 'priest' (*sacerdote*).[47] González, who actually did not land, writes in one of his reports that the word could not be understood; however, from his syntax it is not clear whether he suggests that the indigenous people referred by this name to the Spanish chaplains or to 'hens, chicks and bananas' (*Gallinas, Pollos y Platanos*).[48] I am wondering if the correct transcription and interpretation should not be rather *maika*, which is the Rapanui term for 'banana(s)'. Of course, this is only my provocative hypothesis, which probably would be rejected by every expert; but it is also a food for thought.

Another element indicated by the Edwards: the ceremonial stuffed figure, which allegedly stressed the celebratory atmosphere of the Matariki, probably had a different function. The authors cite Aguera, as translated by Corney, stating that the figure was used by the islanders 'for their amusement'.[49] Nonetheless, in the Spanish narrative by Aguera we find the information that the figure was *dedicado a la Loxuría*,[50] that is, related to sexuality matters. Probably neither Aguera, nor Corney, nor the Edwards are right. Contemporary interpretations also vary. The researchers usually refer to the work by Routledge, where we can read that the figure – called *kopeka* – was a symbol of mourning or even of the revenge for the death of a loved person.[51]

As I have indicated above, the Edwards emphasise that the beginning of the Matariki festivity marked the opening of the season of abundance, and, above all, the deep-sea fishing. I do not dare to deny it; nevertheless, all Europeans who in the 18th century visited Easter Island maintained that

---

[47] Aguera Infanzón, 'Diario de Navegacion', p. 311.
[48] González de Haedo, 'Descripcion de la Isla de San Carlos (alias David)', p. 273.
[49] Edwards and Edwards, *When the Universe Was an Island*, p. 446.
[50] Aguera Infanzón, 'Relación diaria', p. 283.
[51] Routledge, *The Mystery of Easter Island*, p. 234.

the inhabitants possessed only small, ramshackle canoes, made of various pieces of wood, and that the canoses were leaky. Certainly they were not seaworthy enough for catching tuna fish or dolphins. The deep-sea fishing was already history. Below I quote some descriptions of those miserable vessels:

Zijn schuytjen was van kleene stukjes hout gemakt en met eenigh gewas aan malkanderen gehouden, zijnde van binnen met twee (h)outjes voorsien. 't Was soo ligt dat een man het gemakkelijk kon dragen.[52]

Estas Canoas son de cinco pedazos de tablas mui angostas (por no tener en la tierra palos gruesos), como de una cuarta, y por eso son tan zelosas que tienen su contrapeso para no volcarse; y estas creo son las únicas que hay en toda la Ysla: en lugar de clavos, les ponen tarugos de palos.[53]

Their canoe was another curiosity, being patched up of many pieces, each of which was not more than four or five inches wide, and two or three feet long. Its length might be about ten or twelve feet, its head and stern were raised considerably, but its middle was very low. It had an outrigger or balancer made of three slender poles, and each of the men had a paddle, of which the blade was likewise composed of several pieces.[54]

In this moment we can go back to the important question of the calendar. The Rapanui used a lunar calendar which, as we know well, differs from the Gregorian solar calendar of the Europeans. Interestingly, this issue was one of principal motives of a long and famous debate that could be observed in the last decades. It was a dispute between two

---

[52] Bouman, *Sheepsjournaal*, p. 136; cf. 'His canoe had been made of small planks that were held together by some sort of rope; it had two blocks of wood on the inside. It was so light that one man alone could easily carry it.' 'The Complete Journal of Captain Cornelis Bouman', p. 96.

[53] Hervé, 'Derrota del navío', p. 260. 'These canoes are made of five pieces of very narrow planks (because in this land there are no thick trunks), a span wide, therefore they are so unsteady that they are provided with a counterweight in order not to capsize. And I think these are the only canoes on the whole island. Instead of nails they have wooden pegs.'

[54] George Forster, *Voyage Round the World*, p. 558.

anthropologists: Marshall Sahlins and Gananath Obeyesekere,[55] as well as their followers. This debate, hardly mentioned in the book by the Edwards[56] and omitted in their field notes, concerned the status of Captain Cook that was bestowed upon him by the inhabitants of Hawaii, where the great explorer found his death at the hands of the islanders in 1779.

At the heart of the issue was the question whether Cook was deified by the Hawaiians (Sahlins' point of view) or not, and the idea of deification should be then considered as a typical myth of a white European discoverer (Obeyesekere's point of view). Another question that ensued was whether the English captain arrived at Hawaii at the beginning of the Makahiki festivity, which is the equivalent of the Rapanui Matariki. In Sahlins' opinion, the course of events coincided perfectly with the local calendar of festivities: the same as in case of the Edwards and the Spanish expedition to Rapa Nui. However, it turns out that the situation is not so evident. Firstly, the festivity might have been moveable. Moreover, it might have been organised on various dates, according to a particular island. And finally, it is not so easy to establish an exact date – with reference to our present callendar – of a past event regulated by another type of calendar than our own.[57] Both scholars made use of a vast and impressive bibliography and, in spite of that, they could not find a satisfactory solution of the posed problem.

When it comes to Rapa Nui, the matters seem to be even more complicated. Liller, astronomer, indicates that – due to the subtropical localisation of the island – the Pleiades are not so distinctly visible in the night sky as they are in other regions of Polynesia;[58] therefore this star cluster might have been less important than the Edwards claim. According to Liller, solar observations could have been more significant in the local tradition:

---

[55] See e.g. Gananath Obeyesekere, *The Apotheosis of Captain Cook: European Mythmaking in the Pacific*, Princeton, Princeton University Press, 1994; Marshall Sahlins, *How Natives Think: About Captain Cook, For Example*, Chicago and London, The University of Chicago Press, 1995.

[56] Edwards and Edwards, *When the Universe Was an Island*, p. 444.

[57] Cf. e.g. Obeyesekere, *The Apotheosis of Captain Cook*, pp. 58–59, 98–99.

[58] Easter Island is localised on the southern hemisphere, at 27°07'S, 109°21'W. Various other regions of Polynesia lay more to the north and, in case of some islands, the Pleiades can pass through, or close to, the local zenith.

[…] it should be remembered that Rapa Nui is well out of the tropic zone and that the inhabitants do experience seasons and therefore had to be concerned with the best time of year to plant crops such as taro, bananas, and other edibles. So maybe on this special little island, the sun was considered to be the more important celestial body.[59]

To sum up, from all the above analysis one major conclusion should be drawn: it is not easy to interpret past events following a simple formula of apparent analogies and our own convictions. There are too many variables that ought to be taken in consideration. Moreover, we have to remember that an immense body of knowledge about the history and tradition of Rapa Nui was lost forever in the 19th century, when the local community almost vanished, falling victim to the Peruvian slave raids and epidemics of western diseases. These circumstances make the task of reconstructing the past of Easter Island all the more difficult.

Bibliography

Aguera Infanzón, Francisco Antonio, 'Diario de Navegacion del Alferez de fragata y Primer Piloto de la Real Armada don Francisco Antonio, Aguera, Ynfanzon', in Francisco Mellén Blanco, *Manuscritos y documentos españoles para la historia de la isla de Pascua. La expedición del capitán D. Felipe González de Haedo a la isla de David*, Madrid, CEDEX, 1986, pp. 295–347.

Aguera Infanzón, Francisco Antonio, 'Relación diaria de lo mas particular, y acaecido en la navegacion echa en la Fragata *Santa Rosalia*, del mando de su Capitan D. Antonio Domonte, que salio del puerto del Callao el 10 de Octubre de 1770 rn conserva del navio *San Lorenzo*, a hacer la descubierta, y el reconocimiento de la Ysla de David, y otras en estos mares del Sur, siendo su primer Piloto el Alferez de Fragata Don Francisco Antonio Aguera Ynfanzon', in Francisco Mellén Blanco, *Manuscritos y documentos españoles para la historia de la isla de Pascua. La expedición del capitán D. Felipe González de Haedo a la isla de David*, Madrid, CEDEX, 1986, pp. 278–290.

---

[59] Liller, *Review*, p. 77.

Behrens, Carl Friedrich, *Reise nach den unbekandten Süd-Ländern und rund um die Welt, Nebst vielen von ihm angemerckten Seltenheiten und zugestossenen wunderlichen Begebenheiten; Anbey eine warhaffte Nachricht von der Insul und Historie des Robinson Crusoe. In einem Send-Schreiben an einen guten Freund mit Poetischer Feder entworffen*, Frankfurt and Leipzig, [s.n.], 1728.

Behrens, Carl Friedrich, *Carl Friedrich Behrens selbst gethane Reise Und Begebenheiten durch die bekannte und unbekannte Südländer und um die Welt worinnen die Canarische und Saltz Insulen, Brasilien, die Magellanische und Lameerische Strassen, Küste von Chili, die neuentdeckte Insulen, gegen Süden und unterschiedene Plätze in Asia, Africa und America; Wie auch Deren Einwohner Lebens-Art, Policey, Commercien, Gottesdienst und dergleichen beschrieben werden*, Franckfurth, Joachim von Lahnen, 1737.

Belmonte, Juan Antonio and Edmundo Edwards, 'Astronomy and Landscape on Easter Island: New Hints at the Light of the Ethnographical Sources', in Emília Pásztor (ed.), *Archaeoastronomy in Archaeology and Ethnography: Papers from the Annual Meeting of SEAC (European Society for Astronomy in Culture), Held in Kecskemét in Hungary in 2004* (BAR International Series, vol. 1647), Oxford, Archaeopress, 2007, pp. 79–85.

Bouman, Cornelis, *Sheepsjournaal, gehouden op het schip Tienhoven tijdens de ontdekkingsreis van Mr. Jacob Roggeveen, 1721–1722*, ed. F.E. Mulert (Archief; vroegere en latere mededeelingen voornamelijk in betrekking tot Zeeland), Middelburg, Zeeuwsch Genootschap der Wetenschappen, 1911, pp. 52–183.

'Carta del Virrey del Perú al Secretario de Estado para las Indias', in Francisco Mellén Blanco, *Manuscritos y documentos españoles para la historia de la isla de Pascua. La expedición del capitán D. Felipe González de Haedo a la isla de David*, Madrid, CEDEX, 1986, pp. 219–221.

Clark, Malcolm A., 'Solar Observatory Response', *Rapa Nui Journal*, vol. 2, issue 2, Summer 1988, p. 5.

'The Complete Journal of Captain Cornelis Bouman, Master of the Ship *Theinhoven*, Forming Part of the Fleet of Jacob Roggeveen, from 31 March to 13 April 1722 During Their Stay Around Easter Island', transl. Herbert von Saher, *Rapa Nui Journal*, vol. 8, issue 4, December 1994, pp. 95–100.

Corney, Bolton Glanvill (transl. and ed.), *The Voyage of Captain Don Felipe Gonzalez in the Ship of the Line San Lorenzo with the Frigate Santa Rosalia in Company, to Easter Island in 1770–1: Preceded by an Extract from Mynheer Jacon Roggeveen's*

Official Log of His Discovery of and Visit to Easter Island in 1722, Cambridge, Hakluyt Society, 1908.

Edwards, Edmundo and Alexandra Edwards, *Rapanui Archaeoastronomy & Ethnoastronomy: Flag #83 Expedition Report, February–June, 2010*. www.pacificislandsresearchinstitute.org/Flag_83_Report.pdf [accessed 6 February 2013].

Edwards, Edmundo and Alexandra Edwards, *When the Universe Was an Island: Exploring the Cultural and Spiritual Cosmos of Ancient Rapa Nui*, Hanga Roa, Hangaroa Press, 2013.

Englert, Sebastain, *La Tierra de Hotu Matu'a. Historia, Etnología y Lengua de la Isla de Pascua*, Imprenta y Editorial "San Francisco", Rapa Nui, Rapanui Press, 2010 [1st ed. Padre Las Casas, 1948].

Fisher, Steven Roger, *Island at the End of the World: The Turbulent History of Easter Island*, London, Reaktion Books Ltd, 2010.

Forster, George, *A Voyage Round the World, in His Britannic Majesty's Sloop, Resolution, Commanded by Capt. James Cook, during the Years 1772, 3, 4 and 5. By Georg Forster, F.R.S., Member of the Royal Academy of Madrid, and of the Society for Promoting Natural Knowledge at Berlin*, vol. 1, London, printed for B. White, J. Robsen and P. Elmsly, 1777.

Forster, Johann Reinhold, *The Resolution Journal of Johann Reinhold Forster 1772–1775*, ed. Michael E. Hoare, vol. 3, London, Hakluyt Society, 1982.

van Gelder, Roelof, *Naar het aards paradijs. Het rustelose leven van Jacob Roggeveen, ontdekker van Paaseiland. 1659–1729*, Amsterdam, Uitgeverij Balans, 2012.

González de Haedo, Felipe, 'Descripcion de la Isla de San Carlos (alias David), reconocida, de orden del Virrey del Perú, por el Capitan de Fragata Don Felipe Gonzalez, en el año de 1771 [*sic*]. Expresase su circunferencia, producciones, numero de naturales, y demas particularidades que se observaron; con un Plano demonstrativo de ella', in Francisco Mellén Blanco, *Manuscritos y documentos españoles para la historia de la isla de Pascua. La expedición del capitán D. Felipe González de Haedo a la isla de David*, Madrid, CEDEX, 1986, pp. 270–273.

González de Haedo, Felipe, 'Descripcion de la Ysla San Carlos, alias David. Y particularidades que se pudieron observar', in Francisco Mellén Blanco, *Manuscritos y documentos españoles para la historia de la isla de Pascua. La expedición del capitán D. Felipe González de Haedo a la isla de David*, Madrid, CEDEX, 1986, pp. 273–275.

González de Haedo, Felipe, 'Extracto del Diario que ha hecho Don Phelipe Gonzalez de Haedo, Capitan de Fragata y Comandante del Navio de Su Majestad nombrado

San Lorenzo, que a efectos del Real Servicio mandado por el Excelentísimo Señor Don Manuel Amat y Junient, Cavallero de la Orden de San Juan del Consejo de Su Majestad, Gentil hombre de Camara con entrada, Theniente General de sus Reales Exercitos, su Virrey Governador, y Capitan General de estos Reynos y Provincias del Perú y Chile. Salió del Puerto del Callao de Lima en conserva de la Fragata *Santa Rosalia*, su Comandante Don Antonio Domonte, Capitan de Fragata uno y otro Buque con viveres para Seys meses', in Francisco Mellén Blanco, *Manuscritos y documentos españoles para la historia de la isla de Pascua. La expedición del capitán D. Felipe González de Haedo a la isla de David*, Madrid, CEDEX, 1986, pp. 222–226.

[González de Haedo, Felipe], 'Extracto sucinto que acomapaña a la carta n.º 396', in Francisco Mellén Blanco, *Manuscritos y documentos españoles para la historia de la isla de Pascua. La expedición del capitán D. Felipe González de Haedo a la isla de David*, Madrid, CEDEX 1986, pp. 221–222.

Haun, Beverly, *Inventing 'Easter Island'*, Toronto, Bufallo and London, University of Toronto Press, 2008.

Hervé, Juan [?]: 'Derrota del navío de Su Majestad *San Lorenzo* a la isla de David, octubre, 10 de 1770', in Francisco Mellén Blanco, *Manuscritos y documentos españoles para la historia de la isla de Pascua. La expedición del capitán D. Felipe González de Haedo a la isla de David*, Madrid, CEDEX, 1986, pp. 258–263.

Heyerdahl, Thor and Edwin Ferdon Jr. (eds.), *Archaeology of Easter Island: Reports of the Norwegian Archaeological Expedition to Easter Island and the East Pacific*, vol. 1, Stockholm, Forum Publishing House, 1961.

Jakubowska, Zuzanna, 'The Spanish Expedition to Easter Island, 1770: Original Documents and Their Rendition by Bolton Glanvill Corney', in Izabela Handzlik and Łukasz Sorokowski (eds.), *Found in Multiculturalism: Acceptance or Challenge?* (Series: Warsaw Studies in Politics and Society, Vol. 1), Frankfurt am Main, Berlin, Bern, Brussels, New York, Oxford and Vienna, Peter Lang – International Academic Publishers, 2014, pp. 107–119.

Kort en nauwkeurig verhaal, van de reize, door drie schepen in't Jaar 1721 gedaan, op ordre van de Ed. Bewindhebberen vande West-Indische Compagnie in Holland, om eenige tot nog toe onbekende Landen, omtrent de Zuid-zee gelegen, op te zoeken. Waar in alles wat haar op de reize, van haar uitgaan tot haar terugkomste toe, is wedervaren, word aangetoont; als mede veele wonderlyke manieren, gewoontens, en zeden der ontdekte volkeren, &c., Amsterdam, Johannes van Septeren, 1727.

Kyselka, Will, 'On the Rising of the Pleiades', *Hawaiian Journal of History*, vol. 27, 1993, pp. 173–183.

La Pérouse, *Voyage de La Pérouse autour du monde*, ed. M.L.A. Milet-Mureau, vol. 2, Paris, Chez Plassan, Imprimeur-Libraire, 1798.

Liller, William, 'The Ancient Solar Observatories of Rapa Nui', *Rapa Nui Journal*, vol. 1, issue 6, Winter 1987/88, pp. 4–5.

Liller, William, 'Rebuttal', *Rapa Nui Journal*, vol. 2, issue 2, Summer 1988, p. 5.

Liller, William, 'Review: "Astronomy and Landscape in Easter Island: New Hints at the Light of the Ethnographical Sources" and "Megalithic Astronomy of Easter Island: A Re-assessment", by Edmundo Edwards & Juan Antonio Belmonte', *Rapa Nui Journal*, vol. 23, issue 1, May 2009, pp. 76–77.

Mellén Blanco, Francisco, *Manuscritos y documentos españoles para la historia de la isla de Pascua. La expedición del capitán D. Felipe González de Haedo a la isla de David*, Madrid, CEDEX, 1986.

Mellén Blanco, Francisco, 'La Isla de Pascua en el centenario de su incorporación a Chile', *Revista de Marina*, Year CIV, vol. 105, issue 785, 1988, p. 393–402.

Obeyesekere, Gananath, *The Apotheosis of Captain Cook: European Mythmaking in the Pacific*, Princeton, Princeton University Press, 1994.

Roggeveen, Jacob, *Dagverhaal der ontdekkings-reis van Mr. Jacob Roggeveen, met de schepen* Den Arend, Thienhoven *en De Afrikaansche Galei, in de jaren 1721 en 1722. Met toestemming van Zijne Excellentie den Minister van Kolonien uitgegeven door het Zeeuwsch Genootschap der Wetenschappen*, Middelburg, Gebroeders Abrahams, 1838.

Routledge, Katherine, *The Mystery of Easter Island*, Kempton, Adventures Unlimited Press, 1998 [1st ed. 1919].

Sahlins, Marshall, *How Natives Think: About Captain Cook, For Example*, Chicago and London, The University of Chicago Press, 1995.

Seelenfreund, Andrea and Francisca Ramírez, 'El universo textil de Rapa Nui', Ch. II, in A. Seelenfreund (ed.), *Vistiendo Rapa Nui. Textiles vegetales*, Santiago de Chile, Pehuén Editores, 2013, pp. 19–35.

Van Tilburg, Jo Anne, 'Response to "The Ancient Solar Observatories of Rapa Nui"', *Rapa Nui Journal*, vol. 2, issue 2, Summer 1988, p. 4.

The Voyage of La Pérouse Round the World, in the Years 1785, 1786, 1787, and 1788, with the Nautical Tables, ed. M.L.A. Milet Mureau, vol. 1, [no translator given], London, Printed for John Stockdale, Piccadilly, 1798.

'Ynstruccion de lo que han de obserbar las dos embarcaciones de Guerra a saver el Navio nombrado »San Lorenzo«, y la fragata denominada »Santa Rosalia«, en la Campaña que ván á hacer desde el Puerto del Callao, con el fin de rexistrar algunas Yslas y costas de este Mar del Sur, conforme á las ordenes de S.M. y resoluciones de este Superior Govierno del Perú, tomadas por si, y con el dictamen del Real Acuerdo', in Francisco Mellén Blanco, *Manuscritos y documentos españoles para la historia de la isla de Pascua. La expedición del capitán D. Felipe González de Haedo a la isla de David*, CEDEX, Madrid, 1986, pp. 213–219.

Jan Lencznarowicz

The 'Pacific Solution'
in Australian Refugee Policy

In 2001 the Liberal-National Coalition Government led by John Howard introduced the Pacific Strategy, which came to be known as the 'Pacific Solution'. It involved the interception of boats with passengers heading towards Australia and their transfer to Nauru and to Manus Island, belonging to Papua New Guinea (PNG). On these islands, special offshore processing centres were established for asylum seekers or – as they were also called – irregular maritime arrivals. They were not allowed to enter Australia and claim protection there. In 2008 the Labor Government of Kevin Rudd discontinued the Pacific Solution. However, given the sharp rise of unauthorised boat arrivals, the next Labor Prime Minister Julia Gillard re-established the processing of asylum seekers offshore in third countries, that is again in Nauru and PNG. After the Coalition return to power in 2013, true to his election promises Liberal Prime Minister Tony Abbott implemented a much more rigorous policy, known as Operation Sovereign Borders. Since among other measures it also included offshore processing on Nauru and Manus Island, it is seen as the continuation and reinforcement of the previous Coalition's policies towards maritime arrivals.

Since the first boat with five Indochinese landed in Darwin in 1976 the number of boat people had fluctuated. Between 1999 and 2001, 12,179 asylum seekers came to Australian shores, mainly from the Middle East via Malaysia and Indonesia. Their passage was organised by men, described as 'people smugglers', who specialise in the illegal transfer by sea of undocumented travellers.[1] Despite the fact that their operations were increasingly sophisticated, including the use of larger twin-engine vessels with radars and satellite navigation, drownings of many boat people heading for the Australian coast on overcrowded boats, as exemplified by the death of 353 people after one fishing vessel sank on 19 October 2001, caused dismay in Australia.[2]

At the turn of the century the surge in the numbers of unauthorised boats carrying Muslim asylum seekers alarmed public opinion, especially at the time of the 9/11 attack in the United States. With upcoming parliamentary elections in November 2001, Prime Minister John Howard was eager to win back voters who in the previous elections had supported the anti-immigrant One Nation Party led by Pauline Hanson.[3] He declared: 'we will decide who comes to this country and the circumstances in which they come.'[4]

A swift and decisive introduction of the Pacific Solution in September 2001 was triggered by the so-called *Tampa* incident at the end of August of the same year. The *Tampa*, a Norwegian freighter, took on board 433 people from a stricken Indonesian fishing boat, almost all of them Afghans. The *Tampa* set its course for the port of Merak in Indonesia, as the accident had taken place within the Indonesian rescue zone. However, the rescued demanded passage to Australia and threatened to commit suicide if they were not transported there. Since the Australian authorities instructed the captain to avoid Australian territorial waters, he changed his course several times but finally the *Tampa* entered Australian waters

---

[1] Janet Phillips and Harriet Spinks, 'Boat Arrivals in Australia Since 1976', Parliamentary Library, updated 23 July 2013, http://www.aph.gov.au/About_Parliament/Parliamentary_Departments/Parliamentary_Library/pubs/BN/2012-2013/BoatArrivals [accessed 20 October 2017].

[2] Barry York, *Australia and Refugees, 1901–2002: An Annotated Chronology Based on Official Sources*, p. 53, Parliamentary Library, 16 June 2003, https://www.aph.gov.au/About_Parliament/Parliamentary_Departments/Parliamentary_Library/Publications_Archive/online/Refugeescontents [accessed 20 September 2017].

[3] James Jupp, *From White Australia to Woomera: The Story of Australian Immigration*, Cambridge, Cambridge University Press, 2007, pp. 189–190.

[4] John Howard, 'Election Speeches, 2001, Delivered at Sydney, NSW, October 20th', 2001, http://electionspeeches.moadoph.gov.au/speeches/2001-john-howard [accessed 20 October 2017].

near Christmas Island and was boarded by Australian troops. The asylum seekers were not let into Australia. Instead they were sent to Nauru, where their claims for protection were assessed by the Office of the UN High Commissioner for Refugees (UNHCR), and to New Zealand. By the beginning of 2005, 186 of them had returned to their country of origin, while the rest were resettled for the most part in New Zealand.[5] Despite international outcry and some criticism at home, 77 per cent of Australians supported the Government's action[6] and shortly afterwards John Howard won the federal elections.

In the meantime, the Government introduced new legislation to amend the *Migration Act 1958*. Selected islands around the northern mainland were excluded from the 'Australian migration zone' and designated as 'excised offshore places'. Their excision from the 'migration zone' did not result in their removal from Australian sovereign territories. This only meant that unauthorised non-citizens who attempted to enter Australia through these places could not make applications for a protection visa and claim refugee status.[7] In addition, all efforts were made to intercept them at sea and either send them back to their last country of sojourn, in most cases Indonesia, or transfer them to Australian immigration facilities on Christmas Island, excised from the Australian migration zone, or remove them to a third country in the Pacific. And here we touch upon the Pacific Solution in its precise sense.

Agreements signed with the Republic of Nauru and PNG were linked to some additional Australian assistance, which in the case of Nauru was substantial and incorporated into the agreement. More or less formal approaches on the same issue to East Timor, Kiribati, Fiji, Palau, Tuvalu, Tonga and France failed to bring results.[8] On the island of Nauru, which

---

[5] Harriet Spinks, 'Tampa: Ten Years on', Parliamentary Library, 22 August 2011, http://www.aph.gov.au/About_Parliament/Parliamentary_Departments/Parliamentary_Library/FlagPost/2011/August/Tampa_ten_years_on [accessed 20 October 2017].

[6] Katharine Betts, 'Boat People and Public Opinion in Australia', *People and Place*, vol. 9, no. 4, 2001, pp. 40–43.

[7] Moira Coombs, 'Excisions from the Migration Zone – Policy and Practice', Research Note, no. 42, 1 March 2004, http://apo.org.au/system/files/8333/apo-nid8333-60001.pdf [accessed 1 December 2017].

[8] *Select Committee for an Inquiry into a Certain Maritime Incident: Majority Report*, Chapter 1, p. 6 and Chapter 10: *Pacific Solution: Negotiations and Agreements*, Parliamentary Library,

has an area of about 21 square kilometres and about 10,000 residents, two camps were established: the so-called Topside and State House. The facilities in PNG, commonly called the Manus Island Centre, were in fact located in the Lombrum Naval Boat Base on Los Negros Island, off the coast of Manus Island. The centres were managed by the International Organization for Migration (IOM). Refugee claims were assessed by Australian immigration officers, in Nauru in some cases by representatives of the UNHCR, in accordance with the 1951 UN Geneva Convention.[9] However, these claims were processed outside the jurisdiction of the Australian courts, so asylum seekers had no access to legal assistance and judicial review, and no guarantee of resettlement in Australia was given.

The Manus Island facilities ceased to be used in May 2004, and those on Nauru in February 2008, when the Labor Government abolished the 'Pacific Solution'. Out of 1,637 people detained in these centres between 2001 and 2008, 48 per cent had Afghan and 41 per cent Iraqi nationality. 1,153 (or 70 per cent) were resettled in different countries, including 705 people (or 43 per cent) in Australia, whereas 483 (30 per cent) returned to their countries of origin.[10]

The abandonment of the 'Pacific Solution' by the Rudd Government in 2008 was followed by a significant increase in the numbers of undocumented maritime arrivals. Between 2009 and 2013, 841 boats with nearly 52,000 people and 1,700 crew members reached Australian territories.[11] As a result, another Labor Prime Minister, Julia Gillard, on the basis of new agreements with the Governments of Nauru and PNG, reopened the

---

23 October 2002, http://www.aph.gov.au/Parliamentary_Business/Committees/Senate/Former_ Committees/maritimeincident/report/c10 [accessed 1 December 2017].

[9] Department of Immigration and Multicultural and Indigenous Affairs, 'Australian Immigration Fact Sheets: Offshore Processing Arrangements', 2005, http://web.archive.org/ web/20051025182708/http://www.immi.gov.au/facts/76offshore.htm [accessed 1 December 2017].

[10] Janet Phillips, 'The "Pacific Solution" Revisited: A Statistical Guide to the Asylum Seeker Caseloads on Nauru and Manus Island', Background Note, Parliamentary Library, 4 September 2012, http://www.aph.gov.au/About_Parliament/Parliamentary_Departments/Parliamentary_Library/pubs/BN/2012-2013/PacificSolution [accessed 2 December 2017]; Chris Evans, 'Last Refugees Leave Nauru', 8 February 2008, http://parlinfo.aph.gov.au/parlInfo/search/display/ display.w3p;query=Id%3A%22media%2Fpressrel%2FYUNP6%22 [accessed 2 December 2007].

[11] Janet Phillips, 'Boat Arrivals in Australia: A Quick Guide to the Statistics', Parliamentary Library, 23 January 2014, http://www.aph.gov.au/About_Parliament/Parliamentary_Departments/Parliamentary_Library/pubs/rp/rp1314/QG/BoatArrivals [accessed 3 December 2017].

Regional Processing Centres in these countries in September and November 2012. Her government also signed an asylum seekers transfer agreement with the Malaysian Government. However, the High Court of Australia deemed it invalid. When in 2013 Kevin Rudd regained the Prime Minister's office, he announced tough new measures. Now all asylum seekers were to be subjected to offshore processing and even those found to be refugees would not be resettled in Australia.[12]

On coming to power in September 2013, the Abbott Government extended the above-mentioned policies by the immediate implementation of Operation Sovereign Borders, within a wider framework of regional cooperation, particularly with Indonesia. This military-led border protection operation includes such measures as the prevention of people smuggling, the restoration of temporary, instead of permanent, protection visas, denying refugee status for those who deliberately destroyed their identity documentation and, most notably, intercepting and turning back boats, if it is safe to do so. If it is not, boat people rescued at sea are transferred to the offshore processing centres, since another important component of this policy has been the continuation of offshore processing on Nauru and Manus Island.[13] Because of all these measures the number of boat arrivals has plummeted and since July 2014 no boat with asylum seekers has reached Australia.[14] The number of detainees in Regional Processing Centres has been gradually decreasing. From the beginning of Operation

---

[12] Janet Phillips, 'A Comparison of Coalition and Labor Government Asylum Policies in Australia Since 2001', 28 February 2014, http://www.aph.gov.au/About_Parliament/Parliamentary_Departments/Parliamentary_Library/pubs/rp/rp1314/AsylumPolicies#_ftn27 [accessed 3 December 2017].

[13] Tony Abbott, 'Swearing-in of the New Coalition Government', 18 September 2013, http://parlinfo.aph.gov.au/parlInfo/download/media/pressrel/2734797/upload_binary/2734797.pdf;-fileType=application%2Fpdf#search=%22media/pressrel/2734797%22 [accessed 3 December 2017]; The Coalition's Operation Sovereign Borders Policy, July 2013, http://sievx.com/articles/OSB/201307xxTheCoalitionsOSBPolicy.pdf [accessed 3 December 2017].

[14] Janet Phillips, 'Boat Arrivals and Boat "Turnbacks" in Australia Since 1976: A Quick Guide to the Statistics', Parliamentary Library, updated 17 January 2017, http://www.aph.gov.au/About_Parliament/Parliamentary_Departments/Parliamentary_Library/pubs/rp/rp1617/Quick_Guides/BoatTurnbacks [accessed 3 December 2017]; Peter Dutton, 'Opinion: Operation Sovereign Border Has Been an Outstanding Success', 26 July 2017, The Courier-Mail, http://www.couriermail.com.au/news/opinion/opinion-operation-sovereign-borders-has-been-an-outstanding-success/news-story/afb6133ae8faabb88cefab2b7cf08b44 [accessed 3 December 2017].

Sovereign Borders in September 2013 to the end of August 2017, 2,125 irregular maritime arrivals were transferred there (770 to Manus Island, 1,355 to Nauru). Out of this figure 614 voluntarily returned to their countries of origin. As of 31 August 2017, 1,142 were reported to be housed in these centres (773 on Manus Island, 369 on Nauru).[15] By then, the Government of Nauru had taken over the management of the centre located on its territory and given asylum seekers the freedom to move around the island without restrictions.[16]

While the High Court of Australia upheld the legality of the offshore processing of asylum seekers' claims in February 2016, the Supreme Court of Papua New Guinea, in April of the same year, found the functioning of the Manus Centre unconstitutional. As a result, it was formally closed on 31 October 2017. The remaining residents, despite their protests, were moved to accommodation in the local community or a temporary transit centre. Those who failed to gain refugee status are still staying on Manus Island but are expected to return home voluntarily or be removed from PNG. Nobody will be admitted to settle in Australia, not even those who were recognised as refugees.[17] They are to be covered by the US-Australian resettlement deal announced in November 2016 and, despite President Trump's initial reluctance, honoured by his administration. It envisaged the settlement of up to 1,250 refugees from Nauru and Manus Island in the USA in exchange for Australia receiving refugees from camps in Central

---

[15] Australian Border Force. Newsroom, 'Operation Sovereign Borders: Monthly Update: August 2017', 8 September 2017, https://newsroom.abf.gov.au/releases/operation-sovereign-borders-monthly-update-august-3 [accessed 2 December 2017].

[16] The Government of the Republic of Nauru, Government Information Office, Media Release, 'No More Detention for Nauru Asylum Seekers', http://www.naurugov.nr/government-information-office/media-release/no-more-detention-for-nauru-asylum-seekers.aspx [accessed 2 December 2017]; Seweryn Ozdowski, *Relevance of Australian Immigration and Multicultural Experience to Poland and Contemporary Europe*, Poznań, Instytut Historii UAM, 2015, p. 37.

[17] 'Manus Detention Centre to Close on October 31: Dutton', SBS News, 16 May 2017, http://www.sbs.com.au/news/article/2017/05/16/manus-detention-centre-close-october-31-dutton [accessed 26 November 2017]; Stefan Armbruster, 'Refugees Afraid, Confused as Manus Detention Centre Shutdown Begins', SBS News, 9 July 2017, http://www.sbs.com.au/news/article/2017/07/06/refugees-afraid-confused-manus-detention-centre-shutdown-begins [accessed 26 November 2017]; 'Manus Island Asylum Seekers Removed from Detention Centre', *The Telegraph*, 24 November 2017, http://www.telegraph.co.uk/news/2017/11/24/manus-island-asylum-seekers-removed-detention-centre/ [accessed 26 November 2017].

America through its Humanitarian Programme. At the end of September 2017, the first refugees from the Nauru and Manus centres departed to the US.[18]

In terms of border protection, stopping the influx of unauthorised boat arrivals and deterrence of people smugglers the Pacific Solution and Operation Sovereign Borders were successful. However, they attracted severe criticism and fierce protests from international organisations[19] and press as well as from Australian refugee support groups, some academics, journalists and parliamentarians. For instance, serious concerns were raised in the report of the Senate Select Committee for an inquiry into a certain maritime incident,[20] in the *Interim Report* of the Senate Legal and Constitutional Affairs Committee[21] and in the joint report of A Just Australia, Oxfam Australia and Oxfam Novib.[22] These concerns were mostly over the safety

---

[18] Thomas Albrecht, 'Op-ed by Thomas Albrecht, UNHCR Regional Representative in Canberra', 2 October 2017, http://www.unhcr.org/en-au/news/latest/2017/10/59d4786c7/op-ed-by-thomas-albrecht-unhcr-regional-representative-in-canberra.html [accessed 3 December 2017].

[19] UNHCR, 'The UN Refugee Agency, UNHCR Chief Filippo Grandi Calls on Australia to End Harmful Practice of Offshore Processing', 24 July 2017, http://www.unhcr.org/en-au/news/press/2017/7/597217484/unhcr-chief-filippo-grandi-calls-australia-end-harmful-practice-offshore.html [accessed 11 December 2017]; Richard Ewart, 'UNHCR Calls for Immediate Transfer of Refugees out of Manus Island, Nauru to "Humane Conditions"', ABC News, 5 May 2016, http://www.abc.net.au/news/2016-05-05/unhcr-presses-for-transfer-of-refugees-out-of-detention-centres/7385748 [accessed 11 December 2017]; Ashley Hall, 'UNHCR Says Manus Detention Fails International Standards', ABC PM, 12 July 2013, http://www.abc.net.au/pm/content/2013/s3802147.htm [accessed 11 December 2017].

[20] *Select Committee for an Inquiry into a Certain Maritime Incident, Report*, Parliamentary Library, 23 October 2002, http://www.aph.gov.au/Parliamentary_Business/Committees/Senate/Former_Committees/maritimeincident/report/index [accessed 1 December 2017].

[21] Senate Legal and Constitutional Affairs Committee, *Conditions and Treatment of Asylum Seekers and Refugees at the Regional Processing Centres in the Republic of Nauru and Papua New Guinea: Interim Report*, May 2016, http://www.aph.gov.au/Parliamentary_Business/Committees/Senate/Legal_and_Constitutional_Affairs/Offshore_RPCs/Interim_Report [accessed 1 December 2017].

[22] Kazimierz Bem et al., *A Price Too High: The Cost of Australia's Approach to Asylum Seekers*, 2007, http://resources.oxfam.org.au/filestore/originals/OAus-PriceTooHighAsylumSeekers-0807.pdf [accessed 1 December 2017]. For the list of reports and other publications on the topic see Elibritt Karlsen, 'Australia's Offshore Processing of Asylum Seekers in Nauru and PNG: A Quick Guide to Statistics and Resources', Parliamentary Library, 19 December 2016, http://parlinfo.aph.gov.au/parlInfo/download/library/prspub/4129606/upload_binary/4129606.pdf [accessed 1 December 2017].

of asylum seekers, particularly children,[23] and harsh living conditions in detention, their allegedly inhumane treatment, instances of abuse, hunger strikes and self-harm. Such incidents as violence in the Manus Centre in February 2014, were widely reported.[24] Refugee advocates pointed to the prolonged duration of detention and inevitable trauma and mental harm as well as the lack of independent scrutiny and difficulty in obtaining access to the centres. Considerable attention was also given to the financial cost, seen as excessive, and legal issues. It was claimed that Australia failed to fulfil its responsibility to the international refugee system and violated the principle of international law requiring the non-refoulement of refugees.[25]

The Pacific Solution has also impacted on neighbouring islands in the region. In the context of the Australian policy of offshore processing they are seen as 'Australia's dumping ground for refugees', as *The Guardian* dubbed the Republic of Nauru.[26] The withdrawal of Australian financial support for former residents of the Manus centre after its dismantlement was described as 'a bid to turn Pacific Solution into Pacific problem.'[27] Since the *Tampa* crisis aid to Nauru has soared and has been closely tied to the Pacific Solution, critics claim that it was an 'unmitigated bribe', covering short-term costs instead of building for the future.[28] It is also argued that criteria focusing on important issues such as sustainable development and health issues are being ignored. Other Pacific Islands' governments are opposed to the prospect that refugees from outside of the Pacific may be permanently resettled in Papua New Guinea and Nauru. Australia is accused of a neocolonial attitude manifested in the use of its economic and

---

[23] Human Rights and Equal Opportunity Commission, *A Last Resort? National Inquiry into Children in Immigration Detention: Report to the Attorney-General*, Sydney and Canberra 2004, http://www.humanrights.gov.au/sites/default/files/document/publication/alr_complete.pdf [accessed 1 December 2017].

[24] Refugee Action Coalition, 'What Really Happened on Manus Island', 17 March 2014, http://www.refugeeaction.org.au/?p=3179 [accessed 1 December 2017].

[25] Bem et al., *A Price Too High*; Karlsen, 'Australia's Offshore Processing'.

[26] Ben Doherty, 'A Short History of Nauru, Australia's Dumping Ground for Refugees', *The Guardian*, 9 August 2016, https://www.theguardian.com/world/2016/aug/10/a-short-history-of-nauru-australias-dumping-ground-for-refugees [accessed 2 December 2017].

[27] 'UN Refugees' Commission Slams Aust Bid to Turn Pacific Solution into a Pacific Problem', *The National*, 31 August 2017, http://www.thenational.com.pg/un-refugees-commission-slams-aust-bid-turn-pacific-solution-pacific-problem/ [accessed 2 December 2017].

[28] Bem et al., *A Price Too High*.

political leverage in the region to get rid of a troublesome domestic issue. It is alleged that instead of meeting its obligations under international and domestic laws it is trying to solve its internal problems by dumping refugees on poor Pacific Island countries which due to climate change may soon themselves face the prospect of sending out climate refugees.[29]

No doubt, the Pacific Solution, as a fundamental part of the whole range of border protection measures, represents an important change in Australia's refugee policy and the manner in which Canberra is ready to satisfy its obligations under the 1951 UN Geneva Convention Relating to the Status of Refugees. Despite obvious political and PR losses on the international scene, sustained criticism and widespread protests, both at home and overseas, the main political forces, forming alternative governments in Australia, namely the coalition of the Liberal Party and National Party as well as the Australian Labor Party, regardless of their differences, have mostly been ready to pursue this policy. Given its controversial aspects described above, one cannot but wonder as to the reason for this approach. At the end of January 2017, in their first telephone conversation, which was later leaked to the press, Australian Prime Minister Malcolm Turnbull explained his views to President Trump regarding the reasons why the Australian authorities do not allow boat people to reach Australian shores:

> The problem with the boats is that you are basically outsourcing your immigration program to people smugglers and also you get thousands of people drowning at sea. So what we say is, we will decide which people get to come to Australia who are refugees, economic migrants, businessmen, whatever. We decide. That is our decision.

And he pointed to the reason for such a policy, saying 'you cannot maintain popular support for immigration policy, [and] multiculturalism, unless you can control your borders.'[30]

---

[29] Eberhard Weber, 'The Pacific Solution – A Catastrophe for the Pacific!?', *Environment and Ecology Research*, vol. 3, no. 4, 2015, pp. 102–3, http://www.hrpub.org/download/20150620/EER4-14090336.pdf [accessed 2 December 2017].

[30] 'Full Transcript: Donald Trump and Malcolm Turnbull Telephone Conversation', *The Sydney Morning Herald*, 4 August 2017, http://www.smh.com.au/world/full-transcript-donald-

In a similar vein, former PM Tony Abbott in his speech in London at the peak of the migration crisis in October 2015 told his audience:

> Because it's the Australian government rather than people smugglers that now controls our refugee intake, there was massive public support for my government's decision [...] to resettle 12,000 members of persecuted minorities from the Syrian conflict – per capita, the biggest resettlement contribution any country has made.[31]

It appears that in essence the Pacific Solution is an attempt to reconcile, even at considerable political and propaganda cost, adherence to the UN Geneva Convention and continuation of Australia's generous reception of refugees as well as its role in the world refugee system as one of the leading countries of resettlement with, on the other hand, the political will expressed by the majority of Australians to decide who, and in what numbers and circumstances, will be accepted as new residents and prospective citizens.

Bibliography

Literature

Betts, Katharine, 'Boat People and Public Opinion in Australia', *People and Place*, vol. 9, no. 4, 2001, pp. 34–48.

Jupp, James, *From White Australia to Woomera: The Story of Australian Immigration*, Cambridge, Cambridge University Press, 2007.

Ozdowski, Seweryn, *Relevance of Australian Immigration and Multicultural Experience to Poland and Contemporary Europe*, Poznań, Instytut Historii UAM, 2015.

---

trump-and-malcolm-turnbull-telephone-conversation-20170803-gxp13g.html [accessed 2 December 2017].

[31] Tony Abbott, 'We Know How to End the Europe Crisis', *The Daily Telegraph*, 27 October 2015, http://www.dailytelegraph.com.au/news/opinion/we-know-how-to-end-the-europe-crisis/news-story/c8ab6926e933e158e90babb5830d1db2 [accessed 2 December 2017].

Websites

Abbott, Tony, 'Swearing-in of the New Coalition Government', 18 September 2013, http://parlinfo.aph.gov.au/parlInfo/download/media/pressrel/2734797/upload_binary/2734797.pdf;fileType=application%2Fpdf#search=%22media/press-rel/2734797%22 [accessed 3 December 2017].

Abbott, Tony, 'We Know How to End the Europe Crisis', *The Daily Telegraph*, 27 October 2015, http://www.dailytelegraph.com.au/news/opinion/we-know-how-to-end-the-europe-crisis/news-story/c8ab6926e933e158e90babb5830d1db2 [accessed 2 December 2017].

Albrecht, Thomas, 'Op-ed by Thomas Albrecht, UNHCR Regional Representative in Canberra', 2 October 2017, http://www.unhcr.org/en-au/news/latest/2017/10/59d4786c7/op-ed-by-thomas-albrecht-unhcr-regional-representative-in-canberra.html [accessed 3 December 2017].

Armbruster, Stefan, 'Refugees Afraid, Confused as Manus Detention Centre Shutdown Begins', SBS News, 9 July 2017, http://www.sbs.com.au/news/article/2017/07/06/refugees-afraid-confused-manus-detention-centre-shutdown-begins [accessed 26 November 2017].

Australian Border Force. Newsroom, 'Operation Sovereign Borders: Monthly Update: August 2017', 8 September 2017, https://newsroom.abf.gov.au/releases/operation-sovereign-borders-monthly-update-august-3 [accessed 2 December 2017].

Bem, Kazimierz et al., *A Price Too High: The Cost of Australia's Approach to Asylum Seekers*, 2007, http://resources.oxfam.org.au/filestore/originals/OAus-Price-TooHighAsylumSeekers-0807.pdf [accessed 1 December 2017].

The Coalition's Operation Sovereign Borders Policy, July 2013, http://sievx.com/articles/OSB/201307xxTheCoalitionsOSBPolicy.pdf [accessed 3 December 2017].

Coombs, Moira, 'Excisions from the Migration Zone – Policy and Practice', Research Note, no. 42, 1 March 2004, http://apo.org.au/system/files/8333/apo-nid8333-60001.pdf [accessed 1 December 2017].

Department of Immigration and Multicultural and Indigenous Affairs, 'Australian Immigration Fact Sheets: Offshore Processing Arrangements', 2005, http://web.archive.org/web/20051025182708/http://www.immi.gov.au/facts/76offshore.htm [accessed 1 December 2017].

Doherty, Ben, 'A Short History of Nauru, Australia's Dumping Ground for Refugees', *The Guardian*, 9 August 2016, https://www.theguardian.com/world/2016/

aug/10/a-short-history-of-nauru-australias-dumping-ground-for-refugees [accessed 2 December 2017].

Dutton, Peter, 'Opinion: Operation Sovereign Border Has Been an Outstanding Success', 26 July 2017, *The Courier-Mail*, http://www.couriermail.com.au/news/opinion/opinion-operation-sovereign-borders-has-been-an-outstanding-success/news-story/afb6133ae8faabb88cefab2b7cf08b44 [accessed 3 December 2017].

Evans, Chris, 'Last Refugees Leave Nauru', 8 February 2008, http://parlinfo.aph.gov.au/parlInfo/search/display/display.w3p;query=Id%3A%22media%2Fpressrel%-2FYUNP6%22 [accessed 2 December 2007].

Ewart, Richard, 'UNHCR Calls for Immediate Transfer of Refugees out of Manus Island, Nauru to "Humane Conditions"', ABC News, 5 May 2016, http://www.abc.net.au/news/2016-05-05/unhcr-presses-for-transfer-of-refugees-out-of-detention-centres/7385748 [accessed 11 December 2017].

'Full Transcript: Donald Trump and Malcolm Turnbull Telephone Conversation', *The Sydney Morning Herald*, 4 August 2017, http://www.smh.com.au/world/full-transcript-donald-trump-and-malcolm-turnbull-telephone-conversation-20170803-gxp13g.html [accessed 2 December 2017].

The Government of the Republic of Nauru, Government Information Office, Media Release, 'No More Detention for Nauru Asylum Seekers', http://www.naurugov.nr/government-information-office/media-release/no-more-detention-for-nauru-asylum-seekers.aspx [accessed 2 December 2017].

Hall, Ashley, 'UNHCR Says Manus Detention Fails International Standards', ABC PM, 12 July 2013, http://www.abc.net.au/pm/content/2013/s3802147.htm [accessed 11 December 2017].

Howard, John, 'Election Speeches, 2001, Delivered at Sydney, NSW, October 20th', 2001, http://electionspeeches.moadoph.gov.au/speeches/2001-john-howard [accessed 20 October 2017].

Human Rights and Equal Opportunity Commission, *A Last Resort? National Inquiry into Children in Immigration Detention: Report to the Attorney-General*, Sydney and Canberra 2004, http://www.humanrights.gov.au/sites/default/files/document/publication/alr_complete.pdf [accessed 1 December 2017].

Karlsen, Elibritt, 'Australia's Offshore Processing of Asylum Seekers in Nauru and PNG: A Quick Guide to Statistics and Resources', Parliamentary Library, 19 December 2016, http://parlinfo.aph.gov.au/parlInfo/download/library/prspub/4129606/upload_binary/4129606.pdf [accessed 1 December 2017].

'Manus Detention Centre to Close on October 31: Dutton', SBS News, 16 May 2017, http://www.sbs.com.au/news/article/2017/05/16/manus-detention-centre-close-october-31-dutton [accessed 26 November 2017].

'Manus Island Asylum Seekers Removed from Detention Centre', *The Telegraph*, 24 November 2017, http://www.telegraph.co.uk/news/2017/11/24/manus-island-asylum-seekers-removed-detention-centre/ [accessed 26 November 2017].

Phillips, Janet, 'Boat Arrivals and Boat "Turnbacks" in Australia Since 1976: A Quick Guide to the Statistics', Parliamentary Library, updated 17 January 2017, http://www.aph.gov.au/About_Parliament/Parliamentary_Departments/Parliamentary_Library/pubs/rp/rp1617/Quick_Guides/BoatTurnbacks [accessed 3 December 2017].

Phillips, Janet, 'Boat Arrivals in Australia: A Quick Guide to the Statistics', Parliamentary Library, 23 January 2014, http://www.aph.gov.au/About_Parliament/Parliamentary_Departments/Parliamentary_Library/pubs/rp/rp1314/QG/Boat Arrivals [accessed 3 December 2017].

Phillips, Janet, 'A Comparison of Coalition and Labor Government Asylum Policies in Australia Since 2001', Parliamentary Library, 28 February 2014, http://www.aph.gov.au/About_Parliament/Parliamentary_Departments/Parliamentary_Library/pubs/rp/rp1314/AsylumPolicies#_ftn27 [accessed 3 December 2017].

Phillips, Janet, 'The "Pacific Solution" Revisited: A Statistical Guide to the Asylum Seeker Caseloads on Nauru and Manus Island', Background Note, Parliamentary Library, 4 September 2012, http://www.aph.gov.au/About_Parliament/Parliamentary_Departments/Parliamentary_Library/pubs/BN/2012-2013/PacificSolution [accessed 2 December 2017].

Phillips, Janet and Harriet Spinks, 'Boat Arrivals in Australia Since 1976', Parliamentary Library, updated 23 July 2013, http://www.aph.gov.au/About_Parliament/Parliamentary_Departments/Parliamentary_Library/pubs/BN/2012-2013/BoatArrivals [accessed 20 October 2017].

Refugee Action Coalition, 'What Really Happened on Manus Island', 17 March 2014, http://www.refugeeaction.org.au/?p=3179 [accessed 1 December 2017].

Select Committee for an Inquiry into a Certain Maritime Incident, Majority Report, Parliamentary Library, 23 October 2002, http://www.aph.gov.au/Parliamentary_Business/Committees/Senate/Former_Committees/maritimeincident/report/index [accessed 1 December 2017].

Senate Legal and Constitutional Affairs Committee, *Conditions and Treatment of Asylum Seekers and Refugees at the Regional Processing Centres in the Republic of Nauru and Papua New Guinea: Interim Report*, May 2016, http://www.aph.gov.au/Parliamentary_Business/Committees/Senate/Legal_and_Constitutional_Affairs/Offshore_RPCs/Interim_Report [accessed 1 December 2017].

Spinks, Harriet, 'Tampa: Ten Years on', Parliamentary Library, 22 August 2011, http://www.aph.gov.au/About_Parliament/Parliamentary_Departments/Parliamentary_Library/FlagPost/2011/August/Tampa_ten_years_on [accessed 20 October 2017].

UNHCR, 'The UN Refugee Agency, UNHCR Chief Filippo Grandi Calls on Australia to End Harmful Practice of Offshore Processing', 24 July 2017, http://www.unhcr.org/en-au/news/press/2017/7/597217484/unhcr-chief-filippo-grandi-calls-australia-end-harmful-practice-offshore.html [accessed 11 December 2017].

'UN Refugees' Commission Slams Aust Bid to Turn Pacific Solution into a Pacific Problem', *The National*, 31 August 2017, http://www.thenational.com.pg/un-refugees-commission-slams-aust-bid-turn-pacific-solution-pacific-problem/ [accessed 2 December 2017].

Weber, Eberhard, 'The Pacific Solution – A Catastrophe for the Pacific!?', *Environment and Ecology Research*, vol. 3, no. 4, 2015, http://www.hrpub.org/download/20150620/EER4-14090336.pdf [accessed 2 December 2017].

York, Barry, *Australia and Refugees, 1901–2002: An Annotated Chronology Based on Official Sources*, Parliamentary Library, 16 June 2003, https://www.aph.gov.au/About_Parliament/Parliamentary_Departments/Parliamentary_Library/Publications_Archive/online/Refugeescontents [accessed 20 September 2017].

Mieczysław Sprengel

Howard Government Activist Role in the South Pacific

Introduction

Howard's Government during the first five years of the 21st century took on a move as to provide an activist role in the South Pacific region. This was the reaction to terrorist attacks on 11 September 2001 and in Bali. The war on terror allowed on the political intervention in the region. Important areas for Australia were Solomon Islands, Papua New Guinea (PNG) and Nauru.[1]

Australia's protective role in the region has grown during the region's history. In the postcolonial era, Australia become a leader in the region of the South Pacific also due to its role according to Australia's mandate under the League of Nations after the First World War.[2] 'A big responsibility has fallen on Australia in accepting the warden-ship of this great land that is interposed like a shield between our Northern shores and Asia.'[3]

---

[1] Michael O'Keefe, 'Australia and Fragile States in the Pacific', in James Cotton and John Ravenhill, *Trading on Alliance Security*, Melbourne, Oxford University Press, 2007, p. 131.

[2] Por. Mieczysław Sprengel, *Gospodarczo-polityczne współczesne relacje Australii z Japonią – wzorzec dla stosunków międzynarodowych w regionie Azji i Pacyfiku*, Kraków, Avalon, 2012, pp. 49–106.

[3] Frank Clune, *Somewhere in New Guinea*, Sydney, Angus & Robertson, 1951, pp. 347–348.

The Australian taxpayers were not much aware of the country's role in security and therefore it was difficult for the government to explain the expenditures. In the 1980s, the Hawke Government initiated organisation structures for security for example the Defence Cooperation Program with the Pacific Patrol Boat Program.

Australia's tasks in the region were to: solve regional disputes, protect the sovereignty of island states, maintain regional laws and order, provide public goods when natural disorters occur, exclude unwelcome strategic intervention by other powers. In the last two decades of the 20th century Australian Defence Force was operating in Fiji 1989, Vanuatu 1988 and PNG 1989–1990, Bougainville and East Timor 1999.[4]

Generally there was support for Australian interventions in the region but there was also many criticism. Peter King called Australian South Pacific Strategy 'solo forward defence'.[5] Charles Hawksley accused Australia of neglect and heavy-handedness. Other commentators labelled Australia as the USA's deputy-sheriff.[6]

Howard Government intervention in the South Pacific

In the first five years of the 21st century, Australia intervened in two major regional cases, that is in Bougainville and Melanesia. Such period was important to develop Australian role in safe guarding the Pacific islands having problems because of political instability and ethnical fragmentation.[7]

The East-Timor intervention has developed Australian model for this kind of operations in the region. Important aspect was the integration of military, police and aid.[8] The intervention took place before 11 September 2001 while the Australian public opinion supported interventions strongly.

---

[4] Ibid.; O'Keefe, 'Australia and Fragile States in the Pacific', p. 132.

[5] Peter King, 'Australia, Regional Threats and the Arms Race: Everyone Else out of Step?', in Graeme Cheeseman and St John Kettle (eds.), *The New Australian Militarism: Undermining Our Future Security*, Sydney, Pluto Press, 1990.

[6] Ibid.; O'Keefe, 'Australia and Fragile States in the Pacific', p. 133.

[7] O'Keefe, 'Australia and Fragile States in the Pacific', s. 133.

[8] James Cotton, 'The East Timor Commitment and Consequences', in James Cotton and John Ravenhill, *The National Interest in a Global Era: Australia in World Affairs 1996–2000*, Melbourne, Oxford University Press, 2001.

Regional Assistance Mission to Solomon Islands (RAMSI)

The Solomon Islands experienced violence in the year 2000 in spite of the earlier peace agreement which was drafted by Australia. When the Salomon Government asked Australia for intervention, Australia replied that this was on internal offshore and refused help. This was also because of the recent coup in Fiji and fear for disturbance in the region's stability.[9]

By the beginning of 2003 the situation on the Solomon Island had become desperate.[10] The Australian Strategic Policy Institute was asked to report about the situation. The report *Our Failing Neighbour* gave specific recommendations for intervention on a big scale. Politicians and decision-makers followed the report.[11]

To be convinced in the decision for the intervention, the Howard Government had to significantly charge their earlier policy of sovereignty of states. The government had to give priority to humanitarian in case of insecurity and violence for people in the region. The Australian Government worked hard to ensure that the operation in the Solomons would be viewed as legitimate. On 24 June 2000 the Solomons parliament accepted the necessary legislation for the Australian intervention with great public support.[12]

Australia invited the Pacific Islands Forum to take part in this intervention. Sixteen members gave their support and offered troops and police. The local and regional support ensured a legitimate intervention. In July 2003 the peacekeeping forces landed on the Solomons to restore law and order. In total 2,225 people were involved in RAMSI: 1400 Australian Defence Force, 134 Australian Federal Police, 50 Australian Protective Service, as well as people from the Cost Islands, Fiji, Kiribati, New Zealand, Papua New Guinea and Tonga. The military action on the Solomons

---

[9] Ibid.; O'Keefe, 'Australia and Fragile States in the Pacific', p. 133–134.

[10] Sinclair Dinnen, 'Winners and Losers: Politics and Disorder in Solomon Islands', *The Journal of Pacific History*, vol. 37, no. 3, 2002, pp. 285–298.

[11] Elsina Wainright, *Our Failing Neighbour: Australia and the Future of Solomon Islands*, Barton, Australian Strategic Policy Institute, 2003.

[12] Ibid.; O'Keefe, 'Australia and Fragile States in the Pacific', p. 134.

passed quickly. In October the Australian Minister of Defence withdrew 800 soldiers. In August 2004 there were 100 soldiers left to keep the peace.[13]

Howard asked strongly to maintain the intervention 'until, the job was done', although some observes remained more critical. The Comprehensive Package of Strengthened Assistance to Solomon Islands provided physical security, economic development, and long-term state capacity--building (COMPSASI). Australia's experience in peacekeeping was to strengthen governance. Estimate costs were $300 million a year and $2 billion in the following decade. Special coordinator of RAMSI was Nick Warner. The law and order on the islands had improved. More than 3,000 suspects had been arrested.[14]

Including senior government officials and police. 3,700 firearms had been collected and destroyed. Militia leaders had been arrested and faith in Police force was restored. The financial situation was stabilised and basic services were restored too.[15]

Papua New Guinea

Papua New Guinea is a country of great potential but little of it has been used. It has minerals, forestry, agriculture and fisheries. PNG does not have any sustainable development or good governance. It has many problems though: crime, corruption, high unemployed among youth and abuse of public resources. Living conditions are getting worse and efforts to improve have failed.

Political, economic and social indicators prove the fragility of the state. Worse living conditions have led to the violence increase, but also they have affected social and physical security. Also the developing of HIV/AIDS epidemic has caused pressure on law and order and has created societal challenges.[16]

---

[13] Ibid., p. 134–135.

[14] J. Howard, *The Australian*, 23 July 2004, pp. 1, 4.

[15] Ibid.; O'Keefe, 'Australia and Fragile States in the Pacific', p. 136.

[16] Centre for International Economics, *Potential Economic Impacts of an HIV/AIDS Epidemic in Papua New Guinea*, Canberra, Australian Agency for International Development, 2002.

PNG was a natural candidate for intervention because of its domestic problems and the deep relationship with Australia. Many Australian emigrants live and work in PNG. In 2003 Foreign Minister Downer summarised the situation, problems with budgetary management, limited new investment, high population growth, the threat of HIV/AIDS and struggling economy. However the frustration grew when it occurred that there was not any major successes in the aid programme. In early 2004 there was a budget of $800 million to directly improve law and order in PNG. Minister Downer went in September 2004 to Port Moresby with many plans to improve governance in PNG.[17]

The plans were: to send 210 Australian Police, 60 civil servants to be placed in impotent positions of key ministries. Australia connected the ECP – programme to the ether measures of reform and enlarged the annual aid budget with $300 million. Negotiations on agreement between Australia and PNG lasted from December 2003 to June 2004. 'The Joint Agreement on Enhanced Cooperation' was signed and passed by the PNG parliament on 27 July 2004.[18]

On 13 May 2005 the PNG Supreme Court decided that immunity for Australian Police was unconstitutional. Next, Australian Police has deported about 40 remained civil servants as the court's decision has seriously damaged the ECP strategy. Negotiations between governments continued and quickly more officers were deployed in key positions in PNG.[19]

Australia was the most important motivator in the conflict in Bougainville to the end. In the mid-2000's peace was restored. Foreign Minister Downer signed the Bougainville Peace Agreement on 20 August 2001. In the agreement there were details concerning maintenance of law and order organisation of elections especially for local autonomy and allowance for referendum in ten or fifteen years.

Australia was the leader of the peace process in a group called Peace Monitoring Group (PMG). Unarmed military and police monitored the peace. PMG was liquidated on 30 June 2003 and replaced to the end of the year by the Bougainville Transition Team.

---

[17] Ibid.; O'Keefe, 'Australia and Fragile States in the Pacific', p. 136–137.
[18] O'Keefe, 'Australia and Fragile States in the Pacific', p. 137.
[19] Ibid.

The PNG Government published the Constitution for the autonomous Region of Bougainville on 21 December 2004. Election took place from May to June 2005. The new government was sworn in on 15 June 2005. The election was financially supported by Australia and New Zealand. The success has indeed removed the problem in the relations with PNG.[20]

Australian policy and other developments

Besides the problems in PNG and Solomon Island Australia also had to help Nauru. Nauru had serious development problems in the 1990s, it was unsolved and corrupt. Australia sent personnel to the employed in the Nauruan public service in early 2000s. Nauru was also a place of money laundering. Canberra paid $30 million to Nauru to open and maintain detention centres as a part of Pacific Solution.[21] These payments kept Nauru from bankruptcy. The situation at the time of writing of, was so serious that Australian Foreign Minister considered in discussion to relocate the population of Nauru.

In Vanuatu in 2004 Australian pressure played an important role because of party instability and political initiatives were blocked by appeals to court. This led to paralysis of the government. Two federal police officers and two 'Australia AID' advisers were removed and aid was in danger. After Prime Minister's visit to Taipei, to negotiate recognition, he was replaced by the parliament. The new Prime Minister Serge Vohor improved the relations with Australia to secure Australian assistance.[22]

In Fiji it came to tensions as a consequence of the coup in 2000. The Prime Minister's Laisenia Qarase Government planned amnesty for the people who had been responsible for the coup. Chief of military Frank Bainimarama threatened to overthrow the government and the army was divided in pro- and anti-government factions.

---

[20] Ibid., p. 138.

[21] www.abc.net.au/am/content/2004/s1195355.htm [accessed 21 October 2017].

[22] Anita Jowitt, 'Vanuatu', *The Contemporary Pacific: A Journal of Island Affairs*, vol. 17, no. 2, 2005, pp. 456–464.

The intervention in Melanesia in 2000 was similar to the operations in the 1980s and 1990s. The main similarity was to encourage South-West nations to see Australia as a neutral strategic partner and to exclude other powers from the South Pacific.[23] In the 1980s and 1990s Australia tried to protect its regional interest against other powers for example the Soviet Union but also other bodies like the UN.

Several major nations tried to develop relations in the region. France offered assistance to RAMSI but this was refused by Australia. Japan tried to get support in the region to liquidate the ban on whale fishing. Malaysia engaged itself more in PNG but does not have a major role.[24] China had the biggest diplomatic action in the region. It used money and financed big construction projects in different regional capitals. China wanted to exclude Taiwan and limit Australian influence.[25]

Conclusion

On the whole, it cannot be denied that Australia's national strength gains momentum, but needs to be careful and constantly secure its future and means a wide range of geopolitical activities. Accordingly, it must also adhere to its 'peace policymaking' in order to remain reliable to the global market. Unquestionably, Australia has reasons to play an important role in the South Pacific.

---

[23] Department of Defence, *Strategic Review 1993*, Canberra, Australian Government Publishing Services, 1993.

[24] Cotton, 'East Timor', p. 140.

[25] Ibid.

Bibliography

Literature

J. Howard, *The Australian*, 23 July 2004.

Cotton, James, 'The East Timor Commitment and Consequences', in James Cotton and John Ravenhill, *The National Interest in a Global Era: Australia in World Affairs 1996–2000*, Melbourne, Oxford University Press, 2001.

Centre for International Economics, *Potential Economic Impacts of an HIV/AIDS Epidemic in Papua New Guinea*, Canberra, Australian Agency for International Development, 2002.

Clune, Frank, *Somewhere in New Guinea*, Sydney, Angus & Robertson, 1951.

Department of Defence, *Strategic Review 1993*, Canberra, Australian Government Publishing Services, 1993.

Dinnen, Sinclair, 'Winners and Losers: Politics and Disorder in Solomon Islands', *The Journal of Pacific History*, vol. 37, no. 3, 2002, pp. 285–298.

Jowitt, Anita, 'Vanuatu', *The Contemporary Pacific: A Journal of Island Affairs*, vol. 17, no. 2, 2005, pp. 456–463.

King, Peter, 'Australia, Regional Threats and the Arms Race: Everyone Else out of Step?', in: Graeme Cheeseman and St John Kettle (eds.), *The New Australian Militarism: Undermining Our Future Security*, Sydney, Pluto Press, 1990.

O'Keefe, Michael, 'Australia and Fragile States in the Pacific', in James Cotton and John Ravenhill, *Trading on Alliance Security*, Melbourne Oxford University Press, 2007.

Sprengel, Mieczysław, *Gospodarczo-polityczne współczesne relacje Australii z Japonią – wzorzec dla stosunków międzynarodowych w regionie Azji i Pacyfiku*, Kraków, Avalon, 2012.

Wainright, Elsina, *Our Failing Neighbour: Australia and the Future of Solomon Islands*, Barton, Australian Strategic Policy Institute, 2003.

Websites

www.abc.net.au/am/content/2004/s1195355.htm [accessed: 21 October 2017].

Jerzy Grębosz

On the Origin of a Diversity of the Cultural Anthropology of the West Oceania

More than 10 million people live across Oceania. The general public stereotype is of a dark-skinned man of Oceania dressed in a pareo (called sometimes sulu/sarong) lying under a coconut palm or fishing, or dancing. This image is just wrong. First of all the pareo is made of fabric, which is produced in white people's factories – so it is quite a recent fashion. If you look at what types of dress the peoples of Oceania used to wear before the pareo era – you can see how many different distinct and unique cultures are represented there. We may ask: what is the source of this diversity? Perhaps they arrived to Oceania from different parts of the world?

The question of where Oceania's inhabitants come from has been intriguing scientists for a long time. Many people had some ideas of how it could be. One of them was the adventurer Thor Heyerdahl. He noticed human shaped stone sculptures known in Polynesia as *tiki*. He realised that on the west coast of South America you can also encounter human shaped stone sculptures. So he concluded that the people of Polynesia could have arrived from South America. He decided to prove that it was feasible. In 1947 using a raft (called Kon-Tiki) he managed to travel from Peru to the Society Islands in 101 days. This way he proved that such a migration would be possible (but not that it really happened).

Today we know how naïve his idea was and that he had actually proved nothing. Perhaps much more valuable scientific information would come from linguistic research. Luckily, nowadays we have a much better tool – the DNA method. Using it, scientists realised that the first migration of people to this region was 50–65 thousand years ago. These were the people which we call today the Australian Aboriginal people. They came across Indonesia to New Guinea and finally reached Australia. (Note that this was before *homo sapiens* arrived to Europe.)

The next migration which populated the Oceanian islands started around 3,000 BC from east Asia. People crossed the East China Sea and arrived in Taiwan. Then in 2500 BC they migrated to the islands of the Philippines. (This was more or less the time when the Pyramids in Egypt were built.) The next step of migration was to New Guinea – where they arrived circa 1500 BC, while in Europe the Minoan culture (on Crete island) flourished. Then the migration continued, and at 1300 BC they colonised the Solomon Islands and at 1200 BC the New Hebrides. (In Europe, this was the time of the Trojan War.) Five hundred years later New Caledonia was colonised. The Fiji Islands were colonised circa 900 BC, Samoan Islands circa 800 BC. Slowly migration reached the Cook Islands and finally the Society Islands (Tahiti). It took quite a long time until the Polynesians started migrating in three different directions: Hawaii (900 AD), Easter Island/Rapa Nui (900 AD) and New Zealand (1200 AD).[1]

Even if the exact dates mentioned by me above are not quite precise, the conclusion is: people of Oceania all come from the same root. So differences between their cultures should not be so big. Linguists know that for example: at Rapa Nui (Easter Island) for 'hello' you say *iaorana* and on very distant New Zealand the same 'hello' in Maori language is: *kia ora*. So what: are these cultures different or not?

Even on such a very small Archipelago as the New Hebrides you can see very distinct cultures. Hence there are not so many geographic barriers – in the small country of Vanuatu there are around 110 languages. Sometimes in one small island you can have many different languages.

---

[1] See Manfred Kayser et al., 'Melanesian Origin of Polynesian Y Chromosomes', *Current Biology*, vol. 10, no. 20, 2000, pp. 1237–1246; Patrick Vinton Kirch, *On the Road of the Winds: An Archaeological History of the Pacific Islands Before European Contact*, London, University of California Press, 2000.

Let's start from my favourite island called Tanna, because it is closest to my heart. I lived there many times already in a kastom (traditional) village called Yakiel and the chiefs of this village consider me a member of their society. This people told me that on their island there are eight distinct languages and twenty-one dialects.

A culture consist of other factors too. In my opinion, these include art, religion, (science) and technology, and social relations. As part of art is also the dress, let's focus on the dress of Yakiel men. They are almost naked, but having a bunch of fibers called a 'nambas'. We will compare it with nambases worn on different islands.

Let's look at three big islands at the north of the archipelago. They are very close to one another, but the kastom (cultural tradition) there is very different. First let's note how many languages are present on Pentecost Island which is just fifteen kilometres wide and sixty kilometres long. In the south of Pentecost there is a region of the Sa language. Around 3,000 people speak this language. Bunlap is one of the kastom villages where people speak this language. As none of us knows this language, let's concentrate on the other visible features of the kastom. The dress of Bunlap men is a very different nambas – made of leaf or made of a small mat.

If we look at an aerial photo of a village called Rangusuksu, we can see a small river next to the village. The river is so shallow that you can cross it with a car or just walking. This river defines a border between two different kastoms. The language on the other side of the river is called Ske. It is so different from Sa, that knowing one you cannot understand the other. If a boy from one side of the river wants to marry a girl from the other – they have to communicate in Bislama (Pidgin English). The kastom dresses are also very different: here people are dressed in big mats. Again we may ask – why there are such differences if there is no special geographic barrier between these two groups of people?

Let's go to a different island nearby. It is a big island called Espirito Santo. Here there are also many different languages. And what about the dress? As I was informed by the old women in Big Bay, during her childhood all people walked around naked. Old and young, men and women – and there was no problem thinking that it is dirty or a sin. White people

and Christianity brought the feeling of guilt and dirtiness. As she said –
later people started to wear leaves.

During my many visits to Santo I went to a kastom village Marakai (two
days of walking through the bush). The Marakai people are still dressed in
a kastom dress, which is very different from what we have seen on the other islands. Women are not dressed in the usual grass skirts, but in nangaria
leaves. The men are wearing something what they call 'a skin of wood' (of
a melek tree). I also got one from the chief and I was proud to wear it.

Traditional men, who are living closer to civilisation, are wearing *kaliko*. It is like the skin of wood, but made of fabric. Even until now it is
very popular on Santo, because it is more comfortable and easier to made.
I participated in many kastom ceremonies in traditional villages – where
men danced in *kaliko*. Sometimes one can see them coming to a market
in Luganville (the only town on the Santo Island).

Not very far from Santo there is an island called Malekula. It is hard to
find there a true kastom village. However sometimes you can see a dress
of the Big Nambas tribe. I got the (big) nambas dress from Virambat, the
chief of Big Nambas tribe.

Ten to fifteen kilometres north of this place, the dress of the Small
Nambas tribe is very different. It is a nambas made of one leaf, hence
it is very different from a leaf nambas of South Pentecost. Going twenty
kilometres along the North East cost of Melekula you can see even more
different styles of small nambas dress.

Let's return to the question: what made such big differences in kastom
of people who are living so close to each other? In my opinion a factor
which contributed mostly was the fact that these people were constantly
fighting with themselves. They were fighting for territory, for women and
for pigs. In normal situations, after the war comes a period of peace. But
here there was something exceptional. These were cannibal wars. When
you take captives and you eat them, the defeated adversary is not keen
to forgive. The opposite tribe is almost obliged to strike back, take some
captives and eat them as well. There is a weak chance for peace. If there is
constant hostility, there is no chance for convergence of the culture. This
is – in my opinion – the origin of such remarkable cultural diversity on
even the small archipelagos of West Oceania.

Bibliography

Kayser, Manfred et al., 'Melanesian Origin of Polynesian Y Chromosomes', *Current Biology*, vol. 10, no. 20, 2000, pp. 1237–1246.

Kirch, Patrick Vinton, *On the Road of the Winds: An Archaeological History of the Pacific Islands Before European Contact*, London, University of California Press, 2000.

Krzysztof Konstanty Vorbrich

Bass Strait Discovery
and Its Consequences for the British Empire
and Oceania: Little Known Aspects
of Flinders's and Bas's Journals and Maps

This present paper deals with the south-eastern corner of Australia and the island of Tasmania[1] adjacent to it. Australia used to be called Nieuw Holland by the Dutch and its name was under a recommendation from Matthew Flinders. Tasmania used to be called Van Diemen's Land[t][2] by the Dutch and its name was altered on 1 January 1856. Compare newspaper articles. The first cited is[3] introductory and is from 1855:

> [FROM OUR OWN CORRESPONDENT.] Hobarton, 8th August, 1855. BY the arrival of Mr. Rogers, appointed Solicitor General for this colony, we have learned that the Queen has consented to our desired change of name. Van Diemen's Land is to buried in the same grave with convictism, and henceforth our island is only to be known as 'Tasmania'.[4]

---

[1] Named such after its first European discoverer Abel Janszoon Tasman.

[2] 'Tasman wrote in his journal: "[...] we have conferred on it the name of Anthoony Van Diemenslandt in honour of the Honourable Governor-General.", Krzysztof K. Vorbrich, *Memoirs of the Forsters – the Polish-Born Participants of Cook's Expedition: The Same Voyage, Worlds Apart*, extended ed., Poznań, Contact Scientific Publishing House, 2011, p. 237.

[3] Historicus, 'Tale of Tasmania', *Voice* (Hobart, Tasmania), 14 November 1931, p. 8.

[4] Anonymous, *The Sydney Morning Herald*, Tuesday, 14 August 1855, p. 3.

More comprehensive analysis is cited from the newspaper article from 1931:

> A Day Of Days In 1854. Our valued contributor 'Historicus' [...] The initiation of 'the new epoch' in the Tale of Tasmania, which was symbolised by a happy change of name, and the disappearance of 'Van Diemen's Land' except as a more or less untreasured reminiscence. Thus: Shortly after 4 o'clock on the afternoon of October 23rd, 1854, the first step, speedily followed by the other necessary ones, was taken toward the close of one epoch and the opening of another in the history of an outpost of the British Empire. On that day the Legislative Council of Van Diemen's Land, the then sole depository of legislative power in these parts, petitioned Queen Victoria to alter the Island's name to Tasmania. On August 15th, 1855, a favorable answer to the petition was published. On December 27th of the same year Governor Fox Young assented to a Bill, passed by the Council two days before, giving legislative effect to the petitioners' prayer. And so with the dawn of January 1st, 1856, the name Tasmania took the place of the Dutch navigator's appellation, bestowed two hundred and thirteen years before (November 24th, 1642).[5]

My period of time interest in this paper encompasses the end of the 18th century and the first part of the 19th century and the central figures of my story are the people from Great Britain, later the United Kingdom. It is worth remembering that the Aborigines have inhabited Australia for approximately 60,000 years having crossed northward to their homeland over dry land on foot due to the last glaciation. Compare: 'Over the next 60,000 years the land would change dramatically. [...] By 30,000 years ago there were people in Arnhem Land, Cape York, [...] southern New South Wales, Victoria, and the south of Tasmania.'[6]

Humans reached Tasmania from a northerly direction on foot over a dry plane. Tasmania has been populated by humans for 40,000 years. It is important to note that Australia has been separated from other lands, including Tasmania, for approximately the last 12,000–14,000 years, nevertheless there have been places narrow enough to be traversed by a small

---

[5] Historicus, 'Tale of Tasmania', p. 8.
[6] Jackie French, *Let the Land Speak: A History of Australia: How the Land Created Our Nation*, Sydney, Harper Collins, 2013, p. 1.

but seaworthy craft. Scientists state that 'Tasmania became an island separate from the rest of Australia around 14 000 years ago [...]. From that time, Tasmania's cultures developed in isolation [...]. Now [...] the communities on each side of Bass Strait are both identified as Aborigines.'[7]

As far as I am aware, neither Australian nor Tasmanian Aborigines have ever had any sea-going long-distance sailing craft. Over 500 generations of their isolation, Tasmanian and Australian Aborigines almost forgot about each other's existence and about the dry land which connected them approximately 14,000 years previously.[8] However, these memories still remain active in Aboriginal legends. Compare: 'Around 1831, George August Robinson, while locating the tribes of eastern Tasmania, recorded that the Tasmanians "have a tradition that this land was settled by emigrants from a far country, that they came here on land, that the sea was subsequently formed."'[9]

In this context I would like to stress that this paper does not deal with the prehistory (that is without any time enduring records) of sailing crafts of present-day Indonesia, Melanesia and Micronesia nor with the Maori vessels of New Zealand, which technically made the discovery of Australia and/or Tasmania possible. As an aside, compare:

> Devoid of written language or any instruments, guided solely by their senses, the early Polynesians and their Micronesian cousins ranged over an area bigger than all the Soviet Union and China combined [...]. Throughout Oceania I was to find a near identity of navigational techniques which bore witness to the volume of voyaging through something like four thousand years.[10]

In addition, this present paper does not deal with the imaginary or real discoveries of Australia and/or Tasmania made by the Portuguese and the

---

[7] Martin Crotty and David Andrew Roberts, '14,000 BP on Being Alone: The Isolation of the Tasmanians', in iidem (eds.), *Turning Points in Australian History*, Sydney, University of New South Wales Press, 2009, p. 18. [KKV: BP means: Before Present.]

[8] Cf. 'They were alone for five hundred generations', ibid., p. 20. If I take Crotty's data: 14,000 years and 500 generations, this gives me 28 years *per* generation on average.

[9] Ibid., p. 19.

[10] David Levis, *The Voyaging Stars: Secrets of the Pacific Island Navigators*, London, Collins, 1978, p. 14.

Spanish. As an aside, compare: 'The Portuguese sailors set out to reach Eastern Asia by sailing eastward from Europe, landing in such places as Taiwan, Japan, and the island of Timor. They may have also been the first Europeans to *discover Australia* and New Zealand (1522).'[11]

This present paper deals only with the historically documented voyages to Australia and Tasmania. Contrary to popular opinion, James Cook did not discover this continent but he was the first to sight and traverse its eastern coast. It is worth recalling that another Englishman, William Dampier, visited Australia before Cook and on 6 August 1699 his HMS *Roebuck* anchored in Western Australia at the entrance of what Dampier named Shark Bay.[12] Later, he was on the verge of discovering the north-east coast of Australia and sailing southeastwards along its eastern coast when the deteriorating state of his ship prevented these intentions from reaching fruition.[13] The unquestioned historical[14] discoverers of Australia and Tasmania, at least for Europeans, were the Dutch, who mostly referred to their newly discovered land as Nieuw-Holland (New Holland in English). Willem Jansz, in 1606, discovered the north-eastern extremity of New Holland, later called Carpentaria Land[t] by Abel Tasman in 1644.[15] Dirk Hartog, in 1616, discovered the west coast of New Holland, and Thijssen, in 1629, the present-day Great Southern Bight of this continent. In 1642, Abel Tasman discovered the land he named Van Diemen's Land[t], after the name of the governor-general of the Dutch East Indies, Anthony van Diemen, who sent Tasman on his mission, and later he discovered New Zealand. He called the latter Staten Land[t], because he supposed it was connected to an imaginary land which went by the name as the fabled Southern Land which was supposed to have continental dimensions and lie east of the Pacific Ocean and be close to the southern edge of South America.

I mentioned above that Van Diemen's land name changed to Tasmania in 1856. In this present paper, I use both toponyms interchangeably. Two

---

[11] Andrew Targowski, *Informing and Civilization*, Santa Rosa, CA, Informing Science Press, 2016, p. 83.

[12] See Vorbrich, *Memoirs of the Forsters* (2011), p. 232.

[13] Ibid., p. 250.

[14] That is, recorded on paper or any other medium which is difficult to destroy.

[15] Vorbrich, *Memoirs of the Forsters* (2011), p. 222.

years later Tasman reached the southern bottom of the Gulf of Carpentaria. Therefore, by 1644, all the coasts of New Holland apart from its eastern one were, at least partially, known to the Dutch. Cook in his first voyage,[16] in 1770, sailing from New Zealand on board HMS *Endeavour*, aimed to reach Van Diemen's Land known and identified by him as the mainland of New Holland. Due an unfavourable wind, Cook did not reach the land seen by Tasman, but unknowingly, he reached instead the south east tip of continental New Holland, which he called Point Hick. According to Captain James Cook's journal, Zachary Hick[17] was one of Cook's mariners on board HMS *Endeavour* and the first to see land: 'Thursday 19th. [1770] [...] I have named it *Point Hicks*, because Leuitt Hicks was the first who discover'd this land.'[18]

Some contemporary researchers think that Hick and Cook did not see solid land but a cloud formation instead. These researchers consider that Cook first approached the mainland of New Holland close to present-day Cape Cleveland,[19] but not close to present-day Point Hick.[20] In due course Cook sailed along the whole of the eastern coast of New Holland. At the beginning of the traverse he entered Botany Bay but then sailed past the next bay which he named Jackson Bay. The latter was the place where the first capital of the new colony, Sydney, would be located. During his second voyage,[21] James Cook, this time sailing on board HMS *Resolution*, with naturalists Johann and George Forster on board, visited neither Australia nor Tasmania.[22] However, HMS *Resolution's* consort HMS

---

[16] Cook's first voyage (1768–1771), cf. John Cawte Beaglehole (ed.), *The Journals of Captain James Cook on His Voyages of Discovery. Four Volumes and Portfolio. (Edited from the Original Manuscripts)*, vol. 1: *The Voyage of the Endeavour 1768–1771* (Hakluyt Society Works, Extra Series, no. 34), Cambridge, Cambridge University Press for the Hakluyt Society, 1968.

[17] Ibid., p. 667 (Index).

[18] Ibid., p. 299.

[19] Please note the difference in spelling: Point Hick and Cape Everald.

[20] Beaglehole, *Voyage of the Endeavour*, p. 299.

[21] Cf. John Cawte Beaglehole (ed.), *Journals of Captain James Cook*, vol. 2: *The Voyage of the Resolution and Adventure 1772–1775* (Hakluyt Society Works, Extra Series, no. 35), Cambridge, Cambridge University Press for the Hakluyt Society, 1961.

[22] As an aside, on the contribution of the Forsters to Oceania research on board HMS *Resolution* see Krzysztof K. Vorbrich, *Memoirs of the Forsters – the Polish-Born Participants of Cook's Expedition: The Same Voyage, Worlds Apart – Excerpts*, vol. 2: *History of European Oceanic Exploration Discussed in the Forsters' Narrative Writings. Selected Issues*, Poznań, Wydawnictwo

Adventure under the command of Captain Tobias Furneux, touched the southern coast of Tasmania, traversed the eastern coast of this land as well as the islands adjacent the north-east corner of Tasmania in March 1773. Furneaux made a map of this voyage containing the names he bestowed on his discoveries. In his haste to sail eastwards to join Cook in New Zealand, Furneux decided not to sail north to Point Hick and he did not attempt to ascertain what lay westward of Point Hick.[23]

During his third voyage, James Cook, sailing on board HMS *Resolution* was accompanied by HMS *Discovery*; they touched the southern tip of Van Diemen's Land, but did not investigate the waters between Furneaux Islands and Point Hick.[24] The discovery of the interior of Jackson Bay remained unknown until 26 January 1788 when the First Fleet of 11 ships with approximately thousand people including convicts and a group of mariners and officers, as well as the first governor of New South Wales, Arthur Phillip, on board: arrived from England via the southern point of Van Diemen's Land via Botany Bay. 'In sum, out of 1,006 prisoners who sailed from Portsmouth, 267 died at sea and at least another 150 after landing.'[25]

On 11 December 1792, Phillip, on medical grounds, was forced to return to England. On 7 September 1795, HMS *Reliance* arrived in Sydney

Naukowe Contact, 2010; idem, *Memoirs of the Forsters* (2011); idem, 'Three Memoirs of the Forsters – the Polish-Born Participants of Cook's Second Voyage', *Polish AngloSaxon Studies*, vol. 14–15, 2011, pp. 7–47; idem, 'Some Geographical and Geological Aspects in Johann Forster's Posthumous *Journals*… Controversy – HMS *Resolution* Memoirs Never Refined', *Quaestiones Geographicae*, vol. 31, issue 3, 2012, pp. 89–105. In *Memoirs of the Forsters* (2011, p. 6.) I wrote that the research on Australia was mistakenly attributed to the Forsters: 'attributing to Reinhold Forster the discovery in the Australian waters of a genus of fish with the hybrid breathing organs, *Ceratodus (Neoceratodus) forsteri*, is based on a misunderstanding. The Forsters, father and son, had never landed in Australia. *Ceratodus* was named after its nineteenth century discoverer, a certain Australian colonist called William Forster.' Zygmunt Fedorowicz, *Zoologia w Gdańsku w stuleciach XVII i XVIII* (Memorabilia Zoologica, vol. 19), Wrocław, Zakład Narodowy im. Ossolińskich, Wydawnictwo Polskiej Akademii Nauk, 1968, p. 92, my translation – KKV.

[23] Cf. Beaglehole, *Voyage of the Resolution and Adventure*, pp. 161–164, map on Fig. 31, p. 162. Cf. also Vorbrich, *Memoirs of the Forsters* (2011), p. 286.

[24] Cf. painting by Anonymous, *Coast of Van Diemen's Land*. Note: HMS *Resolution* and HMS *Discovery* in 1777. Illustration to the following fragment of Cook's third voyage journals': 'On the 24th [*sic*] January […] we discovered the coast of Van Diemen's Land, and on the 26th [*sic*] we carried the ship into Adventure Bay', cited in M.B. Synge, *Captain Cook's Voyages* […], 1897, quotation and illustration in: Vorbrich, *Memoirs of the Forsters* (2010), 2 p. of the cover.

[25] Robert Hughes, *The Fatal Shore: A History of the Transportation of Convicts to Australia, 1787–1868*, London, Vintage Books, 2003, p. 145.

with her primary aim being the transportation of John Hunter from England to the colony. 'Henry Waterhouse was chosen to command the *Reliance*, under Hunter, at that officer's request.'[26]

John Hunter formally assumed the office of governor four days after HMS *Reliance* arrived and in this way he closed the interregnum which had been in existence since the departure of Governor Phillip to England in December 1792. During this intervening period, the governing of the colony of New South Wales was conducted by a lieutenant-governor and senior military officer. As second governor of New South Wales, Hunter remained in office until 1800. Governor Hunter was no novice when he came to Sydney as he had come there with the First Fleet and written a seminal contribution to the history of the colony.[27] From his journal, the reader learns first hand of the difficulties the colony faced after one of the ships of the First Fleet, HMS *Sirius*, had been lost due to stranding.

This loss was one of the reasons why by 7 September 1795, New South Wales colony was virtually unexplored. Upon taking the office of governor, Hunter was interested in promoting voyages of coastal exploration southwards from Sydney, hoping especially that this would lead to the discovery of a supposed strait between Van Diemen's Land and land West of Point Hick. Governor Hunter was a vigorous proponent of the idea of the existence of such a strait. However, in 1795, he had virtually no ship at his disposal to undertake these voyages of discovery for him. Nonetheless, good luck was to smile upon him in the form of an opportunity presenting itself to fulfill his intentions, albeit not in one go, but by means of the extraordinary efforts of two mariners who succeeded in achieving their and Hunter's objectives over several stages and years. These two people were George Bass and Matthew Flinders who – together with Bass's personal and medical servant William – sailed from England to Sydney with Hunter arriving on 7 September 1795. During their confidence-boosting voyages of exploration, which led to the discovery of Bass Strait, both

---

[26] Ernest Scott, *The Life of Captain Matthew Flinders*, Cambridge, Cambridge University Press, 2011, p. 77 [1st ed. 1914].

[27] Namely, John Hunter – his journal kept on board the *Sirius* during his voyage to New South Wales, May 1787 – March 1791; cf. John Hunter, *An Historical Journal of the Transactions at Port Jackson and Norfolk Island*, London, Printed for John Stockdale, Piccadilly, 1793.

Bass and Flinders wrote journals. These documents are not universally known and some have not been published and remain in manuscript form deposited in the Mitchell Library in Sydney. The aim of this present paper is to discuss the essence of these journals which might be overlooked by a casual reader not familiar with the general maritime output of Bass and Flinders in New South Wales and Bass Strait. It is worth sketching a profile of both of these sailors from England. They were born in the same county of Lincolnshire (Bass in 1771[28] and Flinders in 1774[29]). George Bass was born at Aswarby, close to Boston town and the harbour near Wash, on the east coast of England. His father was a farmer who died when George junior was six years old. His mother Sarah was intellectually orientated and 'resolved that George should get a sound education.'[30] Bass's mother apprenticed him to a Boston surgeon[31] and Bass eventually obtained an M.C.S. diploma (Member of the Company of Surgeons) which entitled him to use the title of Mr.[32]

Matthew Flinders was born at Donnington, 'some eight mile away'[33] from Aswarby. 'Three ancestors of Matthew Flinders in succession had been surgeons. The patronymic indicates a Flemish origin.'[34] Matthew Flinders was to inherit his father's doctor's practice, but he decided to go to sea instead.[35] George Bass and Matthew Flinders may have been related by bonds of blood, however I do not know whether Bass and Flinders ever met before seeing each other on board HMS *Reliance*. This vessel 'was built at South Shields, and bought by the Admiralty in 1783. She was commissioned in March, and was lying in the Thames at Deptford preparing for the voyage to New South Wales. The *Reliance* was an armed vessel [...] she mounted only ten guns and had a crew of only 59 men.'[36]

---

[28] Keith Macrae Bowden, *George Bass 1771–1803: His Discoveries, Romantic Life and Tragic Disappearance*, London, Melbourne, and Wellington, Geofrey Cumberlege Oxford University Press, 1952, p. 2.

[29] Ibid., p. 5.

[30] Ibid., p. 3.

[31] Ibid., p. 5.

[32] Ibid., p. 9.

[33] Ibid., p. 5.

[34] Scott, *Life of Captain Matthew Flinders*, p. 2.

[35] Bowden, *George Bass 1771–1803*, p. 5.

[36] Ibid., p. 25.

George Bass enlisted on board HMS *Reliance* as a surgical assistant. Ernest Scott mentions M. Flinders' function as midshipman on board HMS *Reliance* when she sailed from England: before sailing on HMS *Reliance*, M. Flinders sailed as midshipman with William Blight in 1791 on his second breadfruit expedition to and from Tahiti. He also took part in the naval war with France, particularly in the Battle of the Glorious First of June in 1794.[37] Both Bass and Flinders had a passion for voyages of discovery, which they put to good use aided by the favourable disposition of Governor Hunter. Embarking on HMS *Reliance* in England, George Bass took with him a rowing and sailing dinghy which he named the *Tom Thumb*.[38] The dinghy was of the River Thames design and was small enough to circumvent Governor Hunter's ban on boats. The Governor was afraid that any bigger boat might be 'requisitioned' by prisoners as a means of escape from Sydney, compare: 'Hunter had found it necessary on 9 October 1797 to forbid the building of any boats whatsoever for the use of private persons.'[39]

On 26 October 1795, George Bass, together with Matthew Flinders and his servant, William Martin,[40] in tow, set out on board the *Tom Thumb* in order to find out whether there was any river flowing into Botany Bay, which James Cook chose as the place of his first anchorage in New Holland. They succeeded in discovering a river which flowed into Botany Bay and they named it George's River. Matthew Flinders wrote a journal of their expedition using the plural 'we' and Governor Hunter was so impressed with the Bass and Flinders' positive reports about the suitability of the area by the river for colonisation that he bestowed on one of the places

---

[37] Ernest Scott, *Life of Captain Matthew Flinders*, p. 43 and *passim*; Kenneth Morgan, *Matthew Flinders, Maritime Explorer of Australia*, London and New York, Bloomsbury Publishing, 2016.

[38] Scott, *Life of Captain Matthew Flinders*, p. 77 and *passim*; Keith Bowden (ed.), *Matthew Flinders' Narrative of Tom Thumb's Cruise to Canoe Rivulet*, Brighton, Vic., Australia, South Eastern Historical Association, 1985, p. 1 and *passim*.

[39] Cf. James C.H. Gill, 'Notes on the Sealing Industry of Early Australia', *Journal of the Royal Historical Society of Queensland*, vol. 8, issue 2, 1967, p. 226.

[40] 'Martin came from Dartford in Kent [...] he joined the ship when he was thirteen years old [...] he would have just celebrated his fifteenth birthday before he left with Bass and Flinders on their celebrated second Tom Thumb voyage.' Bowden, *Matthew Flinders' Narrative*, p. XI. Cf. Dan Sprod, 'Flinders and Bass: Coastal Explorations South of Port Jackson, 1795–1798', in idem (ed.), *Van Diemen's Land Revealed: Flinders and Bass and Their Circumnavigation of the Island in the Colonial Sloop Norfolk 1798–1799*, Hobart, Blubber Head Press, 2009, pp. 6–9.

along the river bank, the name Banks town (at present spelled Banks-town), a name that commemorated the naturalist Sir Joseph Banks, who sailed with Captain Cook on his first voyage. It is my belief that Hunter commemorated Banks instead of Bass and Flinders because the former was a very influential naturalist based in London, while Bass and Flinders were completely unknowns at that time. With the successful conclusion of the *Tom Thumb* expedition, the confidence of Governor Hunter in the sailing abilities of Bass and Flinders grew and with it so did their appetite for coastal discoveries. As a result, in March 1796, both sailors departed in another rowing and sailing dinghy, also named the *Tom Thumb*, which was slightly bigger than the *Tom Thumb* from 1795.[41] They set out on another coastal voyage southward. (It is my intention to refer to the boat from the 1795 expedition as the *Tom Thumb I* and the 1796 version as the *Tom Thumb II*.)

The aim of the 1796 voyage was to find a river thought to lie just south of the entrance of Botany Bay. Matthew Flinders wrote journal on the *Tom Thumb II*. In these journal entries he used plural 'we' referring to himself and Bass. From it, can be learnt that from the beginning of the *Tom Thumb II's* voyage difficulties surfaced. Firstly, the sailors underestimated the strength of the coastal current flowing southwards; moreover, they sailed too far from the coast to be able to check their position against the entrance both to Botany Bay and the bay adjacent to it to the south, which – as it turned out later – concealed the suspected mouth of the river they had set out from Port Jackson to seek. As a result, when they were finally able to check their position, it was against a mountain, positioned far south from Sydney; a mountain Flinders knew from a previous voyage on a sea-going ship and he also knew that this mountain had been discovered and named by Cook. Secondly, the sailors had put their fresh water supplies into the wrong kind of (post-wine) caskets. As a result, they quickly realised that they were without fresh water supplies.

This necessitated sailing with a strong wind even further south and further away from the initial aim of the voyage so as to find a fresh water source. Thirdly, the white sailors were so terrified of the Aborigines that

---

[41] Bowden, *Matthew Flinders' Narrative*, pp. 3–19.

contact made with them was so fleeting as to not enable sufficient first ever data of their culture to be garnered.

On the positive side, was the discovery of Lake Illawarra (from the journal it is not altogether clear whether the lake discovered by Bass and Flinders coincides with present day Lake Illawarra); the discovery of several small islands which Cook had missed; the opportunity of detailing observations of the nearby coast (which Cook was not in a position to observe from a greater distance); the discovery of possible coal deposits by the coast[42], and finally, the discovery of the estuary which had been the initial purpose of their expedition in the first place – they named it Port Hacking.

The *Tom Thumb I* and *Tom Thumb II* journals are important as they were the first to emanate from the colony itself without any help from the motherland in Britain. These undertakings kept up the colonists' morale and re-enactments of these voyages are still frequently being conducted.[43] Copies of the *Tom Thumb II* are on display in important maritime museums in Sydney and Tasmania. As far as I am aware, none of these re-enactments have been forced to endure a similar storm as the *Tom Thumb II* had to deal with.

Nevertheless, this storm takes centre stage in illustrations to books about the voyage which are being published to this present day. It is a strange twist of fate that the tragedy of the merchant ship, *Sydney Cove*, triggered a series of events which led to the fulfillment of Governor Hunter's dream of ascertaining whether there was a strait between Van Diemen's Land, north of the islands discovered by Captain Furneaux and south of Point Hick discovered by Captain Cook. The *Sydney Cove* sprang a fatal leak due to a chain of storms and severe gales which persisted during her voyage from Calcutta, and later on while sailing south and east of Van Diemen's

---

[42] George Bass, 'Discovery of Coal. [Extract.] George Bass to Lieutenant-Colonel Paterson (Banks Papers)' [MS 1799], in F.M. Bladen (ed.), *Historical Records of New South Wales*, vol. 3, *Hunter: 1796–1799*, Sydney 1895, pp. 289–290.

[43] George Mackaness, 'Introduction', in Matthew Flinders, *Observations on the Coasts of Van Diemen's Land on Bass's Strait and its Islands and on Part of the Coasts of New South Wales*, Sydney, D.S. Ford, 1946 [reprint of ed. published 1801], pp. 5–12; Bern Cuthbertson, *In the Wake of Bass and Flinders: 200 Years on: The Story of the Re-Enactment Voyages 200 Years on in the Whaleboat Elizabeth and the Replica Sloop Norfolk to Celebrate the Bicentenary of the Voyages of George Bass and Matthew Flinders*, Sandy Bay, Tas., Bern and Jan Cuthbertson, 2001.

Land.[44] As a result she managed to make it to shore on one of the islands
of a group discovered by Furneaux just north-east of Van Diemen's Land.
Apart of a dozen or so mariners set off on board a longboat on a 800 kilometres voyage with the express purpose of aiming to contact Sydney to
seek assistance. If they had managed to achieve this it would have been the
first and bravest sailing of a longboat along the coast from Furneaux Islands to Sydney. However, the longboat was wrecked on the opposite side
of the present-day Bass Strait, on a beach facing the Furneaux Islands resulting in the crew being forced to trek to Sydney. On their way they must
have trekked along the coast of the present-day Twofold Bay; a bay which
had been overlooked by Cook and the First Fleet but was discovered and
named later by Bass. Only two of the sailors trekking from the *Sydney
Cove* longboat reached Port Jackson. They kept a diary which survived
their ordeal. Governor Hunter organised several seaborne rescue expeditions in order to retrieve the sailors and remaining cargo of the wrecked
Sydney Cove.[45] George Bass took part in one of them; he sailed on board
a whaleboat, carrying out a short-range, futile coastal search expedition
for survivors of the trekking party.

At least three rescue missions to the wreck of the *Sydney Cove* were
attempted by the schooner, the *Francis*, under the command of Captain
William Reed (also spelled Reid).[46] (It is worth noting that the *Francis*,
the first ship launched in the colony, was assembled from parts sent from
England and in her first rescue expedition to the *Sydney Cove* her consort
rescue longboat perished in a gale.) In her last and third rescue voyage,
M. Flinders took part in the capacity of passenger and sometime advisor
(to Captain William Reed), hydrographer, observer of tide heights, tidal
currents and fauna and flora.[47]

---

[44] Anonymous, 'Narrative of the Shipwreck of Captain Hamilton and the Crew of the Sydney Cove', reprinted from the *Asiatic Mirror*, Calcutta, [part 1:] 27 December 1797, [part 2:]
10 January 1798, in Bladen, *Hunter: 1796–1799*, Appendix A, pp. 757–768; Michael Nash, *Cargo for the Colony: The Wreck of the Merchant Ship Sydney Cove*, Sydney, Braxus Press, 1996,
pp. 14–48.

[45] John Hunter, 'Governor Hunter to Secretary Nepean. Sydney, New South Wales, 3rd Sept.,
1798', in Bladen, *Hunter: 1796–1799*, p. 474.

[46] Gill, 'Notes on the Sealing Industry', p. 226. On the same page Gill writes: 'Captain Reed
(the name is sometimes spelt "Reid")'.

[47] Hunter, 'Governor Hunter to Secretary Nepean', p. 474.

Flinders also wrote a journal with the aim of presenting it to Governor Hunter. His observations on seals determined the tragic fate which was to befall them when they were exploited by big-money-seeking sealers. However, the first ever accurate observations of birds in the area proved to be of a great scientific value. The tidal observations, which were corroborated by earlier *Sydney Cove*-castaway observations, suggested to Governor Hunter that a strait did indeed exist between the islands discovered by Captain Furneaux and Point Hick.

The above-mentioned tidal observations of the castaways, conducted prior to the *Francis'* third rescue mission, induced Governor Hunter to equip a sound and very seaworthy oar and sail-powered whaleboat to send her on a preliminary coastal voyage to seek the discovery of the strait. (The name of this boat has not been preserved but for the purposes of this paper I refer to her as the *Whaleboat*.) The command of the *Whaleboat* was given to George Bass at the latter's behest.[48] Bass naturally kept a journal of this expedition, which is a priceless account of sailing along the coast of present-day New South Wales first – in the wake of Cook – from Sydney to Point Hick, and then traversing the coast of present-day Victoria as the first ever white man to Western Port,[49] positioned close to present-day Port Phillip and Melbourne. However, Bass's journal is not scientifically or literary-minded and he rarely mentions bird and land animal habits or the beauty of the landscape. He made entries of his discoveries on land and coast very much in line with how they would be of value to future settlers and profit-seeking sealers. He also included in his entries the sheltering capabilities of the coast for the benefit of successors sailing in his wake.

From Point Hick to Western Port and back to Sydney Bass, he sailed very close to the coast with one exception: when he attempted to cross to the wreck of the *Sydney Cove* in waters which were later christened Bass Strait. In the middle of these waters through a combination of a gale-force wind coupled with great waves, the vulnerable and aging *Whaleboat* unexpectedly

---

[48] Scott, *Life of Captain Matthew Flinders*, p. 98 and *passim*; Bladen, 'Introduction', in idem, *Hunter: 1796–1799*, p. xxxii; Hunter, 'Governor Hunter to Secretary Nepean', p. 474; Dan Sprod, 'George Bass and the Discovery of Western Port, 3 December 1797 – 25 February 1798', in idem, *Van Diemen's Land Revealed*, pp. 10–17.

[49] Bladen, 'Introduction', p. xxxii; Sprod, 'George Bass', pp. 10–17.

sprang a dangerous leak. This forced Bass to abandon plans to acquire some additional food supplies stored near the *Sydney Cove* wreck and instead to return northwards, towards the present-day Victorian coast.[50] The fact that Bass was in such dire circumstances in the middle of one of the most dangerous waters in the world (Bass Strait) on an extremely fragile and leaking open-deck boat, is not widely known. On his return northwards no land whatsoever westwards was to be seen. The fact that no land was visible to the west in the middle of this traverse, coupled with the observations of huge waves and of strong tides at Western Port, induced him to believe that he had discovered the strait that in future would be christened with his own name. His entry to this effect in his journal was later confirmed in Bass's letter to Banks: 'Sydney, New South Wales, 27 May 1799. Sir, particularly of one in a whaleboat made in the latter end of 1797 and the beginning of 1797, when, during an absence of three month, I discovered in latitude 39°S a strait which divides Van Diemens's Land from New South Wales.'[51]

The *Whaleboat*'s voyage has been a matter of much romantic debate and commemoration in Australia, and has been re-enacted in a near--replica boat built from private funds. These re-enactments have aroused extreme interest from the modern inhabitants of New South Wales and Victoria's coasts.[52]

George Bass on the *Whaleboat* and Matthew Flinders on the *Francis* returned to Port Jackson almost at the same time.[53] Upon reading their journals and reports, Governor Hunter decided to resolve definitively the issue of the existence of the strait.[54] This decision coincided with the earlier requisition by Hunter of a sloop called the *Norfolk*, built on Norfolk Island. Hunter gave command of the *Norfolk* to M. Flinders, and G. Bass became an officer on the sloop. Hunter's order of the day was to prove the existence of the strait by circumnavigating Van Diemen's Land. Flinders and Bass succeeded in fulfilling their task and so resolved a question which had remained unanswered since Tasman's time. At the beginning of its voyage

---

[50] Hunter, 'Governor Hunter to Secretary Nepean', p. 475.

[51] Bowden, *George Bass 1771–1803*, pp. 82–83.

[52] Cuthbertson, *In the Wake of Bass and Flinders*.

[53] Dan Sprod, 'Matthew Flinders's Voyage to the Wreck of the Sydney Cove in the Schooner Francis 1 February – 9 March 1798', in idem, *Van Diemen's Land Revealed*, pp. 17–22.

[54] Hunter, 'Governor Hunter to Secretary Nepean', p. 475.

from Sydney,[55] the *Norfolk* was accompanied by a seal-whaling sailing ship called the *Nautilus* commanded by an excellent sailor named Charles Bishop. (More will be written later about how excessive seal hunting destroyed the ecological balance of the islands discovered by Furneaux.)

In regard to the *Norfolk*'s circumnavigation, I had at my disposal four versions of Bass and Flinders' journals and one memoir of the latter.[56] These journals will be shortly discussed concentrating on the part of the voyage from the North East tip in Cape Portland to the North West tip of Cape Grim, in Van Diemen's Land; a leg that proved – by various means and without any doubt – the existence of the strait.

One of the versions is a summary of Bass's journal undertaken by a third party.[57] This version will be bypassed as I regard it as less reliable than the original version of Bass's journal. In addition, at my disposal are variants of the journals in the form of hand-written versions (manuscripts) by Bass and Flinders, various published versions and versions deciphered (transcribed) from the manuscripts by myself. Flinders was a professional naval officer with the rank of lieutenant, so – as one might suppose – his two versions of the *Norfolk*'s voyage journal[58] and his memoir called *Observations...*[59] are more navigation- and hydrography-minded than Bass's journal, who – by instinct – was an excellent natural history and geology researcher. For the purposes of this article, I will summarise the voyage of discovery undertaken by the *Norfolk* with regard to the three main versions of the journals, and will explore some differences between them. The *Norfolk* sloop was reconstructed in the 1990s and her epic voyage was re-enacted in 1998/1999 with the voyage's journal receiving publication.[60]

---

[55] Mathew Flinders, 'Narrative of an Expedition in the Colonial Sloop Norfolk [...]' [MS 1799], in Bladen, *Hunter: 1796–1799*, Appendix B, pp. 771–818; Matthew Flinders, 'Introduction. Section IV. Part II [...]', in idem, *A Voyage to Terra Australis* [...], vol. 1, London, Printed by W. Bulmer and Co. Cleveland-Row, and Published by G. and W. Nicol, Booksellers to His Majesty, Pall-Mall, 1895, pp. xcv–cciv.

[56] See Bibliography.

[57] David Collins, 'Abstracted from the Journal of Mr. Bass [...]', in idem, *An Account of the English Colony in New South Wales: From Its First Settlement in 1788, to August 1801* [...], vol. 2, London, Printed by A. Strahan, Printers-Street, for T. Cadell Jun. and W. Davies, in The Strand, 1802.

[58] See Bibliography.

[59] Flinders, *Observations*.

[60] Cuthbertson, *In the Wake of Bass and Flinders*.

From a reading of Bass and Flinders's journals it appears that the original hull often leaked and often required caulking of the tilted vessel. The modern *Norfolk* was also built using only wooden planks, but the technology employed in joining them was modern so the hull did not leak and thus, in this respect the re-enactment was not exact. The basic set consisting of gaff main-sail (here man-sail is the name of the sail); the topsel[61] and single large jib[62] spread on an exceptionally long bowsprit, was augmented by a single rectangular sail fixed on a yard.[63] The latter canvas facilitated sailing with a following wind, especially if the commander wanted forward visibility to be unobstructed by a jib. In the original *Norfolk*, the mast – with reference to its first design on Norfolk Island – was re-fixed well forward. It proved to be a sound decision because as a result, the *Norfolk* was able to sail against the wind with the main sail only, when on one occasion described by Flinders her jib was torn to shreds by a gale force wind. In emergencies, for example, when the wind was too slight and/or the tide too strong, the hull could be propelled by long oars, called 'sweeps' by Flinders. A shallow draught and a straight keel[64] enabled safe sailing to be conducted in unknown waters. Generally, the *Norfolk* sailed as close to the North coast of Van Diemen's Land as possible. Three phases of the *Norfolk's* voyage of discovery along this North coast have been chosen to present to the reader.

During the first phase of the *Norfolk's* voyage of discovery along the north coast of Van Diemen's Land and barely three days after entering virgin waters never before visited by a white man's craft, the *Norfolk* discovered Port Dalrymple, later named the River Tamar, the biggest river on the North coast of Van Diemen's Land. Upon entering the river, the *Norfolk* promptly albeit briefly, touched the bottom of the shallow. Luckily, the bottom was soft and the sloop sailed up river undamaged. Bass and Flinders spent an unplanned long period of one month on the river and its environs. They spent a week replenishing their water supplies, surveying, and mapping. The surveying and mapping they did in light of the

---

[61] A sail placed between the mast and the gaff, and on top of the latter.
[62] A sail which is triangular in shape, placed in front of the mast.
[63] A pole fixed perpendicularly to the mast.
[64] The lowest, stabilizing part of the hull.

possible requirements of future settlers. This done, they wanted to sail further westwards along the north coast of Van Diemen's Land. According to Flinders's journal, a succession of gales, one of which drove the *Norfolk* far back eastwards as far as to the wreck of the *Sydney Cove*, prevented them progressing westwards for another three weeks. (Bass's journal is curiously silent about this episode.)

Eventually, they were able to resume their voyage of discovery westwards. Flinders's memoir *Observations...* and his journals (that is in his manuscript and *A Voyage to Terra Australis...*) include an interesting observations concerning the difference in tidal characteristics between those in the vicinity of Port Dalrymple and Cape Portland in the east and Cape Grim in the far west. In particular Flinders in *Observations...*[65] reports the absence of observable tides between Port Dalrymple Eastwards up to Isle Waterhouse. In *A Voyage...*[66] Flinders reports that observations conducted along the coast demonstrated that the tide was practically non-existent between Port Dalrymple Westwards up to the vicinity of Circular Head. However, as mentioned above, Flinders reveals that at both extremities of the north coast of Van Diemen's Land, namely the north-eastern and north-western, 'the tides run strong...'[67]

Another interesting point in regard to the *Norfolk's* voyage happened when her course westwards was blocked by a mass of land which later proved to be an archipelago. According to Flinders's journal, poor visibility and fear of being embayed did not allow the crew to sail slowly and cautiously westwards in order to verify whether there was any outlet in the mass of land. The *Norfolk* was forced to sail north-westward but at some point her progress was blocked by adverse weather conditions, so bad that, as Flinders wrote in one of his journals,[68] he even gave serious consideration to sailing with a gale-force following wind across what is now called Bass Strait, to seek refuge at a port which had been previously discovered by

---

[65] Flinders, *Observations*, p. 33.
[66] Flinders, 'Introduction', pp. clxvii-clxviii.
[67] Flinders, *Observations*, p. 33.
[68] Matthew Flinders, 'Narrative of the Expedition of the Colonial Sloop Norfolk [...]', in Sprod, *Van Diemen's Land Revealed*, p. 46.

Bass in the *Whaleboat*. Flinders's second journal[69] and Bass's journal make no mention of this idea. However, after a day of arduous tacking against the wind generally in a south-easterly direction, on 8 December 1798, the *Norfolk* managed to regain lost ground and anchor in the shadow of what looked to be a peninsula positioned close to the north coast of Van Diemen's Land (later it turned out to be the last but one island [Three Hummock Island] blocking the *Norfolk*'s path from the Bass Strait). At this anchorage, Bass and Flinders ascertained that the existence of a tidal stream of a certain direction was to be the first clue that the fabled strait was close by. Flinders and Bass noticed that in the place they landed there was a low water or ebb tide. Previously, they had become aware that during the afternoon the outflow of tidal water was from the east. This indicated that the inflow of flood water would come from the west. Therefore, this implied that the inflow of sea water from a westerly direction must be free of obstruction from any solid or uninterrupted land. The next day, 9 December 1798, a combination of other clues helped in turning supposition into reality. Firstly, the oceanic swell was felt and Bass and Flinders reacted with elation, hoping that they had reached the goal of their mission. Then the north western tip of Van Diemen's Land – Cape Grim – was seen and all doubts were removed that the *Norfolk* had reached the strait she had been looking for.

However, only a complete circumnavigation of the island of Van Diemen's Land and *Norfolk*'s safe return to Port Jackson would mark the happy end of the mission. Upon Finders's recommendation, Governor Hunter named the passage of water connecting the Tasman Sea and the Indian Ocean, Bass's Straits. At present it is called Bass Strait. The discovery of Bass Strait was the main, albeit not the only achievement of the *Norfolk*'s mission.

The enormous hydrographic and surveying work undertaken by Flinders and at some point augmented by the cooperation of the hydrographer from the *Nautilus*, who worked in tandem with Flinders, resulted in the compilation of excellent maps with the routes taken by the *Tom Thumb I*, *Tom Thumb II*, the *Whaleboat*, the *Francis*, the *Nautilus*, and the *Norfolk* marked on them. One of these was a map of Twofold Bay discovered by Bass's *Whaleboat* and revisited by the *Norfolk* in the company of

---

[69] Flinders, *Voyage to Terra Australis*.

the *Nautilus*. Another map by Flinders worth mentioning was an accurate map of Port Dalrymple (Tamar River) and also the section of the Furneaux Islands where the *Sydney Cove* was wrecked.

Last but not least, the Bass and Flinders's journals partly revealed the destruction of fauna and flora and the habitat of the Aborigines inflicted by the invading white man. The destruction of the seal population occasioned by the crew of the *Nautilus* which, as mentioned above, arrived on the scene of the Furneaux Islands commanded by Charles Bishop in the company of the *Norfolk*, is what I wish to concentrate on.

Let me start with a description of the extraordinary maritime career of Bishop.[70] After he had served for many years in the British Navy, he engaged in merchant ship speculation in sea otter skins with the American Indians. In this he was moderately successful, enabling him to buy a fifty-seven foot long brig: the *Nautilus* in Calucutta. In due course, in Macao, Captain Roger Simpson, at that time from Canton, was added to the enterprise with the understanding that they were to trade for otter skins with the American Indians. After an unbelievable string of bad luck and even worse gales, the *Nautilus*, following a serious battering and in a lamentable state, ended up in Port Jackson, with Bishop almost financially destitute. Bishop, acting on rumours about profitable sealing opportunities existing at the Furneaux Islands, joined the *Norfolk* on her way there. Flinders described in his journals the way Bishop meticulously had prepared his island-based sealing camp close to the *Sydney Cove* wreck. Both Flinders's journal and Bowden's book illustrate clearly the extent of Bishop's slaughter: at first 'he returned to Sydney in December [1798 – KKV] with a cargo of five thousand seal skins of the best quality.'[71] Further we learn that: 'In the Furneaux Group, Bishop completed a most successful venture, obtaining nine thousand seal skins of the first quality.'[72] The volume of hunted seal skins reported above tallies with the supposition of Gill, who writes as follows: 'what really brought about the near extinction of the seals in this area was the value of their skins.'[73]

---

[70] Bowden, *George Bass 1771–1803*, p. 85 and *passim*.
[71] Ibid., p. 87.
[72] Ibid., p. 88.
[73] Cf. Gill, 'Notes on the Sealing Industry', p. 218.

The number of seals which Bishop killed in the Bass Strait in 1798 and 1799, either of best or inferior quality, is unknown. Profits gained from the venture were huge which means volumes of skin must have been likewise. The income derived from this venture contributed to the later purchase of a brig called *Venus* in Britain in 1800, in a joint venture with Bass and other shareholders.[74] Donald Walker demonstrated the savagery of some of the sea elephant hunters: 'Young Sea Elephants at Macquarie Island. "I myself have seen one of these young females shedding abundant tears, whilst one of our sailors, a mean cruel man amused himself by breaking its teeth with the broad end of one of the oars…" – Peron.'[75]

Bass received sick leave and sailed shortly afterwards to England and back to Sydney and to the Pacific and he was never to see his bosom friend again. Flinders, having circumnavigated the continent, which he proposed to be named Australia, in 1804,[76] was imprisoned for nearly six years on the then French island of Mauritius, and died soon after his return to England because of ill health. Another sealer operating legally in Bass Strait in Bass and Flinders's time was William Reed, who, as mentioned above, was the captain of the *Francis* in a number of rescue voyages to the wreck of the *Sydney Cove*. He is reputed to have been the first to sight land later called King Island, located in the middle of the Western gateway of Bass Strait. If this was the case, Reed might be considered to have been the first discoverer of Bass Strait. In Flinders's map there is an oval shape drawn in an interrupted line close to the place where the present-day King Island is located, with an inscription by Flinders: 'Land of considerable extent has been seen in about this situation.'[77] Flinders may have been in receipt of this information concerning the shape and location from Reed.

After Bass, Flinders, Bishop, and Reed had left, Bass Strait was inundated with sealing boats manned by escaped convicts (some of them criminals who on the mainland were called bushrangers and on the islands of

---

[74] Bowden, *George Bass 1771–1803*, pp. 92–94.

[75] Donald Walker, *Beacons of Hope*, Victoria, Australia, Neptune Press Pty Ltd. Belmont, 1981, p. 15.

[76] Vorbrich, *Memoirs of the Forsters* (2011), p. 235.

[77] Inscription on a map: 'A Chart of Bass's Strait Between New South Wales & Van Diemen's Land Explored by Matt.ʷ Flinders, 2ⁿᵈ Lieut. of His Majesty Ship Reliance by order of His Excellency Gov. Hunter, 1798–9'. Publ. London. Copy in Sprod, *Van Diemen's Land Revealed*, inserted map.

Bass Strait – 'straitmen'). They and free sealers working independently who were not 'straitmen', working from ships cleaned the coast of Bass Strait of seals to such an extent that by the beginning of 1800s there was no sealing business left worth talking about. Compare: 'the industry carried on there [Bass Strait – KKV], but on a progressively lesser scale for the next 25 years until by 1832 it was no longer profitable to engage in it.'[78]

The discovery of the gateway guarding Bass Strait from the West took place not long after Bass and Flinders returned to Port Jackson completing their circumnavigation of Van Diemen's Land. A specially equipped discovery ship, the *Lady Nelson*, was apprehended by the British in the Cape of Good Hope and requested to sail from England via Bass Strait to Sydney from West to East, which she promptly did. In December 1800, on the north-western approaches to Bass Strait, Lieutenant James Grant of the *Lady Nelson* discovered a cape he named Cape Albany Otway, later known as Cape Otway. The above-mentioned King Island was named after Governor Philip Gidley King and was given this name by Captain John Black, who sailed in the direction of King Island on board the brig *Harbringer*. However, according to a short sentence written by Governor King, the island had probably already been discovered by a white man before Black, in 1799. James C.H. Gill writes as follows: 'In a marginal note to a letter from Baudin,[79] written in 1802, Governor King stated that Reed discovered King Island in 1798.'[80]

This refers to a Captain Reed sailing on board the sealer schooner *Martha* although I have not seen or heard of any logbook or diary by Reed which would confirm this supposition. The discoveries of James Grant, William Reed, and John Black initiated a sea route for sailing ships from the United Kingdom to Melbourne and Sydney and back via the gateway formed by Cape Otway on the mainland and Cape Wickham on the northern tip of King Island.[81]

---

[78] Cf. Gill, 'Notes on the Sealing Industry', p. 241.

[79] Ibid., p. 230: '[...] the French exploration ship "*Naturaliste*" (Captain Hamelin), the consort of Baudin's "*Geographe*."'

[80] Ibid., p. 226.

[81] This route has been written about in more detail in: Krzysztof K. Vorbrich, 'Plot and Maritime Metaphors in Sygurd Wiśniowski's Narrative Tales from Mid-19th Century New Zealand and Australia *Ten Years* [...], *Tikera* [...], and *Little Lights* [...] in the Perspective of Joseph Conrad's

There were three phases of passenger carrying services in the period between the First Fleet's arrival in Botany Bay and the wrecking of the ship named *Loch Ard* just east of Cape Otway,[82] which for all intents and purposes marked the end of a canvas propelled passenger service from the UK to Melbourne and Sydney. During the first phase almost approximately 160,000 exiles were carried to the mainland of Australia, as well as to the islands of Tasmania and Norfolk Island.[83] The second phase coincided with the decade of the gold rush in Australia.[84] The third phase mainly brought emigrants, entrepreneurs, scientists, and members of the ruling class to Australia.[85] Each of these phases were characterised by their own wrecking casualties.

At first, captains sailed via Bass Strait very cautiously and wrecking cases were relatively few. Then, haste to reach the destination (time equals money) began to take precedence over the safety and lives of the passengers, resulting in the number of wrecks and associated deaths reaching epic proportions. Even the construction of lighthouses at great human and financial cost at key points along the approaches to Bass Strait, including Cape Otway and Cape Wickham, did not entirely improve the situation. Some extremely tragic wrecks occurred due to human error and ironically, precisely because lighthouses were there. King Island with its western coast, in particular, open to the roaring forties (present-day nautical term), witnessed or rather was the cause of some sixty wrecks[86] and was granted the name of 'graveyard of ships'.

Leaving aside exiles, criminals and gold diggers, not all entrepreneurs who sailed to Australia are remembered by posterity well. A case in point being Benjamin Boyd, who arrived in Sydney in 1842 and who at one time was based in Twofold Bay and the owner of passenger shipping lines connecting the Australian mainland with Tasmania; moreover, he was the

---

and the Forsters' Oeuvre', *Polish AngloSaxon Studies*, vol. 17, 2014, pp. 5–50; idem, 'Introduction: Maritime Aspects in the First Two Chapters of Sygurd Wiśniowski's Book *Światełka w Ciemnym Kraju* (Little Lights in the Dark Country)', *Polish AngloSaxon Studies*, vol. 18, 2015, pp. 79–88.

[82] Cf. Vorbrich, 'Introduction'.

[83] Hughes, *Fatal Shore*, p. 2.

[84] This started in 1851 and the first gold mining site was called 'Ophir'. Cf. Vorbrich, 'Plot and Maritime Metaphors'; idem, 'Introduction'.

[85] For these phases see Vorbrich, 'Plot and Maritime Metaphors'; idem, 'Introduction'.

[86] Cf. Walker, *Beacons of Hope*.

largest landholder in New South Wales, and eventually he had to declare bankruptcy. At a certain point when he was still financially secure, Boyd was engaged in blackbirding, namely bringing indigenous people forcibly from the South Seas to work on his plantations. Finally, the saddest aspect of Bass and Flinders's discovery of Bass Strait and ensuing 'civilisation' of the island of Tasmania, was genocide.

Compare the Tasmanian newspaper article from 1931:

> Those fifteen aborigines were all who remained of at least several thousand of them who roamed the country in tribes […] the barbaric proposal to transfer them to the wind swept Flinders Island […] Their doom had been sealed before 1856, and the death of the last male thirteen years later, followed, at an interval of seven years, by the last survivor of her race, closed the story.[87]

The fact was that at some point, all the indigenous people of Tasmania were forcibly deported by people from the UK to a small island (Flinders Island) nearby, where they all died out from sheer distress. So ended the 40,000-year-epoch of Aborigine presence in Tasmania.

Conclusion

The Aborigines have inhabited present-day Australia for 60,000 years and inhabited present day Tasmania for 40,000. There are still pure blood Aborigines in Australia, but pure blood Aborigines in Tasmania died out. The discovery of Bass Strait had both positive and negative aspects in the long 18th century for all anglophones. To the positive side, belong the increase in strategic value of both Melbourne and Sydney and the increased ease of transportation and communication which took place from and to the United Kingdom and between the Australian colonies themselves. To the negative side, belong the loss of life and property caused by the inherent navigational difficulties of the waters of Bass Strait and by the actions of swashbuckling captains who put profit before the safety of their

---

[87] Historicus, 'Tale of Tasmania', p. 8.

passengers. Others include, indirectly, the almost complete loss of habitat for some fur animals and their decimation. Another negative that the discovery of Bass Strait and the resulting ease of communication brought about was that it enticed a certain type of unscrupulous entrepreneur who was keen on introducing to Australia the enterprise of blackbirding. The saddest part of all was that the discovery of Bass Strait by anglophone people brought about, however indirectly, and only in a few decades, the complete annihilation of the Tasmanian Aborigine population which had endured for 40,000 years.

Notices to maps

Maps were processed in the PC computer from the copies of the originals and using the simple tracing and eliminating software. Only the coast line were generated, the rest was eliminated.

The originals were as follows:

For maps 1 and 2:

'Transport. Roads & Maritime Services. New South Wales Government.

Grid datum is the Geodetic Datum of Australia – 1994, which is approximately equivalent to WGS-84.

Map generated by MapWizard on 19 October 2016 by Mitch Holland. Map Printed November 2016.'

Map 1: Sydney Coastal Area – Map 9.

Map 2: Eden Coastal Area – Map 14.

Map 3: 'A Chart of Bass's Strait Between New South Wales and Van Diemen's Land Explored by Matt.^w Flinders 2nd Lieut. of His Majesty Ship Reliance by order of His Excellency Gov. Hunter, 1798–9', in Matthew Flinders, *Observations on the Coasts of Van Diemen's Land on Bass's Strait and its Islands and on Part of the Coasts of New South Wales by Matthew Flinders*, Sydney, D.S. Ford, 1946, inset after p. 58. A copy of the fold-in map in Dan Sprod (ed.), *Van Diemen's Land Revealed: Flinders and Bass and Their Circumnavigation of the Island in the Colonial Sloop Norfolk 1798–1799*, Hobart, Blubber Head Press, 2009.

Note:

As a rule tracks of the Bass's and Flinders's voyages of discovery were not depicted due to the scale.

Maps were processed by Krzysztof K. Vorbrich and Bartosz Mielnikow.

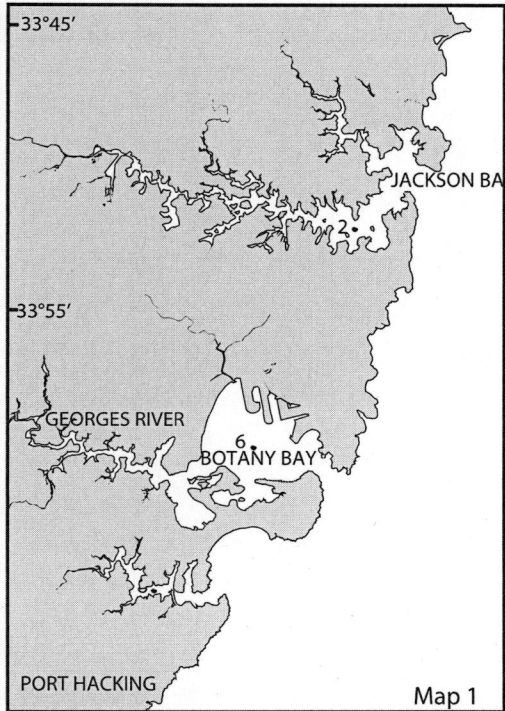

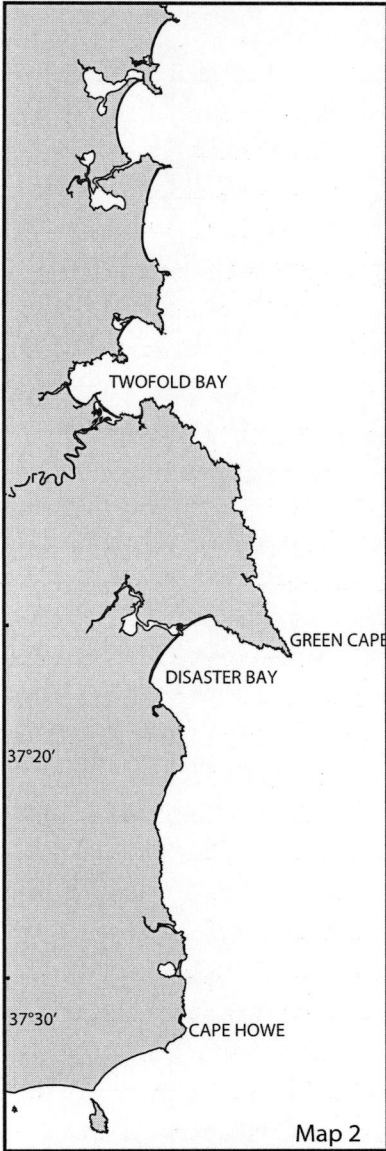

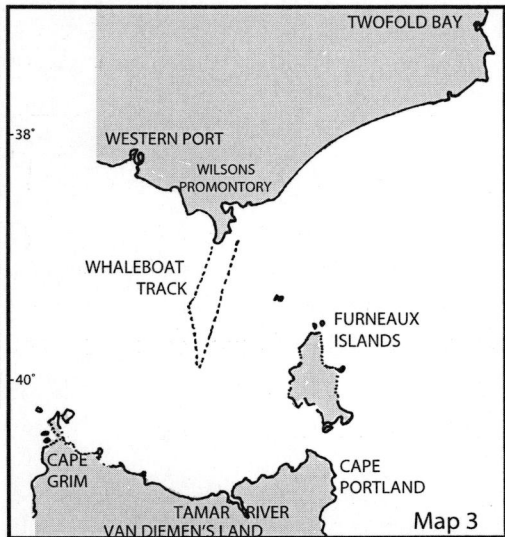

Bibliography

Anonymous, *The Sydney Morning Herald*, Tuesday, 14 August 1855, p. 3.

Anonymous, 'Narrative of the Shipwreck of Captain Hamilton and the Crew of the Sydney Cove', reprinted from the *Asiatic Mirror*, Calcutta, [part 1:] 27 December 1797, [part 2:] 10 January 1798, in F.M. Bladen (ed.), *Historical Records of New South Wales*, vol. 3: *Hunter: 1796–1799*, Sydney, 1895, Appendix A, pp. 757–768.

Anonymous, 'Our First Ship: The Francis: A Sloop in Frame', *Australian Town and Country Journal*, Saturday, 3 April 1897, p. 49.

Anonymous, 'Our Second Ship: The Norfolk: Hard Times', *Australian Town and Country Journal*, Saturday, 29 May 1897, p. 20.

Bass, George, 'The Discovery of Bass Strait: Mr. Bass's Journal in the Whaleboat, between the 3rd of December, 1797, and 25th of February, 1798. Voyage in the Whaleboat' [MS 1799], in F.M. Bladen (ed.), *Historical Records of New South Wales*, vol. 3: *Hunter: 1796–1799*, Sydney 1895, pp. 312–333.

Bass, George, 'Discovery of Coal. [Extract.] George Bass to Lieutenant-Colonel Paterson (Banks Papers)' [MS 1799], in F.M. Bladen (ed.), *Historical Records of New South Wales*, vol. 3: *Hunter: 1796–1799*, Sydney 1895, pp. 289–290.

Bass, George, 'Journal describing Two-Fold Bay in New South Wales, Furneaux's Islands in Bass's Strait and the coast and harbours of Van Diemmen's Land, from notes made on board the Colonial Sloop *Norfolk* in 1798 and 1799', in Dan Sprod (ed.), *Van Diemen's Land Revealed: Flinders and Bass and Their Circumnavigation of the Island in the Colonial Sloop Norfolk 1798–1799*, Hobart, Blubber Head Press, 2009, pp. 71–106.

Beaglehole, John Cawte (ed.), *The Journals of Captain James Cook on His Voyages of Discovery. Four Volumes and Portfolio. (Edited from the Original Manuscripts)*, vol. 2: *The Voyage of the Resolution and Adventure 1772–1775* (Hakluyt Society Works, Extra Series, no. 35), Cambridge, Cambridge University Press for the Hakluyt Society, 1961.

Beaglehole, John Cawte (ed.), *The Journals of Captain James Cook on His Voyages of Discovery. Four Volumes and Portfolio. (Edited from the Original Manuscripts)*, vol. 3: *The Voyage of the Resolution and Discovery 1776–1780. Part One* (Hakluyt Society Works, Extra Series, no. 36a), Cambridge, Cambridge University Press for the Hakluyt Society, 1967.

Beaglehole, John Cawte (ed.), *The Journals of Captain James Cook on His Voyages of Discovery. Four Volumes and Portfolio. (Edited from the Original Manuscripts)*, vol. 3: *The Voyage of the Resolution and Discovery 1776–1780. Part Two* (Hakluyt

Society Works, Extra Series, no. 36b), Cambridge, Cambridge University Press for the Hakluyt Society, 1967.

Beaglehole, John Cawte (ed.), *The Journals of Captain James Cook on His Voyages of Discovery. Four Volumes and Portfolio. (Edited from the Original Manuscripts)*, vol. 1: *The Voyage of the Endeavour 1768–1771* (Hakluyt Society Works, Extra Series, no. 34), Cambridge, Cambridge University Press for the Hakluyt Society, 1968.

Bladen F.M., 'Introduction', in F.M. Bladen (ed.), *Historical Records of New South Wales*, vol. 3: *Hunter: 1796–1799*, Sydney 1895, pp. xxix–xxviii.

Bowden, Keith Macrae, *George Bass 1771–1803: His Discoveries Romantic Life and Tragic Disappearance*, London, Melbourne, and Wellington, Geofrey Cumberlege Oxford University Press, 1952.

Bowden, Keith (ed.), *Matthew Flinders' Narrative of Tom Thumb's Cruise to Canoe Rivulet*, Brighton, Vic., Australia, South Eastern Historical Association, 1985.

Collins, David, 'Abstracted from the Journal of Mr. Bass. By Lieutenant-Colonel Collins, of The Royal Marines, Late Judge Advocate and Secretary of The Colony', in David Collins, *An Account of the English Colony in New South Wales: From Its First Settlement in 1788, To August 1801: With Remarks on the Dispositions, Customs, Manners, etc. of the Native Inhabitants of That Country. To Which Are Added, Some Particulars of New Zealand; Compiled, by Permission, From the Mss. of Lieutenant--Governor King. And an Account of the Voyage Performed by Captain Flinders and Mr. Bass; by Which the Existence of a Strait Separating Van Diemen's Land From the Continent of New Holland Was Ascertained. Abstracted From the Journal of Mr. Bass. By Lieutenant-Colonel Collins, of the Royal Marines, Late Judge Advocate and Secretary of the Colony. Illustrated by Engravings*, vol. 2, London, Printed By A. Strahan, Printers-Street, For T. Cadell Jun. and W. Davies, in The Strand, 1802.

Crotty, Martin and David Andrew Roberts, '14,000 BP on Being Alone: The Isolation of the Tasmanians', in Martin Crotty and David Andrew Roberts (eds.), *Turning Points in Australian History*, Sydney, University of New South Wales Press, 2009.

Cuthbertson, Bern, *In the Wake of Bass and Flinders: 200 Years on: The Story of the Re-Enactment Voyages 200 Years on in the Whaleboat Elizabeth and the Replica Sloop Norfolk to Celebrate the Bicentenary of the Voyages of George Bass and Matthew Flinders*, Sandy Bay, Tas., Bern and Jan Cuthbertson, 2001.

Fedorowicz, Zygmunt, *Zoologia w Gdańsku w stuleciach XVII i XVIII* (Memorabilia Zoologica, vol. 19), Wrocław, Zakład Narodowy im. Ossolińskich, Wydawnictwo Polskiej Akademii Nauk, 1968.

Flinders, Matthew, 'Introduction. Section IV. Part II. (Boat expeditions of Bass and Flinders. Discoveries of Bass to the Southwards of Port Jackson; of Flinders; and of Flinders and Bass'), in Matthew Flinders, *A Voyage to Terra Australis; Undertaken for the Purpose of Completing the Discovery of That Vast Country, and Prosecuted in the Years 1801, 1802, and 1803, in His Majesty's Ship the Investigator, and Subsequently in the Armed Vessel Porpoise and Cumberland Schooner. With an Account of the Shipwreck of the Porpoise, Arrival of the Cumberland at Mauritius, and Imprisonment of the Commander During Six Years and a Half in that Island. By Matthew Flinders, Commander of the Investigator. In Two Volumes, With an Atlas*, vol. 1, London, Printed by W. Bulmer and Co. Cleveland-Row, and Published by G. and W. Nicol, Booksellers to His Majesty, Pall-Mall, 1814, pp. xcv–cciv.

Flinders, Matthew, *A Voyage to Terra Australis; Undertaken for the Purpose of Completing the Discovery of That Vast Country, and Prosecuted in the Years 1801, 1802, and 1803, in His Majesty's Ship the Investigator, and Subsequently in the Armed Vessel Porpoise and Cumberland Schooner. With an Account of the Shipwreck of the Porpoise, Arrival of the Cumberland at Mauritius, and Imprisonment of the Commander During Six Years and a Half in that Island. By Matthew Flinders, Commander of the Investigator. In Two Volumes, With an Atlas*, vol. 1, London, Printed by W. Bulmer and Co. Cleveland-Row, and Published by G. and W. Nicol, Booksellers to His Majesty, Pall-Mall, 1814.

Flinders, Matthew, 'Narrative of an Expedition in the Colonial sloop Norfolk, from Port Jackson, through the Strait which Separates Van Diemen's Land From New Holland, and From Thence Round the South Cape Back to Port Jackson, Completing the Circumnavigation of the Former Island, with Some Remarks on the Coasts and Harbours, by Matthew Flinders, 2nd l't, H.M.S. Reliance' [MS 1799], in F.M. Bladen (ed.), *Historical Records of New South Wales*, vol. 3: *Hunter: 1796–1799*, Sydney 1895, Appendix B, pp. 769–818.

Flinders, Matthew, *Observations on the Coasts of Van Diemen's Land on Bass's Strait and its Islands and on Part of the Coasts of New South Wales*, Sydney, D.S. Ford, 1946 [reprint of ed. published in 1801].

Flinders, Matthew, 'Narrative of the Expedition of the Colonial Sloop Norfolk, From Port Jackson Through the Strait Which Separates Van Diemen's Land from New Holland, and From Thence Round the South Cape Back to Port Jackson, Completing the Circumnavigation of the Former Island. With Some Remarks on the Coasts and Harbours' [MS 1799], in Dan Sprod (ed.), *Van Diemen's Land Revealed:*

Flinders and Bass and Their Circumnavigation of the Island in the Colonial Sloop Norfolk 1798–1799, Hobart, Blubber Head Press, 2009, pp. 23–71.

French, Jackie, *Let the Land Speak: A History of Australia: How the Land Created Our Nation*, Sydney, Harper Collins, 2013.

Gill, James C.H., 'Notes on the Sealing Industry of Early Australia', *Journal of the Royal Historical Society of Queensland*, vol. 8, issue 2, 1967, pp. 218–245.

Historicus, 'Tale of Tasmania', *Voice* (Hobart, Tasmania), 14 November 1931, p. 8.

Hughes, Robert, *The Fatal Shore: A History of the Transportation of Convicts to Australia, 1787–1868*, London, Vintage Books, 2003.

Hunter, John, *An Historical Journal of the Transactions at Port Jackson and Norfolk Island*, London, Printed for John Stockdale, Piccadilly, 1793.

Hunter, John, 'Governor Hunter to Secretary Nepean. Sydney, New South Wales, 3rd Sept., 1798', in F.M. Bladen (ed.), *Historical Records of New South Wales*, vol. 3: *Hunter: 1796–1799*, Sydney 1895, pp. 474–475.

Levis, David, *The Voyaging Stars: Secrets of the Pacific Island Navigators*, London, Collins, 1978.

McDonald, W.G., *The First Footers: Bass and Flinders in Illawarra, 1796–1797*, Wollongong, NSW, Illawarra Historical Society, 1975.

Mackaness, George, 'Introduction', in Matthew Flinders, *Observations on the Coasts of Van Diemen's Land on Bass's Strait and its Islands and on Part of the Coasts of New South Wales*, Sydney, D.S. Ford, 1946 [reprint of ed. published in 1801], pp. 5–12.

Morgan, Kenneth, *Matthew Flinders, Maritime Explorer of Australia*, London and New York, Bloomsbury Publishing, 2016.

Nash, Michael, *Cargo for the Colony: The Wreck of the Merchant Ship Sydney Cove*, Sydney, Braxus Press, 1996.

Scott, Ernest, *The Life of Captain Matthew Flinders*, Cambridge, Cambridge University Press, 2011 [1st ed. 1914].

Sprod, Dan, 'Flinders and Bass: Coastal Explorations South of Port Jackson, 1795–1798', in Dan Sprod (ed.), *Van Diemen's Land Revealed: Flinders and Bass and Their Circumnavigation of the Island in the Colonial Sloop Norfolk 1798–1799*, Hobart, Blubber Head Press, 2009, pp. 6–9.

Sprod, Dan, 'George Bass and the Discovery of Western Port, 3 December 1797 – 25 February 1798', in Dan Sprod (ed.), *Van Diemen's Land Revealed: Flinders and Bass and Their Circumnavigation of the Island in the Colonial Sloop Norfolk 1798–1799*, Hobart, Blubber Head Press, 2009, pp. 10–17.

Sprod, Dan, 'Matthew Flinders's Voyage to the Wreck of the Sydney Cove in the Schooner Francis, 1 February – 9 March 1798', in Dan Sprod (ed.), *Van Diemen's Land Revealed: Flinders and Bass and Their Circumnavigation of the Island in the Colonial Sloop Norfolk 1798–1799*, Hobart, Blubber Head Press, 2009, pp. 17–22.

Sprod, Dan (ed.), *Van Diemen's Land Revealed: Flinders and Bass and Their Circumnavigation of the Island in the Colonial Sloop Norfolk 1798–1799*, Hobart, Blubber Head Press, 2009.

Targowski, Andrew, *Informing and Civilization*, Santa Rosa, CA, Informing Science Press, 2016.

Vorbrich, Krzysztof K., *Memoirs of the Forsters – the Polish-Born Participants of Cook's Expedition: The Same Voyage, Worlds Apart – Excerpts*, vol. 2: *History of European Oceanic Exploration Discussed in the Forsters' Narrative Writings. Selected Issues*, Poznań, Wydawnictwo Naukowe Contact, 2010.

Vorbrich Krzysztof K., *Memoirs of the Forsters – the Polish-Born Participants of Cook's Expedition: The Same Voyage, Worlds Apart*, extended ed., Poznań, Contact Scientific Publishing House, 2011.

Vorbrich, Krzysztof K., 'Three Memoirs of the Forsters – the Polish-Born Participants of Cook's Second Voyage', *Polish AngloSaxon Studies*, vol. 14–15, 2011, pp. 7–47.

Vorbrich, Krzysztof K., 'Some Geographical and Geological Aspects in Johann Forster's Posthumous *Journals*… Controversy – HMS *Resolution* Memoirs Never Refined', *Quaestiones Geographicae*, vol. 31, issue 3, 2012, pp. 89–105.

Vorbrich, Krzysztof K., 'Plot and Maritime Metaphors in Sygurd Wiśniowski's Narrative Tales from Mid-19th Century New Zealand and Australia *Ten Years* […], *Tikera* […], and *Little Lights* […] in the Perspective of Joseph Conrad's and the Forsters' Oeuvre', *Polish AngloSaxon Studies*, vol. 17, 2014, pp. 5–50.

Vorbrich, Krzysztof K., 'Introduction: Maritime Aspects in the First Two Chapters of Sygurd Wiśniowski's Book *Światełka w Ciemnym Kraju* (Little Lights in the Dark Country)', *Polish AngloSaxon Studies*, vol. 18, 2015, pp. 79–88.

Walker, Donald, *Beacons of Hope*, Victoria, Australia, Neptune Press Pty. Ltd. Belmont, 1981.

Cecylia Małgorzata Dziewięcka

'Atenisi Institute for Critical Education in the South Pacific The Kingdom of Tonga

Pauca sed matura

'Atenisi Institute is located in the Kingdom of Tonga it was founded by Futa Helu in 1962. It comprises: 'Atenisi University and 'Atenisi Foundation for the Performing Arts.

Futa Helu was born on a pacific island of Foa in 1934. His family sold copra to send him to Newington College in Australia. He studied physics, mathematics, literature and philosophy for eight years but never completed degree. After his return to Tonga Futa formed an Institute for People, in Nuku'alofa, a night school providing education for civil servants and gave it the Tongan name for Athens – 'Atenisi. It evolved into the high school.

'In the 1960s there were not many high schools in Tonga, and the few that there were catered to either an economic or academic elite. To fill the gap, 'Atenisi's high school' starts to offer 'inexpensive and innovative education. [...] academic standards were high; for example, whereas' government 'schools settled for the modest New Zealand syllabus, 'Atenisi choose the more challenging syllabus'[1] of Australia.

---

[1] 'Atenisi Instutute, Wikipedia, https://en.wikipedia.org/wiki/%CA%BBAtnisi_Institute [accessed 21 October 2017].

The 1970s and 1980s the 'Atenisi had over 800 students; 'however, enrolment began to fall in the 1990s in the face of competition from more than a dozen high schools established by the government or religious organizations. By 2005 school fees were no longer sufficient to cover costs'[2] and 'Atenisi was forced to close by the end of 2009. It reopen two years later. 'Atenisi University is recognised by many countries, it is also accredited in Poland.

> Since the late 1980s, the 'Atenisi Foundation for the Performing Arts has been a component of the Institute, with a mission to preserve the music and dance of traditional Tongan culture, as well as train musicians in European classical music. The Foundation is regarded in Tonga as a national treasure. Its star soprano, 'Atolomake Helu, has performed at Sydney and Auckland Town Halls. For a time 'Atenisi Foundation has toured overseas, performing European classical and operatic excerpts along with traditional Tongan *faiva*.[3]

The 'Atenisi 'was unique in being the only privately funded university in the South Pacific islands, and therefore autonomous from any church or government. The advantage was that the university could freely train critical thought, rather than compel students to conform to bureaucratic obedience or religious dogma.'[4]

Students: *We learn, we have rights to say what we like, do what we want best. Futa knows how to motivate students to study.*[5]

'The disadvantage was'[6] that the university's 'budget was solely supported by modest tuition fees.'[7]

> Because the university regarded method of thought to be its pedagogical priority, philosophy was considered its most important course; facility with the English language and appreciation of English literature was a second key objective. In

---

[2] Ibid.
[3] Ibid.
[4] Ibid.
[5] *Tongan Ark*, the documentary by Paul Janman, PublicFilms, New Zealand, 2012.
[6] 'Atenisi Instutute, Wikipedia.
[7] Ibid.

addition, the university offered core courses in the natural sciences, social sciences, arts, and humanities. Because of its reputation for rigour, most 'Atenisi University students found it relatively easy to obtain scholarships to graduate schools in New Zealand, Australia, and the United States.[8]

Interview with Futa Helu and the 'Atenisi's lecturers from the documentary *Tongan Ark*

'In August 2012 a film on Futa Helu's life and the history of 'Atenisi was screened at the New Zealand International Film Festival. The documentary, *Tongan Ark*, was created, directed, and photographed by Paul Janman,[9] a New Zealand 'anthropologist and former 'Atenisi instructor.'[10]

...and let them see how Futa thinks:

Futa: *First education for criticism, second education for submissiveness. There is no third one. It is why I now tell my students in the last two years when I get older I will go to the old Greek business as I get more and more understanding how the world thinks, how the things are bind together.*

Dr M. Horowitz: *'Atenisi Institute by any rational measure should not exist in Tonga. The idea of an education without any bond of religious orientation or any sponsorship, in opposition to Tongan government over forty years survived.*

Sisi'uno Helu: *Forty years ago my father launched a university here at 'Atenisi. He believed that students should be taught how – not what – to think. He believed the pillars of classical education – philosophy, mathematics, history, literature, and music – remain the most effective facilitators of critical analysis.*

Dr T. Opeti, ex-'Atenisi student: *Students come from small independent plantations. Futa's desire was to combine the western commercial culture values with own cooperative culture. Not carrier objective, the main object of education is how to open students' mind and let them see how Futa thinks.*

---

[8] Ibid.

[9] Ibid.

[10] Ibid.

Nowadays students are not interested in ancient Greeks, but in graduate in cash subjects.[11]

The early years of the university, its emphasis on philosophy was popular with Tonga's independent farmers: their sons might return to their modest plantations and display classical learning at weekend *faikava* (traditional *kava* circles). Yet with growing pressure for vocational success among Tonga's urban middle class, only the most talented students remain attracted to 'Atenisi's classical credo. This has led to a decline in enrolment which limits the small university that Futa Helu built.[12]

Futa in 2009: *'Atenisi is the poorest in the South Pacific, but very brave, it has classical orientation and it strives for quality in everything it does.*
Futa: *Many are drop outs, but we have to work with what we have. The graduates of 'Atenisi have good foundation in scientific methods, in analysing, ethical concept, they reject slavery and falsity, and they develop reliable opinion. I called them 'heavy duty graduates'. Some of these drop outs graduated in 'Atenisi became successful businessmen, university teachers overseas, even clergymen and opera singers.*
Dr T. Opeti, ex-'Atenisi student: *Philosophy: Criticism is what 'Atenisi was very strong, lots of students that time opening my mind, become critical the way see things clear. I am critical the way I see the things, because once you understand the things you are free, you are free man. Adolescence.*
Futa: *I think the freedom reopens us the toleration of publicity, of controversy, be the crown of achievement of society's social and political development.*
Futa: *Glorification of technocracy, legitimization of financial speculation. Look at computer: those who study computer they only have empty knowledge because technology will continue to change. That is why we search for performance, because performance is truth.*[13]
Maxima of 'Atenisi: Learning freedom at the 'Atenisi, is not to follow rules of any.

---

[11] *Tongan Ark.*
[12] 'Atenisi Instutute, Wikipedia.
[13] *Tongan Ark.*

Futa: *Education for criticism applies to everything: there are two points I made: there are not taboo. Taboo is a cover for special demands. Taboo of course can be beneficial in some cases, but it is really destructive to this cowboys. The chiefs put taboo on us. Why certain things not allowed to certain group of people? This way question classes of society. See taboo in religion, tools for control in chief's hands.*[14]

Futa Helu died in 2010.

What and why is thought at the 'Atenisi University?

We teach subjects that are in the core program of the University, and additionally two other own subjects according to our proposal. I, Dr C.M. Dziewięcka, lecture:

1. Civilizations through Time

Objectives: Increase knowledge with understanding; develop imagination; develop a more sophisticated way of thinking, talking about cultural experience; practice the research method of storytelling; learn new words.

2. World Cultural and Natural Heritage of Outstanding Universal Value – UNESCO Conservation and Protection

Objectives: to know more; stimulate enthusiasm of the unique sites of the World and in own country; awake in students respect, responsibility and appreciation of the nature and human expressions across the World.

3. Geography Foundation

Objectives: Geography covers all aspects of Human life; to study geography means to want to know, understand and appreciate Life; to become Geographer means to know, understand and appreciate Life, and to help everyone and everything to live this way.

---

[14] Ibid.

Who are we, 'Atenisi's lecturers

We are lecturers from all over the world. We are attracted to the 'Atenisi Institute not by money but by its idealism, Futa's love for Heraclitus philosophy, Socratic critical thinking, freedom of methods, and the remoteness of Tonga.

The University at 'Atenisi Institute proposes own core subjects and additionally two of lecturer's choice subjects. Students choose the subjects according to their interest. They study the subject for one semester or do whole course. They can study without aiming degree or with intention to graduate. They can be the high schools leavers, drop outs or simply people of any age, nationality or religion interested in knowing, understanding and in free expression.

'Atenisi follows Heraclitus (435BC–475BC) thinking:

1. Everything change and nothing stands still.
2. You could not step twice into the same river.
3. The people must fight for its law as for its walls.
4. Character is destiny.
5. Much learning does not teach understanding.
6. If you do not expect the unexpected you will never find it, for it is not to be reached by search or trail.
7. Good character is not formed in a week or a month. It is created little by little, day by day. Protracted and patient effort is needed to develop good character.
8. The sun is new each day.

Core curricula

There are separate Core Curricula for Arts and Science degrees.

ARTS
English 4 courses
Philosophy 2 courses
Foreign Language 2 courses

Basic Mathematics 1 course
Mathematics 1course
Tongan Dance 1 course

SCIENCE
English 4 courses
Philosophy 2 courses
Foreign Language 2 courses
Science 2 courses
Mathematics 1 course
Tongan Dance 1 course

DEGREES
Both undergraduate and postgraduate study programs are available at the University.
In undergraduate studies four programs are available:
- Associate of Arts (A.A.)
- Associate of Science (A.S.)
- Bachelor of Arts (B.A.)
- Bachelor of Science (B.S.)
In postgraduate studies two programs are available:
- Master of Arts (M.A.)
- Doctor of Philosophy (Ph.D.)

Note of the 'Atenisi's Director:

To prospective under- or postgraduates [...] to Tonga's working people ... to visiting consultants and scholars from overseas, we say talitali lelei: take advantage of 'Atenisi's B.A., B.S., and postgraduate programmes, 3000-volume library, Tongan dance and language instruction, vocal and instrumental coaching, and free evening lectures.

At age 40, 'Atenisi remains wise and innovative. There's simply nothing in the Pacific like it.[15]

---

[15] Message from the Director, 'Atenisi Institute website, https://www.atenisi.edu.to/ [accessed 21 October 2017].

The University at 'Atenisi Institute continues to focus on preparing Tonga's most talented undergraduates for postgraduate study overseas. Since late 2015 'Atenisi graduates have assumed a:
- salaried research assistantship at Northern Illinois University outside Chicago, U.S.;
- fellowship at the University of the Ryukyus in Okinawa, Japan; and
- scholarship at the University of Wroclaw in Poland.

The superior performance of these graduates recently led the Faculty of Arts at the University of Auckland to renew its assessment of 'Atenisi undergraduate degrees as equivalent to UA degrees. This evaluation guarantees prompt postgraduate placement upon admission to a postgraduate programme at UA. Over the past few years 'Atenisi has additionally developed Master of Arts programmes in Communication, Cinematography, and Marine Science.

From the Newsletter No 16 of the Embassy of Republic of Poland in New Zealand, December 2015:

Student from Tonga in Wroclaw: Salise Andrew Faivailo is currently undertaking a Polish language course that will allow him to study geography and music at the University of Wroclaw. This is the first representative of the Tonga studying in Poland. The arrival and study of the student at the School of the Polish language and Culture for Foreigners in Wroclaw was possible greatly through the efforts of Cecylia Dziewięcka PhD, who in 2014 worked as a lecturer at the 'Atenisi University in Tonga.

The first and the only student from Tonga, Salise Andrew Faivailo completed One Year Preparatory Course, at the School of Polish Language and Culture for Foreigners University of Wroclaw, in academic year 2015/2016, and received the Certificate of Completion. The subject of his further study is geography.

Bibliography

Dyck, Dieter, *The Tongan: A South Pacific Adventure*, Auckland, D. Ling Publishing Ltd, 2017.

The Journal of Pacific Studies, vol. 17, no. 3, 1994.

Ledyard, Paricia, *Friendly Islands*, Pacific Publications, Sydney 1974.

Newsletter No 16 of the Embassy of Republic of Poland in New Zealand, December 2015.

Tongan Ark, the documentary by Paul Janman, PublicFilms, New Zealand, 2012.

Websites

'Atenisi Institute, Wikipedia, https://en.wikipedia.org/wiki/%CA%BBAtenisi_Institute [accessed 21 October 2017].

'Atenisi Institute documents, newsletters, https://www.atenisi.edu.to [accessed 21 October 2017].

'Królestwo Tonga. Raj na Ziemi', http://dziendobry.tvn.pl/wideo,2064,n/krolestwo-tonga-raj-na-ziemi,212645.html [accessed 21 October 2017].

Others

Own observations, interviews, conversations, work as lecturer, traveller.

'Atenisi Institute (photo C.M. Dziewięcka)

A flooded street of the capital of Tonga after a cyclone (archive of C.M. Dziewięcka)

Stonehenge of the Pacific – Ha'amonga 'a Maui Trilithon of Tonga
(archive of C.M. Dziewięcka)

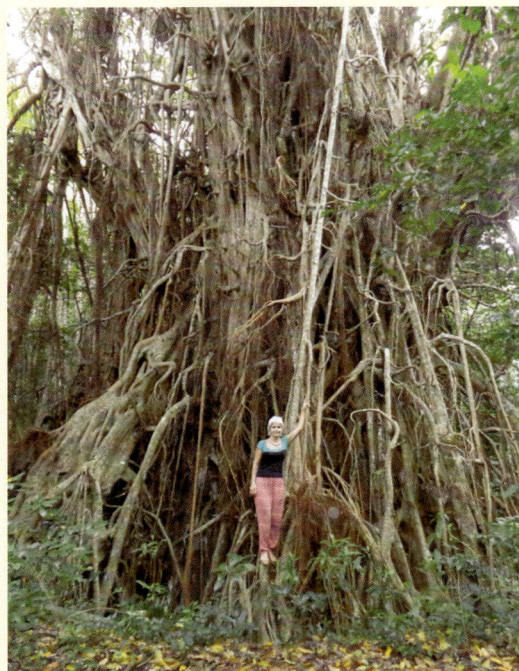

An eight-hundred-year-old fig-tree
on the island of 'Eua in Tonga
(archive of C.M. Dziewięcka)

Piotr Grzybowski

Selected Problems
of Wastes Treatment in Tuvalu

Tuvalu is a young independent country placed on few islands at Equator in the middle of the Pacific Ocean. Poland initiated common relations with Tuvalu. The knowledge about the problems that face this island country, about the life on the islands and real needs was poor by now. To get better understanding about the situation a Technical Mission was organized by the ambassador Zbigniew Gniatkowski. This Mission took place from January 30 to February 2, 2017, and was held in the capital city Vaiaku at the atoll Funafuti. Because of the short stay on the island only some aspect were recognized in detailes. In this paper only some of those problems dealing with the environment protection in Funafuti are presented.

The population of Funafuti is about 5,000 citizens. The consumption goods are being imported to the island mostly from Australia. On the island there is no incineration plant and the package wastes are being collected in the city and transported to the north end of the atoll to the dumpsite. Wastes are being placed there in the holes dug up in the ground and covered later with a layer of the coral soil. In Figure 1 is a picture of the wastes collected at dumpsite.

Such a practice is a cheap method to get rid of the solid wastes. Unfortunately it can be expected that the leaking of impurities from the wastes into the water arises. The soil of the atoll comprises of coral gravel and coral sand and is easily penetrated by the waters. Besides, the atoll itself is elevated only about one meter over the surrounding sea level and strong storms can wash off the wastes from the location and spread them into the inner lagoon. The wastes pieces, specially the floating ones, can drift and reach further the coast and beaches of the whole atoll. A good practice according the solid wastes continued since few years on the island is selective collection of the wastes like glass and metals. These wastes are being separated at homes and from other sources and are being collected in the special containers. They are later exported once a year to the recycling plants overseas because there are no such facilities in Tuvalu. A small local company which deals with these wastes has some incomes. There is no market for selected wastes on the island and the effectiveness of the segregation and collection depends mostly on ecological education of the local community.

On the atoll there is no waste water treatment plant and all the liquid waste reach finally the surrounding waters. Even few ecological toilets, as shown in Figure 2, constructed with the help of foreign organizations, does not play their role efficiently because of the lack of final waste purification step. They are comfortable in use but the wastes from them finally get into the sea. Besides of the liquid wastes produced by the local population there are also farmed pigs and chickens. The pigs are being fed with the imported food and with the local coconuts. On the island there are no fields nor farms where any crops could be produced. Even house gardens are limited in number because of lack of appropriate soil for plants cultivation. Some attempts to produce vegetables have been undertaken but still on a limited scale. There is no demand for manure. The animal droppings are being later washed into the sea also with the use of sea water. A picture of such a simple construction pigpen on the lagoon coast is shown in Figure 3.

The consequence of such situation is marching eutrophication of the inner lagoon waters. The visible result of this eutrophication process are seaweeds washed ashore and collecting on the beaches. It is a new phenomenon on the island and it was not observed few years ago. In Figure 4 is shown a seaweeds deposit on the local beach.

Funafuti atoll has no natural fresh water available. All the fresh water is being collected during rains. Rainwater is being collected and hold on in big plastic containers placed close to the individual houses. There is no waterworks system on the island. The lack of rainwater is being complemented by the fresh water plant operated with reverse osmosis process powered by electricity from generators with diesel engines. This supplementary source of water is used in the case of increased need because it is expensive to operate.

From the technical and technological point of view all described problems in Vaiaku can be effectively solved with some external help. Tuvalu itself has no potential to deal with these problems alone. The ecological problems in Funafuti could be solved or at least decreased with foundation of waste incineration plant. A new project of such incineration facility was already erected at Warsaw University of Technology and search for the financial support is continued. The idea of this facility is to perform complete and safe incineration of solid wastes like cardboard, paper, wood, biomass and plastic and the use the generated heat for sea water desalination. A byproduct of such a method it would be some sea salt for the local needs. Such an incineration facility would be placed fare from the village, e.g. close to the present waste dumping area and the wastes would need to be transported there from the village by truck.

Another suggested improvement of the island infrastructure would be a waste water treatment plant. Construction of such a plant would need to be preceded with the construction of a waste water piping along the whole island. Regarding the lack of fresh water, lack of toilets and bathrooms plugged into the central canalization net a suggestion to use sea water for toilets flushing was presented. There are already technologies based on active sludge process which can operate on sea water based sewages. Another relatively cheap solution would be at least a drainage system which could collect and later send the waste water far into the outer ocean waters where it would dilute and mitigate the lagoon water contamination.

All the ecological aspects of the life on the island are known to the local authorities. We were nicely surprised by the high level of the technological knowledge and ability to compare various methods of waste handling among the government and city hall officials. Regarding to other serious problems the island community meets and due to the lack of enough founds the practical solution of the ecological problems still waits to be solved.

Figure 1. Official dumpsite
at the north end of atoll
(photo P. Grzybowski)

Figure 2. Ecological toilets
in a number of six founded
on the island (photo P. Grzybowski)

Figure 3. A pigpen at the lagoon coast (photo P. Grzybowski)

Figure 4. Seaweeds washed ashore on the beach (photo P. Grzybowski)

Joanna Siekiera

RIMPAC – International Implications of the World's Largest Maritime Exercise

The question of the American interests at the Pacific Ocean was always open and actual. But when it comes to the defence and security matters, the policy of the government in Washington remains precise and clear. It is the United States of America, which are the world's sheriff, the only reliable super power being able to assure peace and stability. Moreover, it refers at the same manner to the unique military (and political, of course) capacities to lead the joint multinational forces. During the Cold War era, that was in fact the Pacific basin, which was the natural border between the two antagonist powers. It was no wonder, then, that the United States Navy had had its main aim to establish the proper means of the maritime cooperation at the North Pacific. And even though it has been already a quarter of a century since the Union of Soviet Socialist Republics collapse, the core motive of the Pacific security system remains the same – armed protection from the Russian aggression on the Western World.[1]

---

[1] Compare the American strategy towards the Asia-Pacific: John C. Dorrance, *The United States and the Pacific Islands*, Westport, Praeger, 1992; Ronald O'Rourke, 'China Naval Modernization: Implications for U.S. Navy Capabilities – Background and Issues for Congress', in Douglas Lovelace (ed.), *Terrorism: Commentary on Security Documents Volume 136: Assessing the Reorientation of U. S. National Security Strategy Toward the Asia-Pacific*, New York, Oxford University Press, 2014, p. 279–285.

Rejection of a common enemy has lead in 1971 to strengthen interoperability at the ocean under the USA leadership and sponsorship. It needs to be underlined that there was no specific establishing document or any memorandum of understanding associated with the exercise.[2] Moreover, the fact of convincing the allied countries to acquire American ships, weapons and aircraft was undeniable. The visible effect of such necessity of establishing an international programme of the maritime collaboration at the Pacific was RIMPAC.[3] The Rim of the Pacific Exercise[4] was launched by the United States Pacific Command, naval forces responsible for the Pacific Ocean zone. At first, there were only five involved countries: Australia, Canada, New Zealand, the United Kingdom and the USA as the founding state.[5]

It is worth mentioning already here the considerable enlargement of the participating forces up to 26 during RIMPAC 2016. Those were Australia, Brunei, Canada, Chile, China, Colombia, Denmark, France, Germany, India, Indonesia, Italy, Japan, Malaysia, Mexico, the Netherlands, New Zealand, Norway, Peru, the Philippines, Singapore, the South Korea, Thailand, Tonga, the United Kingdom and the USA.[6] This was the first time when Denmark, Germany and Italy were participating in the exercise. It shows the first important implication of RIMPAC, namely its grand international potential, which clearly attracts countries far from the Pacific. The governments of the European states and India or Malaysia seem to perceive this maritime cooperation worth engaging. In addition, they decide on close partnership with the USA presenting thereby their approval of the Washington international policy.

RIMPAC 2016 was the 25th exercise in its history. Since 1973 it has been held every two years in and around the Hawaiian Islands in June and July.

---

[2] E-mail to the author from Chuck Bell, Digital Media Director at the U.S. Pacific Fleet Public Affairs from 28 October 2017.

[3] Richard Hunt and Robert Girrier, 'RIMPAC Builds Partnerships that Last', in Sam Tangredi (ed.), *The U.S. Naval Institute on International Naval Cooperation*, Annapolis, Naval Institute Press, 2015, p. 89.

[4] The singular form of a term 'exercise' has been used since the beginning.

[5] 'Pacific War Games', *Micronesia Support Committee Bulletin* (The University of California), 1977, p. vi.

[6] In addition, Brazil was also invited for the first time in history but due to 'unforeseen scheduling commitments' had to resign. See the official website of RIMPAC: http://www.cpf.navy.mil/rimpac/participants/ [accessed 28 October 2017].

The main hosts and logistics organisers are by the joint commandment of the United States Pacific Fleet, led by Vice Admiral Nora W. Tyson, in conjunction with the Coast Guard, Marine Corps and Hawaii National Guard.[7] Having twenty-six nations, forty-five ships, five submarines, more than 200 aircraft and 25,000 personnel participated, there were more countries and personnel in Rim of the Pacific 2016 than in any previous years.

The RIMPAC exercise, due to its participating countries, forms the world's largest multinational maritime training in warfare. In addition, it does provide a unique and globally unprecedented military training to foster and sustain naval cooperation. Such relationships, which are visible and ongoing, are in fact crucial to ensure safety of both oceans and sea lanes.[8] The exercised capabilities range from humanitarian assistance and disaster relief (so-called HADR), maritime security operations to complex war fighting and sea control. Some relevant training can be enumerated too, like learning of various technologies, equipment, tactics, and procedures employed by the leading navies. Those were gunnery, missile, air defence and anti-submarine exercises, counter-piracy, diving and salvage operations, explosive ordnance disposal, and finally mine clearance operations.[9]

Leadership was held internationally, while previously mentioned Admiral Tyson served as the Combined Task Force Commander, Royal Canadian Navy Admiral Scott Bishop was the Deputy Commander, and Japanese Maritime Self Defence Force Admiral Koji Manabe was the Vice Commander. Other leaders of the multinational force included: the maritime component – Commodore Malcolm Wise of the Royal Australian Navy, the air component – Brigadier General Blaise Frawley of the Royal Canadian Air Force, and the amphibious task force – Commodore James Gilmour of the Royal New Zealand Navy.[10]

---

[7] Besides the Hawaiian Islands, for the first time it was the Southern California where some training, such as harpoon missile shoots and mine countermeasures, were upgraded.

[8] E-mail to the author from Lieutenant Lenaya Rotklein, Deputy Public Affairs Office at the U.S. Third Fleet, from 12 December 2014.

[9] Official websites of the America's NAVY: http://www.navy.mil/submit/display.asp?story_id=94978 [accessed 28 October 2017] and the U.S. Pacific Command 'USPACOM': http://www.pacom.mil/Media/News/News-Article-View/Article/788436/27-nations-to-participate-in-worlds-largest-maritime-exercise/ [accessed 28 October 2017].

[10] Ibid. The author has visited one of the Royal New Zealand Navy Battleships during the 75th anniversary of the creation of the service on 14 February 2016 in the Wellington Harbour.

The very original, obvious, but never declared, implication of RIMPAC is demonstration of power, both in military and political sense. Multinational force, by using its main equipment of the largest possible quantity, presents not to undermine warlike capabilities. In other words, RIMPAC under the surveillance of the USA (that is in accordance with their interests) gathers countries, which could be able to fight against the common enemy. In addition, the political perception and reception from any potential threat is also convincing. Such unstated demonstration of power is being made in favour of the Western civilisation along with its values. But against whom? Again, as it was during the Cold War, the Russian Federation appears as the hypothetical opponent. Russia was in fact never invited to RIMPAC.[11] That, however, did not prevent the Kremlin to participate in the exercise. The Russian destroyer ship and an intelligence ship were sent as the spy ships to shadow one of the US ship near Hawaii in 2016.

Still, such international affair is nothing new. During RIMPAC 2014, the Chinese People's Liberation Army Navy has also sent its uninvited spy ship in order to monitor the whole training. In this case, though, China was already participating in the exercise. Likewise in 2016 China expanded its naval delegation despite the formal agreement on how large each national team could be.[12] In conclusion, by coopting China and isolating Russia the US Government sends very clear signal who might be and who is not an ally.[13] That in turn draws sharp border between superpowers, exactly like it was during the Cold War.

She was also guided by Ensign Stacey Turner, with whom she has discussed the role of the New Zealand Navy in providing international peace in the Pacific.

[11] The Russian Navy was invited to RIMPAC 2012 but only as an observer without its military capabilities. While its participation at the following exercise in 2014 was cancelled by the Government in Moscow due to interrupter military collaboration over the territorial dispute in Ukraine. Nonetheless, the actual state of affairs is completely differently described by the Russian side. Compare the website of the Russian news agency Sputnik International: https://sputniknews.com/military/20120719174678625/ [accessed 28 October 2017] and the RT, Russian international television network funded by the Russian Government: https://www.rt.com/usa/348620-china-usa-navy-drills/ [accessed 28 October 2017].

[12] China had therefore one of the most powerful navy during the exercise: Katharina Seibel, Mathieu Duchâtel, and Oliver Bräuner, *US Defence Cooperation in Asia*, in Stockholm International Peace Research Institute, *SIPRI Yearbook 2015: Armaments, Disarmament and International Security*, Oxford, Oxford University Press, 2015, pp. 265–266.

[13] K.R. Bolton, 'US Navy Rim of the Pacific (RIMPAC) War Games, Coopting China, Isolating Russia?', 10 July 2016, website of the Global Research, Centre for Research on Globalization,

Nevertheless working together for the common goal is one thing, but learning from each other and each other's perception is another thing. By building long-lasting partnerships, world's security is being cemented. Knowing each country's capabilities, strengths and most of all weaknesses allows for establishing the proper system of the international maritime security.[14] Bringing people, while not only navies together, must not be forgotten either. Through the wide variety of military and civilian levels, lasting several weeks before heading to sea, naval personnel take part in numerous social and athletic engagements.[15] This could be considered as the second international implication of RIMPAC. In fact, those formal and informal gatherings usually lead to some decision-making. All levels military and diplomatic officials gather in order to discuss the contemporary state of affairs, as well the geopolitical vectors of military cooperation in the nearest future. During the last 2016 exercise, the distinguished guests present at the official and backroom talks were: inter alia Vice President Joe Biden, Hawaii Governor David Ige, the US and foreign ambassadors, generals and admirals from several countries, congressional representatives, as well as civil and business leaders. Such exchanges of thoughts help political and military decision-makers with better understanding how fundamental the maritime environment is and how interdependent the Pacific region is (or ought to be).

Last but not least, the cultural aspect seems also to be very important. Sailors from different nations meet their colleagues during sports and recreation. At the same time, they do represent their navy to Hawaiians and discovered the islands' culture and heritage. Officials and soldiers significantly expand their horizons, foster new experiences and become more aware of the uniqueness of the Pacific basin.[16]

---

https://www.globalresearch.ca/us-sponsored-rim-of-the-pacific-rimpac-war-games-coopting-china-isolating-russia/5535240 [accessed 28 October 2017]; idem, 'World War III? Indo-Pacific Theatre', 20 October 2016, Russian website Geopolitica.ru, https://www.geopolitica.ru/en/article/world-war-iii-indo-pacific-theatre [accessed 28 October 2017].

[14] Jonathan Greenert and James M. Foggo, 'Forging a Global Network of Navies', in Tangredi (ed.), *The U.S. Naval Institute*, p. 38.

[15] Gregory Huffman, 'RIMPAC Builds Relationships; Relationships Make Strong Partners', August 2016, Navy Life, http://navylive.dodlive.mil/2016/08/05/rimpac-builds-relationships-relationships-make-strong-partners/ [accessed 28 October 2017].

[16] Ibid.

Another international implication of RIMPAC is gaining popularity. That is responding to the natural disasters. Besides counterterrorism
(including piracy, widespread on the Pacific) or delivering humanitarian
aid, the multinational forces can be used to combat the effects of climate
change, such as floods, as well as in regard to the phenomenon of 'Ring of
Fire'. On the large territory of the Pacific Rim (countries around the rim
of the Pacific Ocean) there have occurred a great number of earthquakes,
volcanic eruptions, tsunamis and cyclones.[17] As an example, the RIMPAC
organisers state their possible and ready capabilities to bring disaster relief efforts: 'Just recently, while we were engaged in RIMPAC, a typhoon
was barrelling down upon the Philippines. Having just practiced together,
RIMPAC countries could have responded immediately if the call for help
had come in.'[18]

The following international implication of RIMPAC is its influence on
environment, in both good and negative sense. As usual, during the exercise, meteorology and oceanography officers forecasted weather and ocean
conditions. Their task was not only to ensure all participants operate safely
and effectively, but also to consider the real physical environment.[19] The
environmental issues, constantly forgotten during any military activities,
have in turn played the large role in RIMPAC 2016. There was even established special Department of the Navy's Great Green Fleet. Such 'green'
department launched an initiative about making attention effectively how
large is the influence of the exercise on the maritime environment. The
initiative of the US Navy emphasised global operations using alternative
fuel blends along with energy conservation measures. The second effort
was to demonstrate how optimising energy use does increase operational
readiness. RIMPAC has proudly stated that during the last exercise almost
all maritime units functioned using an approved alternate-fuel composite.

---

[17] Bethany D. Rinard Hinga, *Ring of Fire: An Encyclopedia of the Pacific Rim's Earthquakes, Tsunamis, and Volcanoes*, Santa Barbara, ABC-CLIO, 2015.

[18] Gilles Couturier, 'What Exactly is RIMPAC?', 21 July 2014, Navy Live, http://navylive.dodlive.mil/2014/07/21/what-exactly-is-rimpac/ [accessed 28 October 2017].

[19] Tim Gallaudet, 'Naval Meteorology and Oceanography Makes It Real During RIMPAC 2016', 4 August 2016, Navy Live, http://navylive.dodlive.mil/2016/08/04/naval-meteorolo-gy-and-oceanography-makes-it-real-during-rimpac-2016/ [accessed 28 October 2017].

In addition,

> the alternative fuel [...] is derived from waste beef fat from the Midwest. Alternative fuels can be made from animal waste oil, algae, or non-food crops. The fuel must be "drop-in," requiring no modifications to engines or procedures. Having alternative fuel in the supply chain increases operational flexibility by allowing forces to obtain fuel from more sources worldwide.[20]

Nonetheless, the environmental activists working on behalf or the non-governmental organisations underline the huge damage caused by radars, sonar, engines, air and water pollution. They have even delivered the other, bitten meaning of the 'RIMPAC' acronym: Radiating Intense Microwave Pollution Accelerating Corrosion. This international implication of the world's largest exercise emphasises how much do the electrical currents from any radars, electromagnetic antennas or systems destroy calcium and magnesium coral reefs by electrochemical actions.[21]

But RIMPAC is also a well prosperous business. Formal and informal meetings create suitable outlets for bargains at the Hawaiian Islands. As mentioned before, lots of highly distinguished guests, diplomats, high officers with their families stay at the best hotels in Honolulu, spend money in many fancy shops, restaurants or on tourists overpriced activities. Making money on the military exercise is not something new referring to the fact of constant development of weaponry, new technology of defence or deterring enemy. RIMPAC is however becoming an interesting venue, which is shown by establishing trading and collector's items. This occurs not only in the USA, though. There can be found many RIMPAC objects on the Japanese Yahoo website, such as books and expert magazines, posters, games, DVDs.[22]

---

[20] Official statements at the website of RIMPAC: http://www.cpf.navy.mil/news.aspx/110069 [accessed 21 October 2017].

[21] Jeff Wefferson, 'Operation Mahi Tangaroa: Aotearoa's "Rimpac" & Lockheed's "Death Merchant" Conference in "100% Clean and Green New Zealand"', 3 November 2016, Tutunui-Wananga blog, http://tutunui-wananga.blogspot.com.au/2016/11/operation-mahi-tangaroa-aotearoas.html [accessed 28 October 2017].

[22] Compare the Yahoo website: https://auctions.yahoo.co.jp/search/search/RIMPAC/0/ [accessed 28 October 2017].

The next exercise will take place in 2018, as always near Hawaii. The American president Donald Trump invited again China, which caused a tension with the representatives of Taiwan. The USA Government officially does not recognise autonomous powers of the Government in Taipei, however it entirely supports the Beijing's internal policy. This is a very pragmatic approach that nevertheless does not neglect the bilateral relations between Washington and Taipei either. Such relationship arises mainly in the areas of education, business, and global issues, especially in maintaining international security and maritime cooperation.[23] The diplomatic steps towards agreeing both conflicted sides, China and Taiwan, led to inviting China as a participant in RIMPAC 2018, while Taiwan – as an observer.[24]

This articles tries to describe the most vital international implications of the Rim of the Pacific Exercise under the American surveillance. Military, economic, geopolitical, environmental and business factors seem to be prevailing. As the constant development of the size and relevance of the exercise, the leading navies (that is their governing states) have to take into consideration participation in RIMPAC. Due to this fact, countries from Europe and Asia decide on engagement with the US Pacific Command.

Being united and tactically prepared against any hypothetical (or expected by the Government in Washington) threat has led to establishing the world's largest maritime exercise. Russia though, as an assumed threat, seems to underestimate the activities by commenting on adding to the RIMPAC group conflicted countries from Indochina, especially India, China and Taiwan. It is worth remembering the fact of gaining popularity by the Pacific region in the 21st century. The world leaders cross their influences here, what gives this area primacy in geopolitical domination, slowly downgrading the Atlantic Community. And due to this reason, RIMPAC might boost its international implication in the nearest future.

---

[23] Richard C. Bush, 'US Policy Toward Taiwan', *Asian Education and Development Studies*, vol. 5, no. 3, 2016, pp. 266–277; website of the U.S. Department of State: https://www.state.gov/r/pa/ei/bgn/35855.htm [accessed 28 October 2017].

[24] 'US Allows Taiwan Observer Status at RIMPAC Exercise', 22 May 2016, *Taipei Times*, http://www.taipeitimes.com/News/taiwan/archives/2016/05/22/2003646849 [accessed 21 October 2017].

Bibliography

Literature

Dorrance, John C., *The United States and the Pacific Islands*, Westport, Praeger, 1992.

Greenert, Jonathan and James M. Foggo, 'Forging a Global Network of Navies', in Sam Tangredi (ed.), *The U.S. Naval Institute on International Naval Cooperation*, Annapolis, Naval Institute Press, 2015.

Hunt, Richard and Robert Girrier, 'RIMPAC Builds Partnerships that Last', in Sam Tangredi (ed.), *The U.S. Naval Institute on International Naval Cooperation*, Annapolis, Naval Institute Press, 2015.

Lovelace, Douglas (ed.), *Terrorism: Commentary on Security Documents Volume 136: Assessing the Reorientation of U. S. National Security Strategy Toward the Asia-Pacific*, New York, Oxford University Press, 2014.

O'Rourke, Ronald, 'China Naval Modernization: Implications for U.S. Navy Capabilities – Background and Issues for Congress', in Douglas Lovelace (ed.) *Terrorism: Commentary on Security Documents Volume 136: Assessing the Reorientation of U. S. National Security Strategy Toward the Asia-Pacific*, New York, Oxford University Press, 2014, p. 279–285.

'Pacific War Games', *Micronesia Support Committee Bulletin* (The University of California), 1977.

Rinard Hinga, Bethany D., *Ring of Fire: An Encyclopedia of the Pacific Rim's Earthquakes, Tsunamis, and Volcanoes*, Santa Barbara, ABC-CLIO, 2015.

Seibel, Katharina, Mathieu Duchâtel, and Oliver Bräuner, *US Defence Cooperation in Asia*, in Stockholm International Peace Research Institute, *SIPRI Yearbook 2015: Armaments, Disarmament and International Security*, Oxford, Oxford University Press, 2015, pp. 265–266.

Stockholm International Peace Research Institute, *SIPRI Yearbook 2015: Armaments, Disarmament and International Security*, Oxford, Oxford University Press, 2015.

Tangredi, Sam (ed.), *The U.S. Naval Institute on International Naval Cooperation*, Annapolis, Naval Institute Press, 2015.

Websites

Bolton, K.R., 'US Navy Rim of the Pacific (RIMPAC) War Games, Coopting China, Isolating Russia?', 10 July 2016, website of the Global Research, Centre for Research on Globalization, https://www.globalresearch.ca/us-sponsored-rim-of-the-pacific-rimpac-war-games-coopting-china-isolating-russia/5535240 [accessed 28 October 2017].

Bolton, K.R., 'World War III? Indo-Pacific Theatre', 20 October 2016, Geopolitica.ru, https://www.geopolitica.ru/en/article/world-war-iii-indo-pacific-theatre [accessed 28 October 2017].

Bush, Richard C., 'US Policy Toward Taiwan', *Asian Education and Development Studies*, vol. 5, no. 3, 2016, pp. 266–277.

Couturier, Gilles, 'What Eactly is RIMPAC?', 21 July 2014, Navy Live, http://navylive.dodlive.mil/2014/07/21/what-exactly-is-rimpac/ [accessed 28 October 2017].

Gallaudet, Tim, 'Naval Meteorology and Oceanography Makes It Real During RIMPAC 2016', 4 August 2016, Navy Live, http://navylive.dodlive.mil/2016/08/04/naval-meteorology-and-oceanography-makes-it-real-during-rimpac-2016/ [accessed 28 October 2017].

Huffman, Gregory, 'RIMPAC Builds Relationships; Relationships Make Strong Partners', 5 August 2016, Navy Life, http://navylive.dodlive.mil/2016/08/05/rimpac-builds-relationships-relationships-make-strong-partners/ [accessed 28 October 2017].

Official statements at the website of RIMPAC: http://www.cpf.navy.mil/news.aspx/110069 [accessed 21 October 2017].

'US Allows Taiwan Observer Status at RIMPAC Exercise', 22 May 2016, *Taipei Times*, http://www.taipeitimes.com/News/taiwan/archives/2016/05/22/2003646849 [accessed 21 October 2017].

Website of the America's NAVY: http://www.navy.mil/submit/display.asp?story_id=94978 [accessed 28 October 2017].

Website of the Janapese Yahoo: https://auctions.yahoo.co.jp/search/search/RIMPAC/0/ [accessed 28 October 2017].

Website of RIMPAC: http://www.cpf.navy.mil/rimpac/participants/ [accessed 28 October 2017]

Website of the RT: https://www.rt.com/usa/348620-china-usa-navy-drills/ [accessed 28 October 2017].

Website of the Sputnik International: https://sputniknews.com/military/201207 19174678625/ [accessed 28 October 2017].

Website of the U.S. Department of State: https://www.state.gov/r/pa/ei/bgn/35855.htm [accessed 28 October 2017].

Website of the U.S. Pacific Command 'USPACOM': http://www.pacom.mil/Media/
News/News-Article-View/Article/788436/27-nations-to-participate-in-worlds-
largest-maritime-exercise/ [accessed 28 October 2017].

Wefferson, Jeff, 'Operation Mahi Tangaroa: Aotearoa's "Rimpac" & Lockheed's "Death
Merchant" Conference in "100% Clean and Green New Zealand"', 3 November
2016, Tutunui-Wananga blog, http://tutunui-wananga.blogspot.com.au/2016/11/
operation-mahi-tangaroa-aotearoas.html [accessed 28 October 2017].

Others

E-mail to the author from Chuck Bell, Digital Media Director at the U.S. Pacific Fleet
Public Affairs from 28 October 2017.

E-mail to the author from Lieutenant Lenaya Rotklein, Deputy Public Affairs Office
at the U.S. Third Fleet from 12 December 2014.

Pedro Henrique Melchior Nunes da Horta

A Worldwide Nuclear Disarmament Case: The Leading Role of the Marshall Islands at the International Court of Justice Against the United Kingdom in Terms of an International Security

In April 2014, a case was submitted to the International Court of Justice concerning nuclear weapons, and what was decided by the court did not consider everything that was implied in the matter of the case. It had to do with the atomic explosions in a region that was under the United Nations' custody: the Marshall Islands. It is worth pointing out that the matter of nuclear weapons represents a threat to humanity as a whole, and their complete disarmament has always been a challenge that we continue to face and must continue fighting for.

The idea of a worldwide nuclear disarmament goes back to the principle of representativeness and equality among states. Since 1907, at the Second Hague Conference, the Brazilian diplomat Ruy Barbosa started standing for those principles that we now consider undeniable. Without them, there would be no multilateralism, since they express in the international stage the whole purpose of security and democratisation. What Barbosa defended in that context was that the relations between the world's nations could not be based only in balance of power and conflicts for hegemony, but in a way in which they would be routed according to the norms and legal principles of international law, the more reasoned and ethical way of handling all the profound changes in the international stage. Therefore, according to Barbosa, without the principle of equality among states, there would be no reason to exist any international law organisation.

Likewise, the Brazilian judge of the International Court of Justice, Cançado Trindade, was one of the eight judges that stood for the Marshall Islands' application in the court, defending the values and principles that conducts international law. The Marshallese have applied in 2014 in the International Court of Justice against nine nuclear states, that is, China, France, India, Israel, Pakistan, North Korea, Russia, United Kingdom and the United States, accusing them for the non-fulfilment of the article VI in the Non-Proliferation Treaty (NPT): 'Each of the Parties to the Treaty undertakes to pursue negotiations in good faith on effective measures relating to cessation of the nuclear arms race at an early date and to nuclear disarmament, and on a treaty on general and complete disarmament under strict and effective international control.'[1] Only three of the nine accused nuclear states recognise the jurisdiction of the International Court of Justice, that is, India, Pakistan and the United Kingdom, and for this reason sent their representatives to the court.

The historic context that led the Marshall Islands to make this application is that, during the Second World War, the United States have conquered their territory, and have committed to promote the economic advancement and self-sufficiency of their inhabitants. However, during the period of 1946–1958, when the Marshall Islands was under the United States custody, there was a total of sixty-seven nuclear weapons tests in the Marshallese territory. The strongest test series was called *Castle*, with detonations equivalent to a thousand times the bomb that has been launched on Hiroshima. Even though the Marshallese people were required to move away from there, the incidence rates of cancer in the population had increased considerably, as well as other health issues for the population, such as deformations in newborn children and chronic diseases. All of them are results of a high-level exposition to radiation.

---

[1] UNODA, Treaty on the Non-Proliferation of Nuclear Weapons (NPT), 1970, https://www.un.org/disarmament/wmd/nuclear/npt/text [accessed 10 October 2017].

It is worth pointing out that the Marshallese application in the International Court of Justice did not seek financial compensation, but rather only the recognition from the court of the non-fulfilment from the nuclear states of the article VI of the Non-Proliferation Treaty, so that situations like those would cease to happen.

The United Kingdom was the country whose preliminary objection was analysed first by the court. The Marshall Islands, beyond the issue concerning the article VI of the Non-Proliferation Treaty, further accused the United Kingdom to oppose the United Nations General Assembly when they tried to make such negotiations happen, and to have repeatedly declared the United Kingdom's intention to rely on its nuclear arsenal for decades to come.

The British claimed, *inter alia*, that there existed no dispute between the parties, since the treaty did not provide a specific date when the negotiations to a new treaty should take place. Most of the judges accepted this objection, thus they thought it would not be necessary to work on the other countries' preliminary objections.

The court explained that the existence of a dispute between the parties is a condition of its jurisdiction, and 'for a dispute to exist, it must be shown that the claim of one party is positively opposed by the other; the two sides must hold clearly opposite views concerning the question of the performance or non-performance of certain international obligations.'[2]

From the eight court members that stood for the validation of the case, the Brazilian judge Cançado Trindade had the more detailed position in his judgement. He defends an obligation to nuclear disarmament, recalls the principle of equality among states and advocates for an approach focused on the people. According to him, in a case such as the Marshall Islands', the *raison d'humanité* prevails over the *raison d'État*, since humanity as a whole is considered a subject of international law. Cançado Trindade understood that nuclear disarmament, as it affects the whole humanity, is a matter of customary international law, that is, it is *erga omnes*,

---

[2] International Court of Justice, Obligations Concerning Negotiations Relating to Cessation of the Nuclear Arms Race and to Nuclear Disarmament (Marshall Islands v. India), Hague, 2016: Summary of the Judgment of 5 October 2016, p. 2, https://www.icj-cij.org/files/case-related/158/19164.pdf [accessed 10 October 2017].

making the matter obligatory to all states, even to those that are not part of the treaty (in this case, the Non-Proliferation Treaty). He further added that a small group of countries cannot continue to minimise the United Nations resolutions that apply to all the United Nations member states concerning the obligation of nuclear disarmament.

It was thus evidenced the nuclear states contradictions to the public opinion when they make a commitment with the nuclear disarmament goal but do not make efforts to make it happen. Nuclear weapons represent a risk to the world as they could end up on the hands of terrorists' groups, as well as their usage itself, in situations such as nuclear tests, that represent in health issues to a population, or their actual usage in a context of war, which considering their technological improvement since the first explosion in 1945, could be an even greater catastrophe to the world and to humanity.

It is clear how the Marshall Islands with this audacious application in the International Court of Justice gained the world's attention for an important matter, such as the nuclear weapons issue, in what concerns the international security. A small country such as the Marshall Islands is one of those whose action has validated the principle of equality among states and ended up provoking actions in the international stage.

Until now, no nuclear weapon was ever destroyed due to a multilateral agreement. However, on 20 September 2017, the Treaty on the Prohibition of Nuclear Weapons, led by countries such as Brazil, was opened for signature, with more than fifty heads of state having signed it. Although no nuclear states agreed to participate in this treaty, it is always important – in the international community's point of view – to bring any pressure so that the nuclear states could end their nuclear weapons.

In conclusion, it is worth highlighting that it is important that the academia work more on this topic, and that it ponders upon solutions, because it could be said that when one cannot solve the problem, attitudes of conformism become present, even so in face of a great challenge. With more debates and engagement from civil society, it is possible in a medium term to guide authorities to the interest of the majority, or at least to make them fulfil their obligations according to the treaties.

Bibliography

Cançado Trindade, Antônio Augusto, *A Obrigação Universal de Desarmamento Nuclear*, Brasília, FUNAG, 2017.

International Court of Justice, Obligations Concerning Negotiations Relating to Cessation of the Nuclear Arms Race and to Nuclear Disarmament (Marshall Islands v. India), Hague 2016: Summary of the Judgment of 5 October 2016, p. 2, https://www.icj-cij.org/files/case-related/158/19164.pdf [accessed 10 October 2017].

International Court of Justice, Obligations Concerning Negotiations Relating to Cessation of the Nuclear Arms Race and to Nuclear Disarmament (Marshall Islands v. India), Hague, 2016: Dissenting Opinion of Judge Cançado Trindade, https://www.icj-cij.org/files/case-related/158/158-20161005-JUD-01-06-EN.pdf [accessed 10 October 2017].

UNODA, Treaty on the Non-Proliferation of Nuclear Weapons (NPT), 1970, https://www.un.org/disarmament/wmd/nuclear/npt/text [accessed 10 October 2017].

Justyna Eska-Mikołajewska

Stability and Instability in Oceania: The Case of Papua New Guinea, the Solomon Islands and Fiji

Introduction

The problem of state dysfunction is now recognised as one of a number of main threats to stability, in addition to such phenomena as international terrorism, the proliferation of weapons of mass destruction or organised crime. This problem, although perceived primarily from the Eurocentric perspective, is not unique to the continent of Europe. The lack of legitimacy and inefficient government has also been identified in the South Pacific island states. Because of their small size and often distant location from the large centres of power and influence in international politics they are often regarded as belonging to the world's weak and fragile states. The concept of a crisis zone, known as arc of instability, is an Australian idea born at the end of the 1990s. In defining the so-called arc of instability in 1999, the Strategic and Defence Studies Centre's Emeritus Professor Paul Dibb described it as an island chain to the north of Australia, ranging from Indonesia through the Pacific islands to New Zealand.[1] This term

---

[1] Greame Dobell, 'The Pacific "Arc of Instability"', *ABC Correspondent's Report*, 20 August 2006, http://www.abc.net.au/correspondents/content/2006/s1719019.htm [accessed 27 December 2017].

has developed in the Oceania region with reference mainly to three states: Papua New Guinea, the Solomon Islands and Fiji, where there was a lot of internal instability from the 1980s.

A tendency for conflicts that spill over borders and become regional is a main concern of Australia that identifies this arc as the region from or through which a security threat could most easily be posed. Even though the countries of the arc do not like the term, any more than they accept being called 'failing' or 'fragile', Australia has responded to security problems in the arc and is consequently engaged in extensive efforts to support stability of the region by protecting the interests and unique values of the south-west Pacific states.

Fragile states: definitions and reasons for state vulnerability

There are many definitions of the term 'fragile states' or 'state fragility'. Fragile states have been often described as vulnerable to overthrow, to political and economic instability, to 'capture' by unscrupulous neighbours, to be easily 'penetrated' by organised crime. They have been also regarded as more likely to fail because of weak institutions and inexperienced leadership, and to be in need of support and 'rescue' by larger powers of the developed world.[2] One of the most important – the Organisation for Economic Co-operation and Development (OECD) Development Assistance Committee's definition (DAC) from 2007 – indicates that 'states are fragile when state structures lack the political will and/or capacity to provide the basic functions needed for poverty reduction, development and to safeguard the security and human rights of their population.'[3]

According to Department for International Development's definition (DFID) from 2005, fragile states are 'those where the government cannot or will not deliver core functions to the majority of its people, including

---

[2] David Hegarty, 'A Changing Oceania', in David Hegarty and Darrel Tryon (eds.), *Politics, Development and Security in Oceania*, Canberra: The Australian National University Press, 2013, p. 12.

[3] Cited in: Claire Mcloughlin, *Topic Guide on Fragile States*, International Development Department, University of Birmingham, August 2009, p. 8, https://www.files.ethz.ch/isn/113839/CON67.pdf [accessed 27 December 2017].

the poor.'[4] In 2009 the Centre for Research on Inequality and Social Exclusion (CRISE) defined fragile states as 'failing, or at risk of failing, with respect to authority, comprehensive service entitlements or legitimacy.'[5] When we have a brush with state fragility, the state that cannot correct its deficiencies alone is weak. Understanding which factors are responsible for states failing can help in designing appropriate interventions.

Among the main reasons of vulnerability in small island developing states (SIDS) that cover the South Pacific, the Caribbean, the Indian Ocean and West African Coast island groups area special attention is paid to their size. It involves limited natural resource base, high competition between land use, intensity of land-use, immediacy of interdependence in human environment systems and spatial concentration of productive assets. There is an argument for insularity and remoteness what connects with high external transport costs, time delays and high costs in accessing external goods, delays and reduced quality of information flow as well as geopolitical weakness. Third indicator has got an environmental character and it applies both to small exposed interiors and large coastal zones. One of the key components of the vulnerability of small islands is their capability to mitigate disasters. This term should be understood as a limited hazard forecasting ability, complacency and also a little insurance cover.

The grounds for state fragility are also demographic. This group of factors includes a limited human resource base, a small population, rapid population changes, single urban centre, population concentrated on coastal zone, plus dis-economies of scale leading to high per capita costs of infrastructure and services. The cause of vulnerability has also an economic dimension and it refers to small economies, dependence on external finance, small internal market, dependence on natural resources and highly specialised production.[6]

Most factors mentioned above are revealed particularly in the South Pacific. Security in Oceania is threatened by disputes over land, economic disparities, corruption and incompetence in the processes surrounding

---

[4] Ibid.

[5] Ibid.

[6] See Mark Pelling and Juha I. Uitto, 'Small Island Developing States: Natural Distaster Vulnerability and Global Change', *Environmental Hazards*, vol. 3, issue 2, 2001, p. 53.

natural resources exploitation, climate change, natural disasters and poor governance which means lack of confidence in government's ability to solve the basic political, social and economic problems. The key issue concerns two elements that distinguish the small states of Oceania from many small states in other regions of the world: their relative smallness and remote location. It should be added that these states are small, but mostly very extensive like Kiribati, whose islands cover an area of almost 4,000 kilometres around the equator. In addition, they share no land borders with other countries (with the exception of Papua New Guinea), what may have some strategic importance. In fact, their weakness is the practical lack of any influence on international processes taking place in a globalising world. It is referred to as strategic invisibility or even 'strategic neglect' rather than treated as something that positively affects the security and stability in that region.[7]

There are some widely used statistically based indexes which can be helpful in understanding the nature and risk of state fragility. One of the most important is the Fragile States Index (formerly the Failed States Index, FSI) which is an annual report published by the United States think tank the Fund for Peace and the American magazine *Foreign Policy* since 2005. It currently ranks 178 sovereign states with membership in the United Nations across the globe. The lower score indicates an improvement and greater stability, while a higher score indicates greater instability. What is most interesting is that only five Pacific states are on the list: Samoa is ranked as one hundred and eleven in the warning category, Micronesia and Fiji are ranked as eighty and seventy-nine respectively in the elevated warning category, the Solomon Islands and Papua New Guinea are ranked as fifty-six and fifty-one respectively in high warning category. The FSI Index that is a sum of scores for twelve social, economic and political indicators should be treated as an attempt to measure vulnerability to collapse or conflict rather than making prediction of the state's collapse.[8]

---

[7] See Stephanie Lawson, 'Security in Oceania: Perspectives on the Contemporary Agenda', in Eric Shibuya and Jim Rolfe (eds.), *Security in Oceania: In the 21st Century*, Honolulu, Asia--Pacific Center for Security Studies, 2003, pp. 8–12.

[8] See J.J. Messner et al. (eds.), 'Fragile State Index 2018', The Fund for Peace, https://fundforpeace.org/fsi/wp-content/uploads/2018/04/951181805-Fragile-States-Index-Annual-Report-2018.pdf [accessed 25 October 2018].

Another example of the evaluation of the situation in the Pacific is the 'Fragility of Small Island Developing States' produced by Carleton University in Canada's Country Indicators for Foreign Policy (CIFP) Fragility Index (FI). The following analysis draws on the CIFP dataset for the years 2000–2004. This is an index of fragility for small states that in certain circumstances may be more prone to collapse. Among the thirty-seven states ranked in this index from 'Least Fragile' to 'Most Fragile', Samoa, Micronesia and Vanuatu are ranked respectively as ninth, tenth and eleventh, Fiji as sixteenth, Palau and Tonga respectively as twentieth and twenty-first, Papua New Guinea and Kiribati respectively as thirtieth and thirty--first, while the Solomon Islands is ranked as thirty-third.[9]

A 2014 CIFP report provides a global fragility ranking for a total of 197 countries using 2013 data. This composite analysis of fragility uses the Authority (A), Legitimacy (L) and Capacity (C) cluster scores. The initial assuption was that fragile states are influenced by conflict that is a result of development and economic capacity problems, lack of authority as well as weak legitimacy. Based on the report we can conclude that the South Pacific states occupy positions from forty-first (Solomon Islands) to ninety-ninth (Marshall Islands). The least fragile state is Palau ranked as one hundred forty-first.[10]

Human Development Report 2016: Human Development for Everyone is the latest in the series of global Human Development Reports published by the United Nations Development Programme (UNDP) since 1990. It includes all Pacific states with the exception of Marshall Islands, Nauru and Tuvalu. Countries are ranked from number one to number 188 on a four-step scale of Human Development: very high, high, medium and low. None of the Pacific states feature in the top ranking of 'Very High', but four are ranked as 'High': Palau, Fiji, Tonga and Samoa. Three states

---

[9] David Carment, Stewart Prest, and Yiagadeesen Samy, 'Assessing Small Island Developing State Fragility', in Lino Briguglio and Eliawony J. Kisanga (eds.), *Economic Vulnerability and Resilience of Small States*, Msida, University of Malta, 2004, p. 13

[10] David Carment, Simon Langlois-Bertrand, and Yiagadeesen Samy, 'Assessing State Fragility, with a Focus on the Middle East and North Africa Region: A 2014 Country Indicators for Foreign Policy Report', Country Indicators for Foreign Policy, Carleton University, Ottawa, 30 December 2014, https://carleton.ca/cifp/wp-content/uploads/CIFP-2014-Fragility-Report.pdf [accessed 28 December 2017].

fall into the Medium ranking category: Micronesia, Vanuatu and Kiribati. Only Papua New Guinea and Solomon Islands are ranked as 'Low'. Human Development Index trends in 1990–2015 show that almost all Pacific states have risen steadily up the rankings over the last thirty years.[11]

Examples of stability and instability in the South Pacific

The Pacific region is characterised by uncertainty and a high level of risk in many areas. Island states are confronted with such negative phenomena as crises of leadership, political instability, intra-state ethnic conflicts, poverty, drug and people smuggling as well as external threats in the form of threat of force, a change in the balance of forces, including the rivalry of regional superpowers, increased external influences of non-state or potentially hostile actors and the discovery or placement of new strategic assets. All of these key security issues are reflected in three states of Oceania. Their entire political systems and state apparatus remain vulnerable to collapse, so that the potential sources of danger can easily destabilise the situation on a regional scale.

The first example of the state is Papua New Guinea. A war between Bougainville, a part of an independent Papua New Guinea, already an autonomous region, and Papua New Guinea that lasted from 1989 to 1997 degenerated into a civil war that cost about 15,000 lives. The Bougainville peace agreement was negotiated with the significant contribution of New Zealand and finally was signed in April 1998. In 2002 Bougainville Constitutional Commission was established and two years later Bougainville adopted its constitution. The United Nations mission, headed by Australia, led to the destruction of weapons and the establishment of an autonomous, self-governing region, with the prospect of independence in a referendum-based procedure between ten to fifteen years after the election of an autonomous government. This occurred on 15 June 2005, therefore an independence vote must be held before 2019.[12]

---

[11] Selim Jahan et al. (eds.), Human Development Report 2016: Human Development for Everyone, United Nations Development Programme, New York, 2016, http://hdr.undp.org/sites/default/files/2016_human_development_report.pdf [accessed 28 December 2017].

[12] Ben Schaare, 'A Pacific Arc of Instability?', Cogit ASIA, 9 September 2015, https://www.cogitasia.com/a-pacific-arc-of-instability/ [accessed 29 December 2017].

A regional Peace Monitoring Group with military and aid personnel from Australia, New Zealand, as well as Fiji and Vanuatu continues to oversee the peace process. On the one hand, Bougainville region has the greatest likelihood of success, on the other hand, the greatest threat of returning to violence. The reason for this is that the referendum is not binding on the Government of Papua New Guinea, so violence could easily break out should national authorities ignore the will of the people.

The conflict undermined Papua New Guinea's economy and is one of the major causes of its present economic and political instability. Bougainville pointed to another source of insecurity – a deadly lack of nationalism. Instead, they were micronationalism, regionalism and secessionist sentiments in this highly fragmented population that has the greatest linguistic diversity in the world – the number of individual languages listed for Papua New Guinea is 852: among these 840 are living and twelve are extinct.[13]

As the largest of the Pacific states – total area: 462,840 square kilometres and population: 6,909 (July 2017),[14] Papua New Guinea has a substantial resource base with oil, natural gas, copper and gold deposits, forests and fisheries which could provide a solid foundation for long-term income generation and national wealth. However, its main problems are those of political and economic management, high population growth and service delivery across the rugged topography of some parts of the country. The lack of uniformity among the indigenous communities made the institutionalisation of any political or economic system very difficult. The state transformation, which was primarily aimed at enabling the reconciliation of the diversity of the population with the unity of the country, lasted only several dozen years, a process which has required hundreds of years elsewhere.[15]

---

[13] Ethnologue. Languauge of the World, https://www.ethnologue.com/country/PG [accessed 28 December 2017].

[14] CIA, The World Factbook, https://www.cia.gov/library/publications/the-world-factbook/geos/pp.html [accessed 29 December 2017].

[15] Henry Okole, 'Papua New Guinea's Brand of Westminster: Democratic Traditions Overlaying Melanesian Cultures', in Haig Patapan, John Wanna, and Patrick Weller (eds.), *Westminster Legacies: Democracy and Responsible Government in Asia and the Pacific*, Sydney, University of New South Wales Press, 2005, pp. 187, 190–191.

At present, it has a democratic, but very fractious political system. No government has served out a full term of office. This justifies the conclusion that the instability of governing coalitions has become a permanent feature of Papua New Guinea's political system. Politics in which many fluid parties have little consistent platform or ideology means that state/public resources are readily wasted. Papua New Guinea's political leadership, however, is undergoing a generational shift and on both central and provincial level is beginning to develop policy which may announce well for future policy-making and administration.[16] But there is still a serious risk that politicians in this part of Melanesia can easily mobilise local and regional loyalties against national governments. Many 'old problems' like corruption, crime and illegality remain a threat to public order because they have weakened national authority in dealing effectively with them. Currently, there are no terror groups that operate within Papua New Guinea, but the above-mentioned phenomena heighten the possibility of a crime-terror nexus. Their existence provides the ideal conditions to potentially support terrorism in Papua New Guinea. The situation already creates a number of challenges for the national security apparatus, as the state is obliged to rely upon its to counter the effects of a crime-terror convergence.[17]

The second example are the Solomon Islands. It is a small country that belongs to the Small Island Developing States (SIDS) group, what means that it is more vulnerable particularly as a result of its weak economic structures. In fact, it is very dependent on the export of a single primary commodities, such as palm oil, coconut oil, timber and copra. However, the Solomon Islands vulnerability is reflected in immense economic, political and social problems for the state's leadership, which they were inadequately prepared to address.[18] The Solomon Islands have been dramatically disturbed by a period of strain in the ethnic relations for over a decade, which exploded with redoubled strength in the late 1990s. At that time both Australia and New Zealand observed the principle of

---

[16] Hegarty, 'Changing Oceania', p. 10.

[17] See Sean G.L. Jacobs, 'Undermining the State: The "Crime-Terror Nexus" and Papua New Guinea', in Melissa H. Conley Tyler (ed.), *Emerging Scholars 2010–2011*, Australian Institute of International Affairs, June 2011, pp. 8–15.

[18] Carment, Prest and Samy, 'Assessing Small Island', pp. 1–2.

non-involvement. After the Biketawa Declaration, adopted in October 2000 as a response to the *coup d'état* in Fiji and the growing tension in the Solomon Islands,[19] Australia besides donating financial aid, started contributing to the International Peace Monitoring Team deployed in the Solomon Islands.

Serious threats to human security in a situation of internal conflict occurred in 2000, when the constitutional government was forced from office. Those tensions had been building for some years in and around the capital city, Honiara, on the island of Guadalcanal. The points at issue have been land and the control of resources as well as the inability of government to mediate competing claims and deal effectively with grievances held by both the Malaitans and the Guadalcanal people, moreover, people from other groups. That is why forming a cabinet in the Solomon Island has always required the careful harmonising of representation from the island of Malaita with that from Guadalcanal as well as the Western Province.[20]

An intervention by regional forces from the Pacific led by the Australian police, military personnel and several other regional partners including New Zealand through the Regional Assistance Mission to Solomon Islands (RAMSI) began officially in 2003.[21] What is more, it has become an example of a successful cooperation mainly between the two states that did not appear for the first time as the regional peacekeepers.[22] Their efforts were based primarily on elements such as military deployment, a civilian police presence, weapons amnesties and many-sided mediation. These have been combined with initiatives that respond to the unique conditions to the Solomon Islands: technical support for the country's national financial system, a comprehensive anti-corruption campaign extending

---

[19] 'Biketawa Declaration', Pacific Island Forum Secretariat, 2000, http://www.forumsec.org/resources/uploads/attachments/documents/Biketawa%20Declaration,%2028%20October%202000 [accessed 29 December 2017].

[20] Lawson, 'Security in Oceania', pp. 17–18.

[21] Stephen Hoadley, 'Pacific Island Security Management by New Zealand & Australia: Towards a New Paradigm', *Working Paper* (Centre for Strategic Studies, Victoria University of Wellington, New Zealand), no. 20, 2005, pp. 9–10.

[22] See Shaun Goldfinch, 'Australia, New Zealand and the Pacific Island Nations – Interweaved Histories, Shared Futures', *Otemon Journal of Australian Studies*, vol. 31, 2005, pp. 35–36.

throughout the dominant logging industry as well as the political system and efforts to diversify the national economy into areas such as tourism. They paved the way for a transformation in economic and political management. The highest priority were given to initiatives intended to both reduce the state's vulnerability to conflict, to restore law and order and to strengthen all political and economic institutions, so that the state will be better able to cope with any future crises.[23]

The third example of the state is Fiji. Its instability is related to the expanded role of military. Fiji has a polity divided ethnically, communally and geographically, but the state has experienced democratic rule from the time of independence in 1970 and this pattern of civil military relations has worked well enough. However, this did not stop the Royal Fiji Military Forces from taking over democratically elected governments in 1987, 2000 and 2006. The first military coup in 1987 slightly altered the political landscape. A second military coup followed later that year then a brief return to civilian rule was punctuated in 2000.[24] That coup was formally civilian, but military elements were also involved. The civilians tried to form interventionist coalitions or indoctrinate the military with their political ideologies. Since December 2006 Fiji has been under a military government. In 2009, the fourth coup in twenty years took place. It can be argued that a 'coup culture' seems to be developing.[25]

The issue of Fiji's independence has always been an ethnic problem. The potential for political instability is created by tensions between the majority Fiji Indian and minority indigenous Fijian population, and by a contest between two forms of political authority: democratic authority and the authority rooted in Fijian tradition. None of the other Pacific countries was faced with the problem of designing political institutions capable of withstanding bipolar divisions as deep as those experienced in Fiji. Each democratically elected Fijian government should take into account that its authority can be challenged by people who claim to speak in the name of ethnic Fijians and who possess the ability to mobilise Fijian

---

[23] Carment, Prest and Samy, 'Assessing Small Island', p. 2.

[24] Hegarty, 'Changing Oceania', pp. 15–16.

[25] See James Bunce, 'Regional Security and the Major Powers: An Overview' in Hegarty and Tryon, *Politics, Development and Security in Oceania*, p. 208.

public opinion against the government. As the coups of 1987 and 2000 have showed, the military forces, mostly ethnic Fijian in composition, become the final arbiters of politics.[26] Such an extremely dangerous situation for state stability is possible only in a state that has an army comprising only one ethnic group in a multi-ethnic society.[27]

There has long been ambivalence towards democracy and its support by Fiji's communities over the years has always been conditional. All the more so the implications of the Fiji military regime for regional security go much further than the economic implications. If the extensive constitutional and electoral reform in Fiji is carried out under a military rather than civilian government, the future stability of Fiji will be seriously jeopardised. It is significant that no initiative taken by regional or global organisations has had any real effect on the situation in Fiji so far. For example, this state is the least aid dependent among the South Pacific. That is why withholding aid would not seem to be an effective tool.[28] What is more, following the last coup, Fiji has been suspended both from the Pacific Island Forum (PIF) and the Commonwealth. But still a fragile, divided and very unstable state may present security risks especially to Australia and other countries in Oceania. Fiji can quite easily become a haven for a variety of illegal activities such as organised crime, illegal immigration, corruption or terrorism.[29]

Conclusion

A trend in the assertion of ethnic and nationalist identity politics has led to social conflict and political instability in many small islands. This is underpinned by historical processes of development. In the Pacific mass migration between islands during the colonial era, subsequent ethnic competition

---

[26] Stewart Firth, 'Conceptualizing Security in Oceania: New and Enduring Issues', in Shibuya and Rolfe, *Security in Oceania*, pp. 42–43.

[27] Vijay Naidu, 'The Oxymoron of Security Forces in Island States', in Shibuya and Rolfe, *Security in Oceania*, pp. 36–37.

[28] Bunce, 'Regional Security', pp. 207–208.

[29] See Jim Rolfe, 'Oceania and Terrorism: Some Linkages with the Wider Region and the Necessary Responses', *Working Paper* (Centre for Strategic Studies, Victoria University of Wellington, New Zealand), no. 19, 2004, p. 7.

for economic resources and a reluctance on the part of formerly colonial powers to assist in economic development and the strengthening of institutions have led to many conflicts. Currently, independence movements across the region are fuelling destabilisation. All these movements taken together, seriously threaten regional stability. Such disruptions undermine institutional capacity to respond to vulnerability or disaster impacts. These are illustrated by recent examples of Fiji and the Solomon Islands.

The weakness and vulnerabilities of the South Pacific economies are the principal reasons why these nations have increasingly become the scene of transnational organised crime, particularly in the form of migrant trafficking, drug trafficking and money laundering. In times of recession or exhaustion of commercially viable resources, governments have become less careful and in some instances simply ignorant towards the influx of people and foreign investment. It has also to be noted that both human and financial resources are strictly limited in nations with only a few thousand citizens and no major industry.

Furthermore, constitutions in Oceania states were shaped mainly by advisers and ideas working from European colonial models. Almost no one tried to understand the indigenous systems and to incorporate elements of traditional Pacific principles. It is not insignificant that 'Western' democratic form of government and politics are culturally inadequate on Pacific island states. Now is therefore the time for a deep rethink, looking back to those parts of their own culture that still determine behaviour and may have relevance for inclusion in a new model of governance.

We need to be aware that the contemporary perception of the security of the Pacific Islands should take into account its multidimensionality. The most important threats are internal and serious. The solution is based on the good governance that can return the region to the promising prospects it enjoyed in the 1970s. The forms of Pacific governance are likely to be in for radical change in the coming decades. The most important of these is that we cannot ignore the truth of the statement that 'nothing threatens the Pacific Islands security more than trying to ignore ethnic realities.'[30]

---

[30] Ron Crocombe, 'Responding to Threats to the Pacific Islands Region in the South Pacific', in Shibuya and Rolfe, *Security in Oceania*, p. 225.

In other words, building a security in this region means concentrating not on military forces but more accountable, more transparent, more effective and therefore more legitimate and secure forms of government. That is why the new approach for regional security in Oceania is developmental rather than military. To prevent so-called arc of instability forming in the South Pacific, Australia and New Zealand should direct aid toward governance issues, investing in the future stability and prosperity of the region, whose importance has clearly increased in the 21st century.

Bibliography

Literature

Bunce, James, 'Regional Security and the Major Powers: An Overview', in David Hegarty and Darrel Tryon (eds.), *Politics, Development and Security in Oceania*, Canberra, The Australian National University Press, 2013.

Carment, David, Stewart Prest and Yiagadeesen Samy, 'Assessing Small Island Developing State Fragility', in Lino Briguglio and Eliawony J. Kisanga (eds.), *Economic Vulnerability and Resilience of Small States*, Msida, University of Malta, 2004.

Crocombe, Ron, 'Responding to Threats to the Pacific Islands Region in the South Pacific', in Eric Shibuya and Jim Rolfe (eds.), *Security in Oceania: In the 21st Century*, Honolulu, Asia-Pacific Center for Security, 2003.

Firth, Stewart, 'Conceptualizing Security in Oceania: New and Enduring Issues', in Eric Shibuya and Jim Rolfe (eds.), *Security in Oceania: In the 21st Century*, Honolulu, Asia-Pacific Center for Security, 2003.

Goldfinch, Shaun, 'Australia, New Zealand and the Pacific Island Nations – Interweaved Histories, Shared Futures', *Otemon Journal of Australian Studies*, vol. 31, 2005.

Hegarty, David, 'A Changing Oceania', in David Hegarty and Darrel Tryon (eds.), *Politics, Development and Security in Oceania*, Canberra, The Australian National University Press, 2013.

Hoadley, Stephen, 'Pacific Island Security Managemenet by New Zealand & Australia: Towards a New Paradigm', *Working Paper* (Centre for Strategic Studies, Victoria University of Wellington, New Zealand), no. 20, 2005.

Jacobs, Sean G.L., 'Undermining the State: The "Crime-Terror Nexus" and Papua New Guinea', in Melissa H. Conley Tyler (ed.), *Emerging Scholars 2010–2011*, Australian Institute of International Affairs, June 2011.

Lawson, Stephanie, 'Security in Oceania: Perspectives on the Contemporary Agenda', in Eric Shibuya and Jim Rolfe (eds.), *Security in Oceania: In the 21st Century*, Honolulu, Asia-Pacific Center for Security, 2003.

Mcloughlin, Claire, *Topic Guide on Fragile States*, International Development Department, University of Birmingham, August 2009.

Naidu, Vijay, 'The Oxymoron of Security Forces in Island States', in Eric Shibuya and Jim Rolfe (eds.), *Security in Oceania: In the 21st Century*, Honolulu, Asia-Pacific Center for Security, 2003.

Okole, Henry, 'Papua New Guinea's Brand of Westminster: Democratic Traditions Overlaying Melanesian Cultures', in Haig Patapan, John Wanna, and Patrick Weller (eds.), *Westminster Legacies: Democracy and Responsible Government in Asia and the Pacific*, Sydney, University of New South Wales Press, 2005.

Pelling, Mark and Juha I. Uitto, 'Small Island Developing States: Natural Disaster Vulnerability and Global Change', *Environmental Hazards*, vol. 3, issue 2, 2001.

Rolfe, Jim, 'Oceania and Terrorism: Some Linkages with the Wider Region and the Necessary Responses', *Working Paper* (Centre for Strategic Studies, Victoria University of Wellington, New Zealand), no. 19, 2004.

Websites

'Biketawa Declaration', Pacific Island Forum Secretariat, 2000, http://www.forumsec.org/resources/uploads/attachments/documents/Biketawa%20Declaration,%20 28%20October%202000 [accessed 29 December 2017].

Carment, David, Simon Langlois-Bertrand, and Yiagadeesen Samy, 'Assessing State Fragility, with a Focus on the Middle East and North Africa Region: A 2014 Country Indicators for Foreign Policy Report', Country Indicators for Foreign Policy, Carleton University, Ottawa, 30 December 2014, https://carleton.ca/cifp/wp-content/uploads/CIFP-2014-Fragility-Report.pdf [accessed 28 December 2017].

CIA, The World Factbook, https://www.cia.gov/library/publications/the-world-factbook/geos/pp.html [accessed 29 December 2017].

Dobell, Greame, 'The Pacific "Arc of instability"', *ABC Correspondent's Report*, 20 August 2006, http://www.abc.net.au/correspondents/content/2006/s1719019.htm [accessed 27 October 2017].

Ethnologue. Languauge of the World, https://www.ethnologue.com/country/PG [accessed 28 December 2017].

Jahan, Selim et al. (eds.), Human Development Report 2016: Human Development for Everyone, United Nations Development Programme New York, 2016, http://hdr.undp.org/sites/default/files/2016_human_development_report.pdf [accessed 28 December 2017].

Messner JJ., et al. (eds.), 'Fragile State Index 2018', The Fund for Peace, https://fundforpeace.org/fsi/wp-content/uploads/2018/04/951181805-Fragile-States-Index-Annual-Report-2018.pdf [accessed 25 October 2018].

Schaare, Ben, 'A Pacific Arc of Instability?', Cogit ASIA, 9 September 2015, https://www.cogitasia.com/a-pacific-arc-of-instability/ [accessed 29 December 2017].

Jowita Brudnicka

Strategies of the Oceania States in the Prognostic Perspective: Scenarios of Development

The plans are nothing, but the planning is everything

Dwight Eisenhower

The subject of this paper focuses on the strategies of the Oceania countries towards spontaneous forces of the world. A few scenarios will be presented as a prognostic background. The first challenge is to verify the very existence of a strategic culture in this region. Moreover, there is an issue of a human being who is able to experience full empathy with others and also the question concerning people behaving in a certain way remains unspoken. It is impossible to understand their *renuanga*. At the very beginning of the paper let us stress the importance of time and space as a determinant of the local regional situation.

The states of Oceania being so distant from the major center of political and economic powers still operate in the postmodern world and have to adopt to the conditions that are foreign to them. The policies that the countries of Oceania have to adopt are locked in the dilemma of controversial relations between the "conservative" and "progressive" management. The main challenge about the upcoming future is not to discover it, but to be prepared for various options, which we will be forced to face and overcome the unknown and unpredictable faith.

In the modern world the opinion about a fading role of state power has become one of the main tendencies which globalization may bring. Experts and politicians were divided into critics and strong supporters when it comes to the major role of the states in the internal and international politics with the assumption of disabling the military zones of activity. Both groups struggle with imperfections of their judgment, as the role of state could be underestimated, for instance by neoliberal experts, or overestimated by those who do not want to notice the tendencies to oligarchy, corruption or unreasonable bureaucracy. It can be observed that the global trends of the increasing role of a state indicate that neither the role of a state has vanished, nor a state is a sole controller of everything.

In order for the phenomenon of a strategy and a strategic culture to appear there has to be the tradition of general ways and methods that a decision-maker of a certain community prefers to take. Strategic thinking assumes overcoming the unpredictable and spontaneous changes which have occured in the world of anarchy. The term "spontaneous environment" can be explained by dint of a metaphor adopted by Gilles Deleuze, who compares it to a rhizome – a smooth structure devoid of a unified center of power, where participants create their competition and collaboration based on their particular interest.[1] The impotence of control variability of the global systems is the clue of the spontaneous environment. The first question that needs an answer is as follows: can we distinguish a particular form of the Oceania states strategy in the 21st century?

Strategy and strategic culture

Strategy is a praxeological category about the smooth operation of each entity, referring to the most general ways of doing so.[2] The strategy of state may concern Grand Strategy, the strategy of a foreign policy, the strategy

---

[1] See Gilles Deleuze and Félix Guattari, "Kłącze," transl. Bogdan Banasiak, *Colloquia Communia*, no. 1–3, 1988, p. 221.

[2] See Stanisław Koziej, *Wstęp do teorii i historii bezpieczeństwa (skrypt internetowy)*, Warsaw-Ursynów 2010, p. 4, http://koziej.pl/wp-content/uploads/2015/05/Teoria_i_historia_bezpieczenstwa.doc [accessed September 18, 2018]

of a national security or the strategy of a socio-economic development. Nowadays, different kinds of strategies may overlap, which is an effect of fading boundaries between the zones of state activity. Strategy experts agree with the statement that "Real strategy is made in real time."[3]

The process of creating the strategy itself by the state can be perceived, as Max Weber points out, as a monopoly power, which controls the co-ercive measures and where vertical dominance prevails over the society. However, it can be assumed that a state is not one and only, as there are individuals who create the future plans, but its role is to select the config-urations of interests, give superiority to specific group of them and create normative conditions to achieve them. According to Bob Jessop a state is a relation between the social power and its effect on balance or imbal-ance.[4] The process of making a strategy depends on the limits of state pow-er. Power as a term is a symbol for many different things like resources, probabilities and relations. What is more, Joseph S. Nye defined power as a currency, which could be exchanged for binding political decisions.[5] Power is not once given, however authorities have to make sure that their decision-making gains legitimization, otherwise they will be left power-less.[6] Every strategist has to cope with many different obstacles that vary in nature:

- barriers: natural, material, normative ones;
- problem with the lack of restrictions, such as resources, time, space;
- conflict issues: the actions of enemies.

The very existence of such problems proves that a strategy is made un-der conditions of conflict and every strategy has agonistic features.

Strategic culture is essentially an attempt to integrate cultural consider-ations, cumulative historical memory and their influences in the analysis of a states' security policies and international relations. Three elements of strategic culture has been defined by Kerry Longhurst:

---

[3] See Sarah Kaplan and Eric D. Beinhocker, "The Real Value of Strategic Planning," *MIT Sloan Management Review*, vol. 44, issue 2, 2003, p. 72.

[4] See Bob Jessop, "Beyond Developmental States: A Regulationist and State-Theoretical Analysis," *Memoirs of the Institute of Humanities and Social Sciences*, vol. 86, 2006, pp. 145–165.

[5] Joseph S. Nye, *The Future of Power*, New York, Public Affairs, 2011, p. 35.

[6] See Karl W. Deutsch, *The Analysis of International Relations*, Englewood Cliffs (N.J.), Prentice-Hall, 1968, p. 47.

- fundamental values – persistent beliefs regarding the use of force, ways and measures to build the national paradigm;
- decisions concerning the security policy, such as wide acceptable interpretation referring to the ways of achieving a state mission;
- regulations – the most dynamic element which depends on actual political trends.[7]

The strategy of different actors can be implemented on different difficulty levels and it depends on the state power, which is an ability to influence the behavior of others in accordance with their objectives.[8] There are a few components of power, such as geography, population, natural resources, economic capacity, military strength and willingness.

Answering all those questions concerning the Oceania region, allows us to conjecture that the problem remains in inequalities between Oceania countries and the discrepancies seem to be hard to overcome. There are various types of possible inequalities: juridico-political, social and those connected with the equal access and an equal start. Karl Deutsch uses the term "equality in opportunities."[9] Juridico-political equality means that everyone possesses the same legal and political rights, by dint of which the legalized power can resist the political power. In the social context, equality assures protection from discrimination. Everyone ought to have similar opportunities to rise, every contribution should be taken into consideration and initial conditions should let to acquire the same abilities and ranks. However, the access to those opportunities should be equal and relevant to equal abilities (but not to all). Equal start concentrates on the question of how to develop individual potentialities equally. Oceania countries differ from each other at all dimensions of equality. Nevertheless, inequalities *per se* should not be considered only as disadvantages. In the micro scale, in the atomized societies, without the alternative organizations, they undergo centralization. The existence of more powerful players in the macro scale could provide more stability. Analyzing the situation

---

[7] See Kerry Longhurst, *Germany and the Use of Force: The Evolution of German Security Policy 1990–2003*, Manchester, Manchester University Press, 2004, p. 15.

[8] See John W. Spanier and Robert L. Wendzel, *Games Nations Play*, Washington, Congressional Quarterly, 1996, p. 129.

[9] Deutsch, *Analysis*, p. 344.

of the Oceania region, the focus should be placed on a dependency in the macro scale, rather than an interdependence.

What should be emphasized is the importance of collective memory in the strategic culture and contemporary strategic policy of the hierarchy of state-run entities. As Maurice Halbwachs points out "Story is one, collective memory many."[10] As many communities, so many carriers of different interpretations of historical facts. It should also be explained that nowadays a historical research is not only reserved for professionals, but a "renaissance of commemoration" in the public debate can be observed. It is a derivative of the features deviating from a "positive history" to "new history." Culture, also the strategic one, is a product of the historical agency of the whole group of actors operating from different angles. The strategic culture is not obviously a static whole, but it is the derive of a long process which cannot be easily erased from memory.

The strategic culture of Oceania

According to PWN Encyclopedia[11], Oceania is a geographic region comprising of Melanesia, Micronesia and Polynesia. Oceania covers an area of 1.2 million square kilometers and has a population of thirty-two million people, however in many sources this region is called Australasia. The map of the Pacific region reminds the skies full of the shining stars.[12] The center-periphery metaphor provides the right image of a global power relation, although it may be perceived as a colonial period residue. The centers are identified as places which grab attention and have a privileged vantage view. Geographical factor as a determinant of a strategic culture creation can be twofolded: facilitating or obstructing. States with quite a flat area and an access to the sea have better conditions to build

---

[10] Maurice Halbwachs, *Społeczne ramy pamięci*, transl. and introd. Marcin Król, Warsaw, Państwowe Wydawnictwo Naukowe, 1969, pp. 421–422. My translation – JB.

[11] "Oceania," Encyklopedia PWN online, https://encyklopedia.pwn.pl/haslo/Oceania;4019539.html [accessed September 19, 2018].

[12] Aleksander Posern-Zieliński, *Polinezja świat nieznany*, Warsaw, Książka i Wiedza, 1972, p. 5.

communication infrastructure. Mountainous area and tropical climate or lack of natural resources in general, require major capital expenditures to create a functional political system. Pre-colonial period in Oceania islands can be characterized by the development of a tribal system. Such an archetype of a state can be taken as the beginning of creation of political culture. Geography was the main factor which influenced the creation of a mechanism of balancing interest groups. We can make an assumption that geographical differences between various parts of Oceania are important elements of the differences of states when considering a political development and a strategic culture. Taking into account the pre-colonial period, the political situation in Papua New Guinea seemed to be more complex and chaotic than the situation in Tonga, which evidently had an impact on hitherto strategic situation.

Firstly, let us analyze an archetype that is common for all. The cultures of Oceania states are so diverse when it comes to political roles of military force, chiefs, warriors, heroes and dictators. In all tribal communities warriors were mainly needed to implement the chiefly power. War was the natural occupation of men who were supposed to protect the community. Confrontations with enemies were numerous, although usually short and with a limited number of casualties. The symbolic victory was sufficient, as the main goal was to establish the power in the longer term, not to exterminate the opponents.[13] Nonetheless, it is very hard to opt for uniform style of fight and war. First of all, in Oceania there were many different attitudes to the phenomenon of cannibalism. In Europe there is a possibility to define a common codex of a noble knight in general, but there is no unity about a cannibalistic practice. In ethnographic literature, there is an evidence that cannibalism were practiced in New Zealand, Fiji, New Guinea, Vanuatu, New Caledonia, Gambiers and on Easter Island. Cannibalism was not practiced on a couple of Polynesia islands. Also it has been reported by some European visitors of Melanesia that this ritual was not practiced by *all* people there. Many of the tribes were headhunters,

---

[13] Hélène Goiran, "The Political Roles of the Fiji Military: A Brief History of the Chiefs' Warriors, Heroes of the World Wars, Peacekeepers and Dictators," in David Hegarty and Darrell Tyron (eds.), *Politics, Development and Security in Oceania*, Canberra, ANU Press, 2013, p. 60.

as they killed men, women and kids to gain their heads. Also, the aim of cannibalism differed in various places. Eating human meat served many purposes, as it satisfied the appetite for meat in general, it was treated as a punishment and contempt directed at an enemy, and a magical ritual of acquisition of somebody's virtue.[14]

Secondly, what constitutes a strategic culture is its colonial heritage. Primarily, the colonial powers tried to divide a population into already scattered island archipelagos. The location of colonial capitals on small offshore islands, such as Tulagi in Solomon Islands, Jaluit in the German Marshall Islands proved a restricted influence of the largest and the most populous islands. European models of governing were highly influential in creating rule systems in the Pacific islands. In turn, Southern Pacific remains under European hemisphere. French Polynesia, Wallis and Futuna and New Caledonia are under the francophone system of law, having a full participation in elections to the National Assembly in Paris and presidential elections.[15] In former British colonies, an electoral system has been expressed in the form of Westminster system or has evolved to reach a final compromise between the British and French authorities, such as Vanuatu. The 21st century state-building process differs extremely from the process dating back to the 19th century.

Oceania was first explored by Europeans from the 16th century onwards. Competition for the South Pacific space begun in the 17th century and ceased in 1906, when New Zealand proclaimed sovereignty. The proper analysis of the situation of postcolonial states needs a significant insight. In analytical research, the term "postcolonial" should be referred to the countries which remained under the colonial dependence, however nowadays, also in their structure, there are significant social, economic, political or ideological after-effects. Contemporary socio-political situation in Oceania shows different outcomes of the colonial times. Clearly identified categories of "allies" and "enemies" constitute the source of power which

---

[14] Douglas L. Oliver, *The Pacific Islands*, Honolulu, University of Hawaii Press, 1989, pp. 316–317.

[15] Jon Fraenkel, "How Relevant are European Models of Government to Pacific Islands States," in Hegarty and Tyron, *Politics, Development and Security*, p. 198.

unites the whole community.[16] These days, the former colonial states are not directly perceived as enemies. For French Polynesia, despite all centrifugal tendencies, France is not a main power posing a threat for the national interest. The enemy is defined more like an external force that may craftily inhibit internal abilities to create a sovereign policy. The colonial heritage left not only different state governance styles, but it also influenced the inclination to unite around common objectives.

It is vital to note that the main external threats, such as those from the 21st century are not military threats, but rather economic ones. The main strategic aim that constitutes a common denominator for all the Oceania countries is to ensure the state economic security. The term "economic security" in Security Studies assumes the maintenance of integrity and politico-military abilities enabling the state to overcome various risks, which are a result of global economic systems.[17] The largest element of spontaneity can be found in economy. Still religious, tribal and traditional threats reproduce themselves and remain a challenge for states, however in the face of the world economical crisis it seems that financial markets gain the most of unpredictable processes. In order to understand the economic situation that is to be analyzed, we need to take into account the complexity of macroeconomic indicators, as they mostly remain in the very interest of aid organizations. In the short-term perspective it is not a catastrophe when a state takes loans, but during that time they have to preserve the economic growth. Lack of inflation is the first macroeconomic indicator favorable for the further aid programs. When countries are not able to manage the economy as a system, they would not be able to manage a foreign aid. The economic factor as a symbol of unification with the people of Oceania would be too far-stretched. As long as main players in the region show no interest in the expansion of countries as a whole, there will not be enough pull factors to unite.

It may seem that in the face of encompassing climate changes and vanishing coral islands processes, the inescapable fear will gather peoples'

---

[16] Paweł Kaczorowski, *My i oni. Państwo jako jedność polityczna. Filozofia polityczna Carla Schmitta w okresie republiki weimarskiej*, Warsaw, Szkoła Główna Handlowa, 1998, p. 103.

[17] Alan Collins, *Contemporary Security Studies*, Oxford, Oxford University Press, 2007, p. 210.

hearts and minds. In combination with bad market and lack of economic maneuverability, the vision of migration seems to be the best answer for the community of the Oceania small island.

When considering the military security, the largest unprecedented event, after the Second World War, was a military operation known under the name RAMSI (Regional Assistance Mission to Solomon Islands). The multinational mission was an answer to the deepening destabilization in Solomon Islands. In the public debate it is very easy to find uncomplimentary opinions about RAMSI. Many of the arguments seem to be acceptable, however the disputes are very often burdened with a poor understanding of security studies and as a result the interlocutors are divided into opponents and supporters of international military interventions. First of all, a military intervention does not imply that the strategic objective is to kill potential enemies. Moreover, the military is formed from soldiers and skilled civilians. Secondly, despite all bad associations people may have due to Iraqi Freedom, there is no simple scheme for a military operation, as the term is constituted from various kinds of missions: state-building, peace building/keeping/enforcement etc. Thirdly, the strategic, operational and tactical aim of the mission is in the process of a permanent redefinition and it depends on leadership if it is well recognized and implemented without any obstacles. Fourthly, the question of legality of military operations appears. Everyone regarded in international organizations mostly is created as an answer for help from states authorities. RAMSI was not a military operation. It can be regarded as a crisis management operation. It was a civilian-led mission, an initiative of PIF (Pacific Islands Forum) along with the invitation of Solomon Islands Government.

Negative opinions appear when it comes to the general political situation in Solomon Islands, however one should not be so naïve to believe that due to the foreign forces it is possible to establish the rule of law and democracy in its best scenario. Militaries are CIMIC (Civil-military cooperation), which is not projected to make politics, but to create favorable conditions to leave the crisis area and let them make their own governance without tensions. If communities are able to take advantage in the long term, they can stabilize a socio-political situation on their own. Lack of the strategic culture, geographical dispersion, ineffective market do not help in creating safe environment in the region. Potential lack of RAMSI during those years could provoke deepening the collapse of states and make the rest of the region even more fragile than it is now. Analyzing military missions there are a lot of factors that should be taken into account and the following question may be asked: why did they sometimes fail in achieving their objectives and what are the conditions under which they succeed?

Strategic situation of Oceania

Strategic scene is a field of rivalry, whereas a strategic situation is a scene and the dynamism of interactions between the players. To be more precise, a strategic situation is composed of the fundamental and actual strategic context. It may happen that they are contradictory. History and historical values constitute the most stable strategic categories. Time and a real situation are the most dynamic categories of the whole strategic analysis. Nowadays, states face bigger possibilities of contact with spontaneous rhizome, which is the reason why they have to recognize more and more side stages in strategies (peripheral scene). The research could refer to every single state understood as a strategic player, but in this paper we shall focus on the conglomerate of Oceania states as a main strategic player.

The Oceania states region is our main strategic scene, as there is a high resemblance between particular countries, so that they have a common strategic culture. Stating that the unification of every single Oceania state is possible can be controversial. In this particular research, being aware of the complexity of conditions which have to be filled, it can be assumed that the main scene is composed of the whole Oceania or a part of it. The group of states should have such a significant potential so that they would be able to create a local strategic scene.

There are some peripheral stages which may have a direct impact on the strategies of Oceania countries:

- Oceania + Australia and New Zealand – the closest to the main scene.
- Peripheral scenes: Australia, New Zealand, Indonesia, the USA, the EU (and particular countries of the EU), China, India, Antarctica.

The key questions for Oceania states are:

- What is our position in the global system and what constitutes that?
- Who is the most powerful and the weakest link in our close surroundings?
- What strategies do the countries in our close and further surroundings have?
- Are there any possibilities to take advantage of their strategies?

The answers to this catalogue of questions may provide the basis for creating the unique geopolitical code. As it is claimed by Julian Skrzyp, there are some states in their strategies that never transcend the borders of the home region. For smaller states every Grand Strategy of the global power is a challenge, as it requires revising the existing goals.[18] At every level of both geopolitical and geostrategic aspects should be taken into consideration. When analyzing the situation of Oceania countries there are as follows: geography, lack of natural resources (problems with export as a main way to generate wealth), ecological changes, internal diversity of political development (lack of pre-colonial prototype of state), the colonial past (turbulent political systems, lack of trust to institutions), internal financial capital, private property problems, migration of the educated people. These are the reasons why it is so difficult to establish the economic security in this region. As it can be observed, ecological security[19] is considered to be a subordinate category to the economic security.

Geostrategic aspects include geopolitical competition over the South Pacific space being in contradiction with other actors' strategies: they refer to close surroundings, such as the American hemisphere, and further surroundings – Chinese attempts to empower their military abilities, which refer mainly to the conflict on the South China Sea.

Oceania states' peripheral position of power is a result of most of the above-mentioned factors, due to the economically unattractive area which

---

[18] Julian Skrzyp, *Geopolityka. Przeszłość przyszłości*, Warsaw, AON, 2016, p. 11.

[19] A catalogue of actions protecting people and the environment from ecological threats and such shaping of natural and social relations in the biosphere of Earth, which creates the right conditions for all humanity. More: Wojciech Łepkowski (ed.), *Słownik terminów z zakresu bezpieczeństwa narodowego*, Warsaw, AON, 2008.

inhibits a relative self-sufficiency and an inability to urge other players to economic undertakings, potentially beneficial for both parties.

While the first cause seems to be quite clear as it refers to natural conditions, the second reason is very complex. Oceania states should have an elaborated project with strong and weak sides of their position. Then it can be understood that they cannot improve their position relative to other players, mostly towards Australia and New Zealand, which generated wealth and despite a close geographic location a different strategic culture. In fact, the differences between states' potentials wither for the Oceania states. In such circumstances, the main actor (Oceania countries) has to share with other players with the possessed advantages. In this case geopolitical and geostrategic maritime possibilities shall be considered. In other words, these are exclusive economic zones, sea routes and tropical conditions attractive for the tourism sector.

The key factor to create an appropriate strategy for any player is to identify the opportunities aptly in particular time. Time may be perceived as the unified process at an equal pace and range of moments. The first approach is characterized by a simple extrapolation of trends and it can be stated that trends vanish and rise. Spontaneous surroundings are filled with unexpected and rare phenomena sometimes identified in literature as "black swans." To create a strategy under postmodern global trends it is hard to identify a permanent regularity. The asymmetrical relation between causes and results exists. Such nonlinearity may take the form of "the Butterfly Effect"[20] or a "Mountain Effect."[21] What can be identified as a main trend impact on states' strategies is concerned with getting rid of the belief of the states' equality. In case of Oceania, in the creation of a strategy is limited at the very beginning, due to the fact that global powers such as the USA, China, India and the UE with various degress of severity still tend to create the strategies for others.

---

[20] A small cause has huge consequences. More: Wojciech Lamentowicz, *Strategia państwa. Teoria państwa aktywnego wobec sił spontanicznych*, Warsaw, Dom Wydawniczy Elipsa, 2016, pp. 155–156.

[21] A spectacular event brings about minor changes. More: ibid.

Oceania region scenarios – conservative management or progressive management

Scenario is a description of the future, possible situations in which the actor can find himself. It shows that a certain kind of event development can be a condition for objecting a further behavior. A division between the possible scenario and the desirable scenario has to be made.

Descriptive scenario[22]

Oceania region has a diverse mix of economies. The smallest Pacific nations rely on the trade with Australia, New Zealand and the United States for exporting goods and accessing other products. Australia and New Zealand's trading arrangements are known as Closer Economic Relations. Australia and New Zealand, along with other countries, are members of Asia-Pacific Economic Cooperation (APEC) and the East Asia Summit (EAS), which may become trade blocs in the future, particularly EAS. They do not have large land space areas and financial capital to invest, however small island countries still remain monopolistic when it comes to the market structures. Assuming that small states do not change rapidly, the production conditions and market situations could be illustrated as a monopoly competition. Market is in peculiar relations between demand and supply. Products do not differ from one another and companies can count on profits from demand when they are loyal to the brand. Opening the market makes the products much cheaper, but a company still can sell more.[23]

In many countries a political system is unstable and has a military *coup d'état*. Archipelagos are in danger because of rising water levels. The region is bordered by Australian and New Zealand strategic culture – among which New Zealand seems to be more similar to the Oceania culture.

---

[22] Relative objective and neutral sequences of possible events. More: Halina Świeboda, *Prognozowanie zagrożeń bezpieczeństwa narodowego Rzeczypospolitej Polskiej*, Warsaw, Akademia Sztuki Wojennej, 2017.

[23] Adam Budnikowski, *Ekonomia międzynarodowa*, Warsaw, Polskie Wydawnictwo Ekonomiczne, 2017, p. 112.

Military situation in the Oceania region is complex, as the states pay attention to the military security in different ways. While Fiji tries to develop their military abilities through retrofitting their equipment, other states consider strategic challenges elsewhere, for instance in developing tourism. Internal security is determined by various features, namely the migration of young and educated people, lack of economic infrastructure, also the tourism infrastructure. What singles out Oceania states is having incomparably larger exclusive economic zones.

We can assume that the phenomenon of Oceania strategic culture does exist, but only in comparison with other global strategic cultures, as the "inside pull factors" cannot constitute a peculiar strategic culture. Empathy as the ability to participate in a person's feelings or ideas varies not only between three subregions, but also within the subregions in general. The whole variety of attitudes are exacerbated by economic inequalities. The Banaban people are able to understand feelings of others, but they do not equate themselves, as they feel socially and economically better positioned than the strangers.[24] The conception of self within the Banabans has undergone a historically specific shaping and created a self-perception as *titebo ma kaokoro*: same but different.[25] In this case adding the ethnic component helped to ensure a wide-ranging autonomy for their home islands: Rabi and Banaba.[26]

Normative scenario/forecasting scenario[27]

The most desirable scenario assumes that Oceania states gain such a financial capital to independently secure their self economic security, understood as a secured internal business environment, and create possibilities

---

[24] Nancy Scheper-Hughes, *Death Without Weeping: The Violence of Everyday Life in Brazil*, Berkeley, University of California Press, 1992.

[25] Elfriede Hermann, "Manifold Identifications Within Differentiations: Shaping of Self Among Relocated Banabans of Fiji," in Toon van Meijl and Henk Driessen (eds.), *Multiple Identifications and the Self*, Utrecht, Stichting Focaal, 2003.

[26] Elfriede Hermann, "Empathy, Ethnicity and the Self among the Banabans in Fiji," in Douglas W. Hollan and C. Jason Throop (eds.), *The Anthropology of Empathy: Experiencing the Lives of Others in Pacific Societes*, New York and Oxford, Berghahn Books, 2011, p. 36.

[27] Normative and forecasting scenarios can be supplemented. More: Świeboda, *Prognozowanie zagrożeń*.

to develop also in the foreign countries. To do so, it is necessary to find an innovative way to bring the foreign capital into the state. It could happen by the market privatization of a part of the national economy. With the gradual development of a human being, Oceania states can gain time to build a well-perceived political status and calm down the social tensions. Opportunities possessed by the states should be viewed as positive. These are: maritime communication routes, attractive and still undiscovered areas and land lease possibilities. At this point, a huge potential for cultural diplomacy should be spotted. As it is pointed out by Charles Fankel, the states always used culture to promote their political, economic and social values.[28]

In a normative scenario methodology the worst-case scenario should also be described. It may happen when there is no willingness to create a platform of agreement between Oceania countries, which unfortunately is highly possible. In international relations taking actions completely out of rational way of thinking is a common practice. In the Security Studies it is called "The Prisoner's Dilemma" and it is a standard example of a game analyzed in the game theory that gives an explanation why two "rational" individuals might not want to cooperate, even if it appears to be in their best interest to do so. Such a mutual misunderstanding and a deep distrust can paralyze the inventions of decision makers. If such a regional cooperation is possible, a multitude of threats may appear. They can have an internal (cultural and political tensions) and external character (aggressive external "partnership" based more on neocolonial expansion than on simple "sale and purchase" relation).

To improve growth a couple of rules should be adopted. First of all, neutralizing the geographical dispersal through connectivity of people, information and goods. In the macro scale, it would be better if regions diversify their export using creative economies, based on traditional industries and start to develop the infrastructure, also by dint of a foreign financial capital. What should also be taken into consideration is projecting "creative" cities according to the global tourism sector. There are

---

[28] Charles Frankel, "Educational and Cultural Diplomacy, Department of State, Office of Media Service, Bureau of Public Affairs [1963]," in Theodore M. Vestal, *International Education: Its History and Promise for Today*, Westport (Conn.), Praeger Publishers, 1994, p. 33.

places being more accessible to foreign visitors which let them get to know foreign tradition and the local culture. If foreign tour companies start to invest in the local infrastructure, it will be easier to establish international found in case of natural disasters.

Every case scenario requires a specific management style. Management in general is a process concerning society, which is deeply rooted in the strategic culture. Moreover, it requires simple and clear values that unite people, as well as communication between society and administration.[29] State management is characterized by the uncertain environment, which in this research is called the "spontaneous environment." The unpredictability is expressed in an inability of resolving problems, also those which are known: lack of information network, bad information management skills and the ambiguity of legal regulations. Progressive management stimulates independent and spontaneous troubleshooting and taking risks to go beyond schemes. The motto of such a management model is as follows: "Better prevent than remove the effects of any crisis: economic or social." Conservative management does not exclude the elements of a progressive management, but it is characterized by a state of attachment to the established rules and values. It is more appropriate to deal with an actual crisis than with the situation of a relative stability. Reasoning about the suitability of a conservative management during the actual crisis is based on life wisdom presupposing that crisis is the worst period for experiments.

The comparison between those two management styles seems to be clear and non-controversial. According to the theory, Oceania states should first stabilize the socio-political situation of the internal states and start to look at global challenges in which they could be a helpful element in the strategies of international actors. A conservative attitude should be maintained in the preservation of a strategic culture, but it also should be present in a new and generally acceptable way of political thinking. In order to compete on the ground of potential incomes, a subtle game of diplomacy should be launched. It seems that dedication to provide home markets for foreigners could be the simplest way to gain financial capital inland. The

---

[29] Peter Drucker, *The Coming of the New Organization*, Boston (Mass.), Harvard Business School Press, 1988, pp. 75–76.

highest threat to Oceania states may come from within the region and take the character of an all-encompassing distrust – citizens to institutions, institutions to governments and governments to the foreign actors. Other problems can also be identified in Oceania states, one of which is an unwilling attitude to unite around the common goal of which there is prosperity and the possibility to face threats, such as ecological ones.

Changeable attitude which is so characteristic of Oceania states paradoxically lowers the possibilities of the development of every single country. It may be the case that common strategic culture values are not so obvious to every politician in Oceania islands, or they cannot be identified as a sufficient factor to unite people of Oceania. Undoubtedly, geographical dispersion is a factor that influences the division of a society. To finish off, let us give an example of a question for the further research: do intensified communication possibilities between the regional states can serve the Oceania cultural identity?

Conclusion

The role of a state in the 21st century has declined due to intensification of the globalization processes. The states of Oceania open opportunities to "see far back" into the past and, in consequence, bring unique opportunities of how communities has been organized. Only environment determining the security system of Oceania has been changed. The process of a global modernization is quicker than internally established capacities of a local adaptation. There are many determinants of such a situation. The first one discussed in this paper is concerned with geographic isolation and contradictive incompatibility in the following capacities: territorial, substantial, demographic. It seems that geographic distance is equal to the cultural consciousness. The perception of the conglomerate of Oceania states as a single, autonomous of international relations unit apparently seems to be a mistake, since there is no sufficient socio-political coherency to see a regional reality as a single strategic cultural unite. In the case being discussed a possible economic and political cooperation should be reduced to the limited amount of stakeholders and rational goals to be achieved. As a result, it allows to reduce the level of uncertainty and hazard. Previous analysis depict that every single state of Oceania will search for adequate partners from the region (the choice is very limited: Australia or New Zealand), or states from the outside of the region: China, Russia, India, the USA etc. Strategic dispersion of small states may bring profits to them, while most of the challenges of the 21st century are connected with certain problems common for all of them: climate changes, migration and Oceanic competition of superpowers.

Bibliography

Literature

Budnikowski, Adam, *Ekonomia międzynarodowa*, Warsaw, Polskie Wydawnictwo Ekonomiczne, 2017.

Collins, Alan, *Contemporary Security Studies*, Oxford, Oxford University Press, 2007.

Deleuze, Gilles and Félix Guattari, "Kłącze," transl. Bogdan Banasiak, *Colloquia Communia*, no. 1–3, 1988, pp. 221–238.

Deutsch, Karl W., *The Analysis of International Relations*, Englewood Cliffs (N.J.), Prentice-Hall, 1968.

Drucker, Peter, *The Coming of the New Organization*, Boston (Mass.), Harvard Business School Press, 1988.

Fraenkel, Jon, "How Relevant are European Models of Government to Pacific Islands States," in David Hegarty and Darrell Tyron (eds.), *Politics, Development and Security in Oceania* (pp. 195–204), Canberra, ANU Press, 2013.

Frankel, Charles, "Educational and Cultural Diplomacy, Department of State, Office of Media Service, Bureau of Public Affairs [1963]," in Theodore M. Vestal, *International Education: Its History and Promise for Today*, Westport (Conn.), Praeger Publishers, 1994.

Goiran, Hélène, "The Political Roles of the Fiji Military: A Brief History of the Chiefs' Warriors, Heroes of the World Wars, Peacekeepers and Dictators," in David Hegarty and Darrell Tyron (eds.), *Politics, Development and Security in Oceania* (p. 57–69), Canberra, ANU Press, 2013.

Halbwachs, Maurice, *Społeczne ramy pamięci*, transl. and introd. Marcin Król, Warsaw, Państwowe Wydawnictwo Naukowe, 1969.

Hermann, Elfriede, "Manifold Identifications Within Differentiations: Shaping of Self Among Relocated Banabans of Fiji," in Toon van Meijl and Henk Driessen (eds.), *Multiple Identifications and the Self*, Utrecht, Stichting Focaal, 2003.

Hermann, Elfriede, "Empathy, Ethnicity and the Self among the Banabans in Fiji," in Douglas W. Hollan and C. Jason Throop (eds.), *The Anthropology of Empathy: Experiencing the Lives of Others in Pacific Societes* (p. 25–41), New York and Oxford, Berghahn Books, 2011.

Jessop, Bob, "Beyond Developmental States: A Regulationist and State-Theoretical Analysis," *Memoirs of the Institute of Humanities and Social Sciences*, vol. 86, 2006, pp. 1–36.

Kaczorowski, Paweł, *My i oni. Państwo jako jedność polityczna. Filozofia polityczna Carla Schmitta w okresie republiki weimarskiej*, Warsaw, Szkoła Główna Handlowa, 1998.

Kaplan, Sarah and Eric D. Beinhocker, "The Real Value of Strategic Planning," *MIT Sloan Management Review*, vol. 44, issue 2, 2003, 71–76.

Lamentowicz, Wojciech, *Strategia państwa. Teoria państwa aktywnego wobec sił spontanicznych*, Warsaw, Dom Wydawniczy Elipsa, 2015.

Longhurst, Kerry, *Germany and the Use of Force: The Evolution of German Security Policy 1990–2003*, Manchester, Manchester University Press, 2004.

Łepkowski, Wojciech (ed.), *Słownik terminów z zakresu bezpieczeństwa narodowego*, Warsaw, AON, 2008.

Nye, Joseph S., *The Future of Power*, New York, Public Affairs, 2011.

Oliver, Douglas L., *The Pacific Islands*, Honolulu, University of Hawaii Press, 1989.

Posern-Zieliński, Aleksander, *Polinezja świat nieznany*, Warsaw, Książka i Wiedza, 1972.

Scheper-Hughes, Nancy, *Death Without Weeping: The Violence of Everyday Life in Brazil*, Berkeley, University of California Press, 1992.

Skrzyp, Julian, *Geopolityka. Przeszłość przeszłości*, Warsaw, AON, 2016.

Spanier, John W. and Robert L. Wendzel, *Games Nations Play*, Washington, Congressional Quarterly, 1996.

Świeboda, Halina, *Prognozowanie zagrożeń bezpieczeństwa narodowego Rzeczypospolitej Polskiej*, Warsaw, Akademia Sztuki Wojennej, 2017.

Websites

Encyklopedia PWN online, https://encyklopedia.pwn.pl/haslo/Oceania;4019539. html [accessed September 19, 2018].

Koziej, Stanisław, *Wstęp do teorii i historii bezpieczeństwa (skrypt internetowy)*, Warsaw-Ursynów 2010, http://koziej.pl/wp-content/uploads/2015/05/Teoria_i_historia_bezpieczenstwa.doc [accessed September 18, 2018].

Masum Billah

Constitutional Property Clause: A Comment on the Bangladeshi, New Zealand and Polish Approach

Introduction

Constitutional guarantees of property rights are the subject of continued popular and political interests. Nonetheless, it has always been a big question how to treat property rights within a constitutional framework. There are different approaches to the issue. Many countries have constitutional-ised property protection (i.e. Bangladesh, South Africa, Poland and USA), a few others have not (i.e. New Zealand and Canada). Some countries have taken a balancing approach to the issue (i.e. India).

In my PhD thesis, I investigated the postcolonial land reform of Bangladesh. One of the related issues of the thesis was to examine how a post-colonial 'Lancaster House' type of constitution like Bangladesh addresses the property issue, land reform in particular. The country inserted right to property in its constitution of 1972 as one of the fundamental rights of the citizens. However, after forty-five years of such incorporation, it appears that Bangladesh has not been able to create a just property system. A wide-spread gap between the rich and the poor is apparent and poverty due to landlessness is rampant in Bangladesh. Therefore, my idea was to revisit the constitutionalisation of property issue and examine its implications in shaping a textual and structural framework where pro-poor land reform can take place.

Constitutionalisation of property rights issue may be indeed an appropriate topic when discussing the Oceania. The approach to property protection largely depends on the historical and cultural background of a country. However, there are certain common issues which need to be tested in every jurisdiction. In this short note, I comment on the property clause of the Bangladesh Constitution in the light of other experiences, i.e. New Zealand and Poland. My point is that constitutional property clause should aim to establish a coherent relationship between property rights, constitutionalism and state's power.

Bangladesh

Bangladesh inserted a property clause in its 1972 Constitution like this:

> Article 42: (1) Subject to any restrictions imposed by law, every citizen shall have the right to acquire, hold, transfer or otherwise dispose of property, and no property shall be compulsorily acquired, nationalised or requisitioned save by authority of law.
>
> (2) A law made under clause (1) of this article shall provide for the acquisition, nationalisation or requisition with compensation and shall fix the amount of compensation or specify the principles on which, and the manner in which, the compensation is to be assessed and paid; but no such law shall be called in question in any court on the ground that any provision of the law in respect of such compensation is not adequate.[1]

The insertion of this property clause in the Constitution implies that its framers were conscious about the significance of right to property. The clause affords a protection to people's economic liberty as well as recognises state's relationship with its property system. In legal theory, such

---

[1] The Constitution of the People's Republic of Bangladesh, http://bdlaws.minlaw.gov.bd/sections_detail.php?id=367&sections_id=24590 [accessed 19 November 2017].

a clause serves as a basis of the state's property law that helps achieving the purposes of social justice. However, Bangladesh seemingly failed to create a just property regime in the post-independence settings irrespective of its social and aspirational egalitarian ethos. Here, the loopholes in land reform law are dominant, land distribution is grossly unequal, tenurial security is fragile and in many cases undefined. As a result, the promise for land reform remains merely a political rhetoric since the day of partition in 1947.

Bangladesh Constitution puts property rights and other fundamental rights in the same order. There is a view that property rights should not be equated with first-order values (life, liberty, equality, speech). According to this view, property is a means to attain these values, not one of the values itself.[2] People exercise the first-order values without any cost of another. In contrast, right to property has its uniqueness in it. When property is meant some external finite resources (which in Bangladesh is culturally understood as *sompatti,* i.e. land[3]), it should be placed in a different order of rights. If a person's right of possession over land is protected, it implies that other person's right over it is denied. This peculiarity of property rights invites a different role to be played by the state.[4] From this point of view, the property clause of the Bangladesh Constitution upsets the order of fundamental rights. This leads us to raise the question that whether *equality* should be made accountable to property or *property* should be made accountable to equality.[5]

The property clause empowers the state to acquire private property under the notion of *eminent domain.* The state usually enacts acquisition law to acquire private property for public purposes. In order to facilitate

---

[2] Jennifer Nedelsky, 'Should Property be Constitutionalised: A Relational and Comparative Approach', in Gerrit E. van Maneen and André J. van der Walt (eds.), *Property Law on the Threshold of the 21st Century*, Antwerp, Maklu, 1996, p. 417.

[3] Article 42 at first refers the term 'property' and then quickly starts talking about 'acquisition', 'nationalisation' and 'expropriation', etc. It gives the impression that the constitutional framers predominantly took the meaning of property in its tangible or immovable sense.

[4] Laura S. Underkuffler, *The Idea of Property: Its Meaning and Power*, Oxford, Oxford University Press, 2003, p. 141.

[5] Underkuffler forwards an illuminating reasoning. She argues that the notion of property cannot be analytically and physically separated from the maintenance of life itself and should be the substance of this right. Ibid., p. 148.

the greater public welfare, the property clause limits the scope of judicial review of acquisition legislation. It debars challenging an acquisition law on the ground of inadequacy of compensation. However, it obliges the state to follow certain basic principles with a view to prevent the misuse of eminent domain power. The principles are as follows:

i)   the acquisition must be by authority of law;
ii) the affected person must be compensated, adequate or inadequate;
iii) the acquisition law must either fix the amount of the compensation or specify the principles and manner of fixing and handing over the compensation;
iv) the acquisition must be done for a 'public purpose'.

Of these four principles, the principle of public purpose has not received any express treatment in the property clause. Perhaps, it was a deliberate oversight, as the presence of such purpose is 'inherent' in acquisition. Therefore it is settled that public purpose is a feature of the acquisition power itself.[6] The Constitution does not define the term 'public purpose'. The statutory law has also not demarcated the scope of the doctrine. Case laws view the term liberally.[7] Therefore, statutory, judicial and juristic commentary in Bangladesh fails to set an intellectually compelling interpretation of public purpose. This failure makes the state's power of eminent domain enormous, because it is knotted with the breadth or narrowness assigned to the definition of 'public purpose'.

The New Zealand and Polish approach

New Zealand has no written constitution. The rights of the citizens are recognised by the Bill of Rights Act 1990. However, right to property was kept out of the ambit of the list of the rights. The property protection is afforded by Public Works Act 1981, Magna Carta 1215 and the principles established by case laws. These protections are inadequate and at times

---

[6] *State of Bihar* v *Kameshwar Singh* [1952], AIR 252 (SC) (Patanjali Sastri CJ).
[7] S.M. Masum Billah, 'How Eminent is Eminent Domain: A Critique of Bangladeshi Acquisition Law', in Mizanur Rahman and Rahmat Ullah (eds.), *Human Rights and Displacement* (ELCOP Yearbook of Human Rights 2016), ELCOP, 2016, p. 139.

impeded by the doctrine of parliamentary supremacy. As such there is an argument that it should be included in the Bill of Rights Act 1990.[8] Several attempts were made subsequently to incorporate the right in to the 1990 Act. The generation of litigation was one of the fears why the initiative to include right to property in New Zealand Bill of Rights was frustrated in 1998 and 2005. There were other reasons, however: i) ambit and scope of the Bill was unclear, ii) apprehension of complicating legal interpretation, iii) incurring extra cost on government and local authorities, and iv) court's involvement in matters of economic policy. At present, a Constitutional Review Panel is considering the inclusion of property rights in the Bill.

The 1997 Polish Constitution has spared several clauses on property matters. Article 64(1)(2) of the Constitution has envisaged that 'Everyone shall have the right to ownership, other property rights and the rights of succession. And everyone, on an equal basis, shall receive legal protection regarding ownership, other property rights and the right of succession.'[9]

The Polish Constitution has made the right to property subject to social consideration.[10] The Constitutional Court ruled that the ownership is limited by statute, principles of morality and the socio-economic purpose of the right as set out in the Constitution. The Polish Constitution has also granted the state the power of eminent domain in wider terms. Article 21 states that 'expropriation may be allowed solely for public purposes and for just compensation.' The constitutional court has declared that the term expropriation embraces all forms of takings. However, the two important safeguards are that the property must be taken for a public purpose and just compensation must be provided upon expropriation. The term 'public purpose' has not received any definition and the just compensation rule has been compromised by insufficient compensation suggested

---

[8] Karyn Pulley, 'To Write the Right to Property: The Right to Property in New Zealand and Its Possible Inclusion in The Bill of Rights Act 1990', LLB Hons Research Paper, Victoria University of Wellington, 2003, p. 52.

[9] Poland's Constitution of 1997, https://www.constituteproject.org/constitution/Poland_1997.pdf [accessed: 19 November 2017].

[10] Rachelle Alterman, *Takings International: A Comparative Perspective on Land Use Regulations and Compensation Rights*, Chicago, American Bar Association, 2010, p. 225.

by other statutory laws. The Constitutional Court has advised that just compensation is much more an appropriate term than full compensation as situation may demand to grant less compensation.

Conclusion

Majority jurisdictions in the world have constitutionalised property rights. I have mentioned in this note that Bangladesh and Poland belong to the constitutionalist group. New Zealand is yet to recognise property rights from the perspective of constitutional ideology. But there is the prevailing opinion in the New Zealand society that the common law protection is often uncertain and there is always an educative effect of the constitutionalising the right to property. There is more or less uneasiness in the state of property rights in Bangladesh, Poland and New Zealand. In Bangladesh, there was never a serious political debate about the inclusion or exclusion of property clause in the constitution. The absence of such a debate suggests the existence of a political compromise on the land question. A rereading of the Bangladeshi clause is necessary to understand the ambiguities lurk in it with regard to notion of property, acquisition, just compensation and public purpose. The New Zealand also has to define these terms should it go for a written constitution in future.

The Polish case is also not fundamentally different. The debate relating to just compensation upon expropriation, the principle of social obligation of the state and the extent of public purpose should have to be clarified and fashioned. A sound property clause with emphasis both on land reform and public purpose one the one hand, and private property on the other hand may function as an important tool for the transformation of property law and changing the existing patterns of property rights. A degree of political commitment and a level of legal creativity are necessary for this purpose.

Bibliography

Literature

Alterman, Rachelle, *Takings International: A Comparative Perspective on Land Use Regulations and Compensation Rights*, Chicago, American Bar Association, 2010.

Billah, S.M. Masum, 'How Eminent is Eminent Domain: A Critique of Bangladeshi Acquisition Law', in Mizanur Rahman and Rahmat Ullah (eds.), *Human Rights and Displacement* (ELCOP Yearbook of Human Rights 2016), ELCOP, 2016.

Nedelsky, Jennifer, 'Should Property be Constitutionalised: A Relational and Comparative Approach', in Gerrit E. van Maneen and André J. van der Walt (eds.), *Property Law on the Threshold of the 21st Century*, Antwerp, Maklu, 1996.

Pulley, Karyn, 'To Write the Right to Property: The Right to Property in New Zealand and Its Possible Inclusion in The Bill of Rights Act 1990', LLB Hons Research Paper, Victoria University of Wellington, 2003.

State of Bihar v Kameshwar Singh [1952], AIR 252 (SC) (Patanjali Sastri CJ).

Underkuffler, Laura S., *The Idea of Property: Its Meaning and Power*, Oxford, Oxford University Press, 2003.

Websites

The Constitution of the People's Republic of Bangladesh, http://bdlaws.minlaw.gov.bd/sections_detail.php?id=367&sections_id=24590 [accessed 19 November 2017].

Poland's Constitution of 1997, https://www.constituteproject.org/constitution/Poland_1997.pdf [accessed: 19 November 2017].

Adam Jakuszewicz

Endangered Statehood of Sinking Island States: A Legal Challenge to the International Community

Introduction

Climate change presents a unique threat to the territorial integrity of some coastal and island states, as they will be affected by permanent loss of land through shoreline erosion, inundations and submersions caused by extreme weather events and sea-level rise. The effects of these phenomena are particularly severe to small island states situated on the Pacific Ocean. It has been suggested that by the end of this century a number of low-lying islands may be rendered totally uninhabitable or completely submerged.[1] As noted by the Intergovernmental Panel on Climate Change, '[s]ea-level rise impacts on the low-lying Pacific Island atoll States of Kiribati, Tuvalu, Tokelau and the Marshall Islands may, at some threshold, pose risks to their sovereignty or existence.'[2]

---

[1] Rosmary Rayfuse and Emily Crawford, 'Climate Change, Sovereignty and Statehood', *Sidney Law School Legal Studies Research Paper*, no. 11/59, 2011, p. 1 et seq, https://papers.ssrn.com/sol3/papers.cfm?abstract_id=1931466 [accessed 10 October 2017].

[2] Intergovernmental Panel on Climate Change (IPCC), *Climate Change 2007*, Fourth assessment report, 'Report of the International Working Group II: "Impacts, Adaptation and Vulnerability"', http://www.ipcc.ch/pdf/assessment-report/ar4/wg2/ar4-wg2-chapter17.pdf, p. 736 [accessed 10 October 2017]. The IPCC is a scientific intergovernmental body set up by the World

The small island nations are among those least able to take counter-measures against climate changes and the least culpable for contributing to warming trends.[3] Nonetheless, the peoples living on small island state will have to suffer their worst consequences. In the event that their territories are submerged they will lose everything they have, including their culture and identity, ancestral property, state and rights attached to it, especially the citizenship.[4] Apart from moral responsibility of the international community, the plight of small islands peoples raises several unresolved legal issues: is it legally possible (and desirable) for the small island states to retain their statehood in the case of loss of their territory? What would the status and scope of powers of a 'deterritorialised' small island state be? What kind of challenges would such a state face? Are there any legal alternatives to continued statehood that would be appropriate (and politically viable) for securing legitimate interests of the relocated peoples? Can the right to self-determination play a role in this respect? What are legal implications of each outcomes for the legal status of the affected peoples?

For the time being, both national and international legal systems are unprepared and ill-equipped to deal with these unprecedented challenges. As this paper shows, their solution will need courageous political decisions at both national and international level that in turn may bring about dramatic changes in basic concepts and institutions of international law.

The concept of state under international law and its implications for the statehood of sinking island states

The definition of a state under international law is laid down in Article 1 of the Montevideo Convention on the Rights and Duties of States which provides that the State as a person of international law should possess the

---

Meteorological Organization (WMO) and by the United Nations Environment Programme (UNEP). It was established to provide decision-makers and other stakeholders with an objective source of information about climate change.

[3] Sumudu Atapaltu, *Human Rights Approaches to Climate Changes: Challenges and Opportunities*, London, Routledge, 2016, p. 230.

[4] Ibid., p. 157.

following qualifications: a permanent population, a defined territory, government and capacity to enter into relations with other states. Although
the Montevideo Convention is a regional treaty with limited number of
signatories, the criteria laid down therein are generally accepted as repre-
senting customary international law.[5] All the criteria for statehood should
occur simultaneously. However, the absence of some of them over a period
of time does not necessarily deprive a state of its international personality.[6]

The requirement of a permanent population refers to a stable community, whereas no minimum is set for numbers. For instance, when Nauru
became independent, its estimated population was 6,500 people. As the
case of Vatican City shows, it is legally possible for an entity to be qualified
as a state even if its population numbers less than one thousand.[7] The law
likewise does not prescribe the physical scope of territory necessary as
a physical basis of a state: 'infinitesimal smallness has never been seen as
a reason to deny self-determination to a population.'[8]

The requirement of 'government' is understood as the existence of an
effective government, i.e. capable of exercising jurisdiction over a population on a given territory and independent from the influence or control of
other states. Finally, capacity to enter into relations with other states is an
amalgam of government and independence, namely the ability to operate as
an independent entity on the global stage, able to engage in legal relations

---

[5] See, for example, Arbitration Commission of the European Conference on Yugoslavia
(Badinter Commission), Opinion No. 1 (1992), in: Alain Pellet, 'The Opinions of the Badinter
Arbitration Committe: A Second Breath for the Self-Determination of Peoples', *European Journal of International Law*, vol. 3, 1992, pp. 182–183, www.ejil.org/pdfs/3/1/1175.pdf [accessed
28 December 2017].

[6] See Alina Kaczorowska, *Public International Law*, London, Routledge-Cavendish, 2008,
p. 186.

[7] The matter whether a very limited population will preclude the creation of a state was ex-
amined by the UN Special Committee of Twenty-Four which was asked to interpret the right to
self-determination of colonial people in the context of extremely small colonial populations. The
smallest entity which was discussed by the Committee was Pitcairn Island with a population of
(then) ninety inhabitants occupying an area of five square kilometres. The Committee reaffirmed
the right of the people of Pitcairn Island to self-determination but warned them that in deciding
their political future they should take into consideration the tiny size of the territory, its small
and decreasing population and economic dependence on other states. See UN Doc A/9623/Add
5 (Part III) (1974), pp. 6–7.

[8] Thomas M. Franck and Paul Hoffman, 'The Right of Self-Determination in Very Small
Places', *New York University Journal of International Law and Politics*, no. 8, 1976, pp. 383–384.

with other entities under international law. This requirement has been challenged by many authors as being a consequence of statehood and not its prerequisite. Indeed, the capacity of an entity to enter into relations with other states derives from the control the government exercises over a given territory, which in turn is based on the actual independence of that state.[9]

The discussion about the phenomenon of sinking island states is based on the assumption that at some point the territories of states such as Kiribati and Tuvalu will disappear, either completely, or to the point that they can no longer sustain permanent populations. However, the focus on loss of territory as the indicator of a state's disappearance may be unfounded since small island states will become uninhabitable long before they physically disappear. It is therefore more probable that the other criteria for statehood, namely a permanent population, an effective government, and the capacity to enter into relations with other states, will have been challenged prior to the disappearance of the territory.

The most probable reason for rendering the countries in question uninhabitable is insufficient fresh water and consequently food scarcity. Sea water is infusing underground water wells with salt water and thus renders the stored water undrinkable. At the same time, it causes salination of the soil. Moreover, exposures to recurring droughts undermines water sanitation and brings about disease outbreaks. It is predicted that the scarcity of potable water will adversely affect agricultural capacity and, in turn, lead to greater urbanisation and increased pressure on an already poor labour market. Internal migration from outer islands to the higher-lying islands already causes population pressures and are likely to cause resource fights in the future. Furthermore, due to the climate change the small island states are exposed to severe weather conditions that include increasing flooding, drought, and wind/storm surges from tropical cyclones. Disaster losses can seriously impede economic and social development. For instance, tourism infrastructure at the coasts may be destroyed, putting the economy of a whole country at risk as tourism represents a major portion of GDP for many small islands states.[10]

---

[9] Kaczorowska, *Public International Law*, p. 186.

[10] Cosmin Corendea, *Legal Protection of the Sinking Islands Refugees*, Lake Mary, Vandeplas Publishing, 2016, p. 12.

The ability to respond to climate change (adaptive ability) of small island states is limited by geographical and economic factors. Another disadvantages arise from their small size. It is to be noted that small economies are generally more exposed to external shocks, such as extreme events or climate change, than larger countries, because many of them rely on one or few economic activities, such as tourism or fisheries. The adaptation can be very difficult due to limited resources, the concentration of population and infrastructure in coastal areas in limited land area, as well as limited financial, technical and institutional capacities. It is therefore likely that long before the land disappears, the majority of the population will have moved. The relevant question is whether a state ceases to meet the criteria of statehood when the overwhelming majority or all of its population lives outside the state's territory.[11]

Extinction of states in international law vs. the presumption in favour of continuance of statehood of sinking island states

Both the existence and disappearance of a state is a matter of fact to which international law attaches legal consequences. While it is not unusual for governments to disappear, it is rather rare for states to become extinct.[12] Extinction of a state may take place as a consequence of merger, absorption or, historically, annexation. It may also occur as a result of the disintegration of an existing state. As these examples show, the extinction of a state has always occurred in the context of succession, whereby another state replaced the extinct one. In response to political reality of changing a sovereign authority over a territory, international community created provisions on state succession. The situation of low-lying island states, however, would be different and unique in the sense, that in the event of their disappearance there would, in principle, be no successor state. Inter-

---

[11] Jane McAdam, "'Disappearing States', Statelessness and the Boundaries of International Law", 21 January 2010, *UNSW Law Research Paper*, no. 2, 2010, https://ssrn.com/abstract=1539766 [accessed 10 November 2017], p. 8.

[12] Malcolm N. Shaw, *International Law*, Cambridge, Cambridge University Press, 2008, p. 208.

national community has not developed any rules that would apply to such a case, simply because it has never faced it before. It is presumed that the existing lacuna will have to be filled by casuistic political practice, rather than by general and abstract legal norms.

Furthermore, under international law there is a presumption of the continuance of a state in some form, that is either as a part of another, pre-existing state, or as an entirely new successor state.[13] The presumption of continuity applies also to existing states even if the criteria of statehood are met only to a limited extent. There is, however, no precedent for loss of the entire territory of a state or the exile of its entire population.[14] According to Rosmary Rayfuse and Emily Crawford two alternatives suggest themselves in the latter situation. One option is that the population of a disappearing state is relocated to the territory of another sovereign state, and either naturalised, i.e. granted the nationality of that state, or conceded a portion of land within the immigration state and given some degree of autonomous jurisdictional control over it. Another option would be to create artificial islands, which is technically possible.[15]

All of these options are of political character, since there is no legal obligation to admit immigrants into a state's territory, to grant them nationality or to provide financial and technical means to construct artificial islands where populations of disappearing states could live. Hopefully, in an emergency case the entire populations will be displaced elsewhere, even if such displacement is politically difficult to carry out. The option of constructing artificial islands, in turn, seems utopian for economic reasons. By the way, UN Convention on the Law of the Sea does not provide for artificial islands to have their own territorial waters or exclusive economic zones, so that the adoption of this measure would require a change in international to that effect.

The presumption of the continuity of a government in exile of a sinking island state will probably continue until the other states no longer recognise

---

[13] Rayfuse and Crawford, 'Climate', p. 5.

[14] Susin Park, *Climate Change and the Risk of Statelessness: The Situation of Low-Lying Island States* (Legal and Protection Policy Research Series), Geneva 2011, p. 6, http://www.unhcr.org/4df9cb0c9.pdf#zoom=95 [accessed 5 October 2017].

[15] Rayfuse and Crawford, 'Climate', p. 9 et seq.

it. The recognition of such a government is facilitated by the fact that there is no state against which this measure would be unlawful. In this sense the political and legal position of a government in exile of a state whose territory has become inhabitable or disappeared would be more advantageous to the position of a seceding state. Whereas the latter has to establish its adverse claim against a state from which it wishes to secede by demonstrating that it exercise effective and stable control over a territory, the former does not have to meet this condition. For its recognition it may suffice that it just makes a claim to continuity and the other states defer to it.[16]

As rightly noted by R. Rayfuse and E. Crawford, the criteria for statehood as enshrined in the Montevideo Convention do not constitute a rigid set of rules to be complied with. They should rather be interpreted as admitting some degree of flexibility and leeway in their application. Consequently, neither territory nor effective government should be deemed necessary for statehood, at least when a political entity has established itself in international community as a state. In order to corroborate this thesis, the authors give the example of governments in exile during the Second World War that were recognised although they did not exercise effective control over their territories and populations. They also make reference to the so-called failed states where all form of government and civil order have disappeared. In the authors' opinion, these examples lead to the conclusion that 'if it is possible to conceive of governments in exile, or states that remain states, even in the absence of key criteria, it may therefore be possible to conceive of "States in exile" – theoretical constructs without dominion over their original territory, because such territory have been lost.'[17]

This statement, however, does not seem sustainable. The authors do not take into account that the presumption in favour of continuity of a state or a government in exile is limited to situations where its territory has been lost temporarily. It is assumed that the government in exile sooner or later will regain the control over its territory and population. The loss of independence continued over an extended period would become a *fait*

---

[16] McAdam, "Disappearing States", p. 9 et seq.
[17] Rayfuse and Crawford, 'Climate', p. 5.

accompli that could not be disregarded by international community. Sooner or later, it would lead to withdrawal of recognition to the former state, which would be tantamount to its legal extinction.[18] The same reasoning applies to states whose territory disappears physically and irretrievably, as it is likely to happen in the case of some sinking island states. Under current international law permanent loss of a territory implies the loss of statehood irrespective of whether that loss is caused by political factors (permanent loss of independence) or natural factors (submergence of an island state). It is thus hard to agree with the statement that

> [g]iven the preponderance of practice and theory that suggests that states are essentially robust entities once properly constituted, questions of state 'extinction' due to climate change seem somewhat premature [...]. Whatever practical solutions are settled on for saving the Maldives, Tuvalu and Kiribati, this states will still be states, just in slightly altered physical form.[19]

It is inconceivable to describe a state whose territory has disappeared as continuing in 'slightly altered physical form'. It is rather to be assumed that if the territory of a state becomes uninhabitable or is submerged through rising sea-levels, and no other territory is ceded (which is the most probable scenario), it will be difficult to argue that the constitutive elements of statehood continue to exist, even when the presumption of continuity applicable for states already in existence is interpreted in a flexible way. Despite the fact that the air space and the territorial sea would physically remain, these are regarded as mere appurtenances to the land territory, that is why they would cease to exist with the land territory.[20]

The disappearance of small island states (or their conversion into *sui generis* entities equipped with some degree of international personality) would present a heightened risk of statelessness of their peoples. Article 1 of the 1954 Convention relating to the Status of Stateless Persons defines a stateless person as 'a person who is not considered as a national by any

---

[18] Park, *Climate Change*, p. 7.
[19] Rayfuse and Crawford, 'Climate', p. 11.
[20] Park, *Climate Change*, p. 14.

State under the operation of its law.' [21] This definition 'can no doubt be considered as having acquired a customary nature.'[22] Should a state cease to exist, citizenship of that state would then cease too, as there would no longer be a state of which a person could be a citizen. In such a case states parties to the 1954 Convention would be obliged to facilitate as far as possible the relocated persons' assimilation and naturalisation.[23] Nevertheless, under international law there is no right to nationality.[24] There is only a rule that in case of change of nationality, statelessness is to be prevented.

For this reason, the issue of relocation of a population affected by the loss of their homeland cannot be reduced to securing a territory where they could settle. Ideally, they should acquire the nationality of the host state, otherwise they would be exposed to the risk of being expelled, should the host country wish to do so.

State in exile: a realistic option for disappearing island states?

Athought the criteria for statehood as enshrined in the Montevideo Convention are regarded as customary international law, some scholars argue that the notion of statehood should evolve so as to accommodate the novel situation of uninhabitable small island states. In case a nation loses its state without its own fault, it should be provided with the possibility to continue to enjoy rights and privileges associated with statehood in a form or another. Since the notion of state is a legal fiction, international lawyers should devise another fiction to cover the phenomenon of sinking islands.[25] Should the statehood of submerged island states be continued, the international community would have to reconceptualise the very

---

[21] 'Draft Articles on Diplomatic Protection (with Commentaries)', in *Report of the International Law Commission: Fifty-Eighth' Session (1 May–9 June and 3 July–11 August 2006)*, UN Doc. A/61/10, p. 49.

[22] Ibid.

[23] McAdam, "Disappearing States", p. 24.

[24] It is noteworthy that Article 15 of the Universal Declaration of Human Rights enshrines the right to nationality. It lacks, however, a correlative duty on the state to confer nationality. The states were unable to agree on inclusion of this right into the International Covenant on Civil and Political Rights.

[25] Atapaltu, *Human Rights*, p. 237.

concept of statehood to that effect. This may take the form of a series of *sui generis* treaties with the 'new' states recreated due to climate change, in which the international community recognises their enduring statehood, despite their altered circumstances.[26] However, the modalities of that continuance will have to be worked out because even 'a state in exile' or 'an *ex situ* state' will have to be physically located somewhere.[27]

The demand for a recognition of the continuance of a submerged state in exile is a moral or political appeal rather than a legal obligation. The crucial issue is whether the other states will be prone to continue to recognise a state in the absence of permanent population on the diminishing territory. Even if such a deterritorialised state is initially recognised, it does not seem realistic that this recognition will continue *ad infinitum*. It is rather more appropriate to envisage such status as transitional, lasting perhaps one generation (around thirty years) or one human lifetime (100 years). Meanwhile it is likely that international law applicable to the case of sinking islands (for instance, the law of the sea) will have to be reconsidered and reconfigured.[28]

Furthermore, if the international community agreed to create a concept of a deterritorialised state, such an entity would have to be administered by a government in exile. However, the powers of such a government would be considerably restricted. Firstly, the principle of sovereignty means that a government may act as a government in exile only with the consent, express or implied, of the host state. For this reason the powers of the government in exile are necessarily more limited than when it operates within its own territory. Given that the population relocated from their sinking homelands will be subject to the laws and jurisdiction of the host state, a government in exile will only be able to extend diplomatic and consular protection and will largely lack capacity to enforce its own laws. Moreover, lack of funds could prove an important obstacle to its functioning in practice.

Theoretically, the governments in question could continue to claim some income from exploiting the former territorial sea and exclusive

---

[26] Rayfuse and Crawford, 'Climate', p. 12.
[27] Atapaltu, *Human Rights*, p. 167.
[28] McAdam, "Disappearing States", p. 23, note 90.

economic zones, for instance by means of agreements with other states on fishing rights, this option would be feasible if states agreed to create appropriate legal arrangements aimed at providing economic basis for the continued states in exile. Unless measures such as the maintenance of current exclusive economic zones were adopted, the government in exile could become dependent on funding provided by other states. In such circumstances the government in exile would struggle to guarantee even basic rights or services to its citizens. Additional problems would emerge if nationals of a state in exile were displaced to a country different from that of its government or if they were dispersed in many countries. Then the exercise by the government in exile of protection would depend on another state's (states') acceptance. The population holding the citizenship of a state in exile but residing in a state different from the state where the government in exile is based, could find itself without access to the protection of the state. In such circumstances, it could be considered as *de facto* stateless.[29]

The *raison d'être* of the government in exile would become doubtful if the population were granted the nationality of the host state, which is desirable for the sake of their integration with the community of their new homeland. The utility of maintaining a government in exile is also questionable in a situation, where (for symbolic reasons) peoples of the disappearing states were to retain their nationality and at the same time granted nationality of the host state. Since in case of dual nationality the principle of an effective nationality applies, the presumption of competencies with regard to diplomatic protection would favour a state where a person resides. In any case, the function of a government in exile would wane over time.[30] Furthermore, should the government in exile merge with authorities of the host state, than the state it represented would definitely become extinct, unless there was another internationally recognised interest in its continuity.

Finally, it is possible to envisage the termination of statehood of a submerged island state as such but to provide for its continued existence as

---

[29] Park, *Climate Change*, p. 14.
[30] McAdam, "Disappearing States", p. 13.

an entity endowed with international personality. A similar solution has been adopted with regard to Sovereign Order of Malta that in 1798 lost the Maltese island by surrendering to France and settled definitively in Rome. Although the Order does not have any territory, it is considered the subject of international law. It maintains diplomatic relations with 107 states, enters into treaties and enjoys the status of permanent observer to the United Nations. Its premises in Rome, similar to embassies, enjoy extraterritoriality (immunity from the jurisdiction of the hosting state).

However, as far as the sinking island states are concerned, it does not seem probable that they will ever be converted into another entities equipped with personality under international law. It is because states sometimes continue to recognise a state even if criteria for statehood are only vestigial. On the other hand, such a solution presumably would not satisfy the aspirations of the displaced peoples and/or their governments in exile.[31]

Loss of statehood vs. the right of peoples to self-determination

Alternatively to the government *ex situ* discussed in the previous section, some scholars advocate setting up a governing body that would exercise authority over the displaced peoples patterned after the former trusteeship system of the UN. Such authority could also administer (the former) territorial seas and exclusive economic zones for the benefit of the relocated populations. This claim, however, is premised on the assumption that these maritime zones will not disappear when the island states have submerged.[32] Under the international law as it stands today the exclusive economic zones are created up to 200 nautical miles from the territorial sea baselines. States that have exclusive economic zones enjoy sovereign rights over natural their resources,[33] which is of vital economic significance espe-

---

[31] Ibid., p. 24.

[32] Atapaltu, *Human Rights*, p. 239.

[33] Under article 56 of the Convention on the Law of the Sea, the coastal state in the economic zone has *inter alia*: (a) sovereign rights for the purpose of exploring and exploiting, conserving and managing the natural resources, whether living or non-living, of the waters superjacent to the seabed and of the seabed and its subsoil and with regard to other activities for the economic exploitation and exploration of the zone, such as the production of energy from the water, cur-

cially to the small island states reliant on fishing and exploitation of other maritime resources.[34] Total loss of the land territory by an island state is tantamount to losing the maritime territory and exclusive economic zone of that state.[35] When the whole land territory of a state disappears and the population is displaced onto the territory of other states, the sovereignty over its exclusive economic zone will be absorbed by the rights of all states in international waters.

To remedy this outcome, some scholars resort to the right to self-determination of peoples.[36] This right has been placed at the forefront of the international human rights law, namely in Article 1 of both the International Covenant on Civil and Political Rights and the International Covenant on Social, Economic and Cultural Rights that reads as follows:

1. All peoples have the right of self-determination. By virtue of that right they freely determine their political status and freely pursue their economic, social and cultural development.

2. All peoples may, for their own ends, freely dispose of their natural wealth and resources without prejudice to any obligations arising out of international economic cooperation, based upon the principle of mutual benefit, and international law. In no case may a people be deprived of its own means of subsistence.

3. The States Parties to the present Covenant, including those having responsibility for the administration of Non-Self-Governing

---

rents and winds; (b) jurisdiction with regard to (i) the architecture and use of artificial islands, installations and structures; 126 (ii) marine scientific research; (iii) the protection and preservation of the marine environment.

[34] For instance, Federated States of Micronesia controls a sizable portion of the Pacific rich in marine resources. It controls near 3 million square kilometres of Pacific Ocean – an area that generates fisheries and aquaculture production valued annually approximately at $225 million. See Clement Yow Mulalap, 'Islands in the Stream: Addressing Climate Change from a Small Island Developing State Perspective', in Randall S. Abate and Elizabeth Ann Kronk (eds.), *Climate Change and Indigenous Peoples: The Search for Legal Remedies*, Cheltenham, Elgar, 2013, p. 379.

[35] Even a partial loss of the territory of an island state, for example due to the submergence of an outer island that forms an archipelago, would have adverse economic implications for the affected population as it would bring about respective loss of a part of its exclusive economic zone.

[36] Cameron Moore, 'Waterworld: Climate Change, Statehood and the Right to Self-Determination', in Ottavio Quirico and Mouloud Boumghar (eds.), *Climate Change and Human Rights: An International and Comparative Law Perspective*, London and New York, Routledge, 2016, p. 111.

and Trust Territories, shall promote the realisation of the right of self-determination, and shall respect that right, in conformity with the provisions of the Charter of the United Nations.[37]

In particular, it is argued that the right to self-determination could have a role to play in enabling peoples of small island states to support their claim that they still should enjoy their sovereign rights over natural resources, even when the territorial basis for asserting those rights literally disappears beneath the waters. This is due to the fact that the right to self-determination is enjoyed by the peoples and not by the states. Moreover, the loss of natural resources would be contrary to the spirit of the original self-determination process, as those people would *de facto* become subject once again.[38]

It should therefore be assumed, so the argument goes, that failure to meet the conditions for statehood should not frustrate the right to self--determination which is a peremptory claim, preliminary to the idea of state itself, especially when a people enjoys such a right and is threatened to lose it through no fault of their own. In this context it is interesting to note that the Committee on Economic, Social and Cultural Rights invited Israel to respect Palestinians' rights to natural resources in the territorial sea and the exclusive economic zone of the Gaza Strip,[39] although Palestinians have no state. So it is possible to maintain the right of people over natural resources without any relation to the concept of state.

Nevertheless, the recourse to the right to self-determination of peoples in order to support the idea of recognising states *ex situ* that would be a continuation of disappeared small islands states and the demand of preserving the exclusive economic zones of the submerged states for the benefit of their relocated populations does not seem to be legally viable. In its political aspect, the right to self-determination is subordinate to the

---

[37] International Covenant on Civil and Political Rights, adopted and opened for signature, ratification and accession by General Assembly resolution 2200A (XXI) of 16 December 1966, https://www.ohchr.org/en/professionalinterest/pages/ccpr.aspx [accessed 1 October 2018]; International Covenant on Social, Cultural and Economic Rights, adopted and opened for signature, ratification and accession by General Assembly resolution 2200A (XXI) of 16 December 1966, https://www.ohchr.org/en/professionalinterest/pages/cescr.aspx [accessed 1 October 2018].

[38] Ibid., p. 108.

[39] Concluding observations of the Committee on Economic, Social and Cultural Rights, Israel, E/C.12/ISR/CO/3, 16 December 2011, https://unispal.un.org/DPA/DPR/unispal.nsf/0/B6A80AE59FA1F7C78525796F00520D03 [accessed 15 December 2017].

principle of territorial integrity. Its relevance is confined to colonised or occupied peoples, the vast majority of whom has gained independence. In its economic aspect, the right to self-determination, understood as a right to exercise control over the nations' resources and the right to economic development on equitable terms failed to bring about any fundamental changes in global economic relations. First and foremost, attempts to reduce the wealth disparity between North and South made little progress, notwithstanding the concept of 'the common heritage of mankind' that has been introduced into the Convention on the Law of the Sea of 1982, and in spite of the adoption of a UN General Assembly Declaration recognising a 'human right to development'. 'All these attempts to argue for economic redress for the debilitating effects of colonialism by way of fair trade and development, while very successful in obtaining widespread support in the UN, had little practical impact.'[40] Given these developments it is difficult to defend the thesis that invoking the right to self-determination would help the peoples displaced from their submerged homelands to secure any political or economic benefits.

Conclusion

International law has developed as a response to recurring needs of the international community. In this sense it seems to be reactive rather than proactive. It is therefore not surprising that it does not provide for satisfactory solutions to novel challenges related to the phenomenon of disappearing states. For this reason, the ensuing legal problems, such as the issue of the continued statehood, nationality of the displaced populations or maritime boundaries require political measures. It is highly improbable that a state would be willing to cede a fraction of its land in order to provide a disappearing island state with a territorial basis for their continued existence, so that it is to be assumed that the latter will cease to exist when its territory becomes uninhabitable or is completely submerged. It

---

[40] Wade Mansell and Karen Openshaw, *International Law: A Critical Introduction*, Oxford, Hart Publishing, 2013, p. 62.

is advisable to set up an independent authority that would in the interim be entrusted with protecting rights and interests of the displaced populations. However, the option of creating a permanent government in exile that would represent the displaced populations does not seem viable for economic and practical reasons. The *raison d'être* of such a government would become highly questionable once the displaced populations is naturalised and fully integrated into the societies of the receiving state. Should relocation of the entire population from a small sinking states be necessary, it should be carried out in a planned and systematic manner. This could be achieved by means of gradual strengthening of multifaceted (i.e. economic, social, cultural) relations between a state whose population is supposed to be displaced and a potential receiving state so that rights and interests of both parties are effectively safeguarded. Given that there is no legal obligation to admit immigrants or grant them nationality resulting from universal or regional international law, bilateral agreements seems to be the most suitable instrument for that purpose.

Bibliography

Literature

Atapaltu, Somudu, *Human Rights Approaches to Climate Changes: Challenges and Opportunities*, London, Routledge, 2016.

Corendea, Cosmin, *Legal Protection of the Sinking Islands Refugees*, Lake Mary, Vandeplas Publishing, 2016.

Franck, Thomas M. and Paul Hoffman, 'The Right of Self-Determination in Very Small Places', *New York University Journal of International Law and Politics*, no. 8, 1976.

Kaczorowska, Alina, *Public International Law*, London, Routledge-Cavendish, 2008.

Mansell, Wade and Karen Openshaw, *International Law: A Critical Introduction*, Oxford, Hart Publishing, 2013.

Moore, Cameron, 'Waterworld: Climate Change, Statehood and the Right to Self--Determination', in Ottavio Quirico and Mouloud Boumghar (eds.), *Climate Change and Human Rights: An International and Comparative Law Perspective*, London and New York, Routledge, 2016.

Pellet, Alain, 'The Opinions of the Badinter Arbitration Committe: A Second Breath for the Self-Determination of Peoples', *European Journal of International Law*, vol. 3, 1992, pp. 182–183, www.ejil.org/pdfs/3/1/1175.pdf [accessed 28 December 2017].

Shaw, Malcolm N., *International Law*, Cambridge, Cambridge University Press, 2008.

Yow Mulalap, Clement, 'Islands in the Stream: Addressing Climate Change from a Small Island Developing State Perspective', in Randall S. Abate and Elizabeth Ann Kronk (eds.), *Climate Change and Indigenous Peoples: The Search for Legal Remedies*, Cheltenham, Elgar, 2013.

Documents

Concluding observations of the Committee on Economic, Social and Cultural Rights, Israel, E/C.12/ISR/CO/3, 16 December 2011, https://unispal.un.org/DPA/DPR/unispal.nsf/0/B6A80AE59FA1F7C78525796F00520D03 [accessed 15 December 2017].

'Draft Articles on Diplomatic Protection (with Commentaries)', in *Report of the International Law Commission: Fifty-Eighth' Session (1 May–9 June and 3 July– 11 August 2006)*, UN Doc. A/61/10.

Intergovernmental Panel on Climate Change (IPCC), Climate Change 2007, Fourth assessment report, 'Report of the International Working Group II: "Impacts, Adaptation and Vulnerability"', http://www.ipcc.ch/pdf/assessment-report/ar4/wg2/ar4-wg2-chapter17.pdf [accessed 10 October 2017].

International Covenant on Civil and Political Rights, adopted and opened for signature, ratification and accession by General Assembly resolution 2200A (XXI) of 16 December 1966, https://www.ohchr.org/en/professionalinterest/pages/ccpr.aspx [accessed 1 October 2018].

International Covenant on Social, Cultural and Economic Rights, adopted and opened for signature, ratification and accession by General Assembly resolution 2200A (XXI) of 16 December 1966, https://www.ohchr.org/en/professionalinterest/pages/cescr.aspx [accessed 1.October 2018].

UN Doc A/9623/Add 5 (Part III) (1974).

Websites

McAdam, Jane, "'Disappearing States", Statelessness and the Boundaries of International Law', January 21, 2010, *UNSW Law Research Paper*, no. 2, 2010, https://ssrn.com/abstract=1539766 [accessed 10 October 2017].

Park, Susin, *Climate Change and the Risk of Statelessness: The Situation of Low-Lying Island States* (Legal and Protection Policy Research Series), Geneva 2011, http://www.unhcr.org/4df9cb0c9.pdf#zoom=95 [accessed 5 October 2017].

Rayfuse, Rosmary and Emily Crawford, 'Climate Change, Sovereignty and Statehood', *Sidney Law School Legal Studies Research Paper*, no. 11/59, 2011, https://papers.ssrn.com/sol3/papers.cfm?abstract_id=1931466 [accessed 10 October 2017].

Przemysław Osóbka

International Responsibility of States on Climate Change Consequences in the Frame of Public International Law

However experts and scientists have different opinions on the causes of this phenomenon, climate change is a fact. Regardless of whether the cause of this phenomenon is deemed to be human activity or natural process, its effects are objective. Regardless of our assessment of climate change, its results and often associated with them natural disasters will force the world to face the problem of the so-called climate refugees and the states that will disappear from the surface of the Earth, or have already begun to lose their territories under the influence of climate change.

Sometimes extreme emotions that accompany media messages on the inflow of refugees to Europe mean that the international community gradually begins to lose the initial sensitivity to the needs of people who face the threat of losing their lives or loved ones, property, place of work or study, etc.

This makes it even more likely the possibility that mankind will remain indifferent to the needs of those whose existence will be threatened in the near future due to climate change which take place on the Earth. Unfortunately, sometimes it is favoured by the transferring to the international community conflicting information on global warming and its consequences for the various spheres of life.

The president of Kiribati, an island microstate located in the Pacific Ocean has repeatedly called for the assistance of the international community in the fight for the survival of the entire population at risk of regular flooding of its territory by the waters of the ocean.

Tuvalu, other microstate of this region of the world, is plagued with similar problem. Tuvalu's government in 2008 asked the Australia and New Zealand to assist in the resettlement to these countries all the inhabitants Tuvalu islands. This country is situated so low above sea level, that – if the rate of rising water in the oceans will be kept – Tuvalu will be flooded within the next fifty years. Already threatened are also Solomon Islands, Marshall Islands and Vanuatu. Similar processes occur not only in the South Pacific, but also in the Indian Ocean, where for example territory of the Maldives is threatened by the same reasons.

Natural disasters which are consequences of climate change, like cyclones and tsunamis, are the direct causes of the threat of existence of human populations in many other parts of the world (South Atlantic, Caribbean Sea).

Presented risks with regards to individuals and entire communities as well as to sovereign states bring with them a whole range of issues to be settled by international law, with particular emphasis on the challenges for the international protection of human rights.

Climate change is more often considered in the context of ensuring of international security and conflict prevention. Scientists predict that in the 21st century major changes will happen in the land areas: retreating of the coastline and submergence of large areas including entire countries such as small island states. We can expect more conflicts because of land and maritime borders and other territorial rights. It will be needed to introduce changes to the existing rules of international law, in particular the law of the sea, relating to the settlement of territorial disputes and borders.

Social groups that already suffer from poverty, health conditions, unemployment or social exclusion, they are more susceptible to the effects of climate change, which could increase or trigger migration within a country or between different countries.

United Nations predicts that in 2020 there will be millions of 'environmental' migrants, and climate change will be one of the main factors intensifying this phenomenon.

Some countries particularly vulnerable to the effects of climate change are already calling for international recognition of such migration associated with environment changes. Such migration may increase conflicts in transit and in destination. Europe must expect substantially increased migratory pressure.

Climate change and lack of international legal regulations may significantly increase instability in weak or failing states, stretching the already limited capacity of governments to cope with facing them challenges. Inability to meet the needs of governing the whole society or providing them protection against difficulties resulting from climate change could cause frustration, lead to tensions between different ethnic and religious groups within the country and to political radicalisation. This could lead to destabilisation in some countries and even entire regions of the world.

If the international community fails to address the risks described above, the multilateral system will be compromised. The climate change impact will be fuel to the antipathy between those who bear the greatest responsibility for climate change and those affected by these changes.

Policies aimed at mitigating the impact of climate change (or policy ineffective) will therefore cause political tensions within individual countries and internationally. The potential rift not only North and South, but also divide the South because of sharing global emissions. The already burdened international security architecture will be put under increasing pressure.

In this context, there are legitimate questions about based on existing principles of international law the responsibility of states for damages caused by climate change taking place before our eyes.

Matters relating to environmental protection have been taken for the first time at the United Nations forum and by its specialised agencies (e.g. UNESCO, FAO, WHO) in the 1960s in the framework of the so--called First Development Decade launched in 1961. However, for many years the issue of state responsibility for the natural environment was ignored by international community. Only the United Nations Conference on the Human Environment, held in Stockholm on 5–16 June 1972, took the first attempt to face this challenge.[1]

---

[1] See Declaration of the United Nations Conference on the human environment, Stockholm, 1972, in Report of the United Nations Conference on the Human Environment, UN Doc.A/CONF.48/14/Rev. 1.

Stockholm Declaration consists of a preamble included in seven points and twenty-six principles, among which in the context of the international responsibility of states particular importance was gained by rule no. 21, which provides:

States have the sovereign right to exploit their own resources pursuant to their own environmental policies, and the responsibility to ensure that activities within their jurisdiction or control do not cause damage to the environment of other States or of areas beyond the limits of national jurisdiction.[2]

Also important seems to be the rule no. 22, which states that: 'States shall cooperate to develop further the international law regarding liability and compensation for the victims of pollution and other environmental damage.'[3]

Similar provisions were included in the content of the United Nations Framework Convention on Climate Change of 9 May 1992,[4] as well as in the Rio Declaration on Environment and Development of 14 June 1992,[5] which was the culmination of the so-called Earth Summit.

Framework Convention confirmed a large extent the provisions of the Stockholm Declaration, reiterating *inter alia*, the principle according to which states have: 'the responsibility to ensure that activities within their jurisdiction or control do not cause damage to the environment of other States or of areas beyond the limits of national jurisdiction.'[6]

Echoes of the provisions of the Stockholm Declaration can be also found in the second of the indicated acts:

States shall develop national law regarding liability and compensation for the victims of pollution and other environmental damage. States shall also cooperate in an expeditious and more determined manner to develop further international law

---

[2] Ibid.

[3] Ibid.

[4] United Nations Framework Convention on Climate Change (hereafter: UNFCCC) 1992, FCC/INFORMAL/84/Rev.1.

[5] Rio Declaration on Environment and Development, 1992, A/CONF.151/26.

[6] UNFCCC, 1992, FCC/INFORMAL/84/Rev.1.

regarding liability and compensation for adverse effects of environmental damage caused by activities within their jurisdiction or control to areas beyond their jurisdiction.[7]

The way from defining the rules to codify the provisions relating to the international responsibility of states has proved to be extremely difficult. It is enough to mention that long-term efforts of the UN International Law Commission in this area led only to the adoption of Draft Articles on Responsibility of States for Internationally Wrongful Acts.[8]

The principle of international responsibility of states in the frame of international law have not been codified in the form of international agreement. That is why it shall be described generally by referring to the common law and to mentioned above project. Also it should not be surprising that the issue of liability for damages caused as a result of climate change has been also duly resolved neither in the Protocol to the United Nations Framework Convention on Climate Change concluded in Kyoto on 11 December 1997,[9] nor in the Paris Agreement, 12 December 2015.[10]

Some laconic wording used in the Kyoto Protocol emphasizing the 'common but differentiated responsibilities' of States Parties for the implementation of its provisions still leave much to be desired and raise even more doubts about the intentions that accompanied its authors.

Some progress in the field of international responsibility of states for detriments caused by climate change brought only the already mentioned Paris Agreement which art. 8 stipulates that 'Parties recognize the importance of averting, minimizing and addressing loss and damage associated with the adverse effects of climate change, including extreme weather events and slow onset events, and the role of sustainable development in reducing the risk of loss and damage.'[11]

---

[7] Rio Declaration.

[8] Draft Articles on Responsibility of States for Internationally Wrongful Acts with commentaries 2001, text adopted by the International Law Commission at its fifty-third session, in 2001, and submitted to the General Assembly as a part of the Commission's report covering the work of that session (A/56/10).

[9] Kyoto Protocol to the United Nations Framework Convention on Climate Change, 1997.

[10] Paris Agreement, *Official Journal of the European Union*, L 282/4 EN, 2015.

[11] Ibid.

At the same time art. 2 of the Paris Agreement includes a provision according to which: 'Agreement will be implemented to reflect equity and the principle of common but differentiated responsibilities and respective capabilities, in the light of different national circumstances.'[12]

At the moment it is reasonable to ask a question if the cited legal bases are sufficient for states affected by the negative effects of climate change to formulate claims and start investigations in this respect of any reparations? Let's try to consider this issue on the example of countries located in the South Pacific region.

In 2003 Roda Verheyen, attorney from Hamburg, passsed her doctoral thesis on the perception of climate change in international law. At the beginning no one treated her ideas too seriously. Also Verheyen from the beginning categorically rejected the possibility of receiving by endangered microstates compensation for degraded environment. The reason seems to be very simple: no one could be blamed. Today, more and more lawyers claim that bringing this type of actions is justified, and the subject taken by Roda Verheyen meets with growing interest.[13]

The question who should pay for the damage caused by climate change and who should compensate for 'climate refugees' because of loss of their health and previously owned property until recently was considered only in the context of morality.[14]

Changing this approach became possible thanks to the involvement of researchers from scientific centres around the world, among which the great contributions have laid scientists from the School of Law of the University of the South Pacific established in Vanuatu.[15]

Vanuatu is one of the island countries in Oceania, located in the South Pacific, occupying an area of 12,290 square kilometres, situated on eighty--five islands with twenty uninhabited islands. On 13 March 2015 population of Vanuatu was painfully experienced by devastating impact of

---

[12] Ibid.

[13] See Roda Verheyen, *Climate Change Damage and International Law: Prevention Duties and State Responsibility*, Leiden, Martinus Nijhoff, 2005.

[14] Richard S.J. Tol and Roda Verheyen, 'State Responsibility and Compensation for Climate Change Damages – a Legal and Economic Assessment', *Energy Policy*, vol. 32, issue 9, 2004, pp. 1109–1130.

[15] See 'School of Law', website of the University of the South Pacific, http://www.usp.ac.fj/index.php?id=6193 [accessed 14 March 2017].

tropical cyclone Pam, which was recognised by the state authorities as the greatest disaster in its history.[16]

The cyclone caused the death of twenty-four persons and destroyed large part of the infrastructure of the state and farmland, cutting off from the rest of the world inhabitants about sixty islands and depriving them of drinking water supply.[17]

In the context of the international responsibility of states, the case of Vanuatu indicates the need to investigate possible links of anthropogenic character of climate change with the emergence of phenomena such as cyclones and their devastating consequences.

On the basis of the United Nations Framework Convention on Climate Change of 9 May 1992 'climate change' is defined as follows: '[...] change of climate which is attributed directly or indirectly to human activity that alters the composition of the global atmosphere and which is in addition to natural climate variability observed over comparable time periods.'[18]

On the other hand, the fifth report of the Intergovernmental Panel on Climate Change from 2014 indicated on the 95-per cent probability that human activity is the cause of global warming.[19]

Even among researchers behaving well understood scientific skepticism there is a perception that the scientific evidence on anthropogenic character of climate change is stronger than ever.[20]

---

[16] See Joshua Robertson, 'Cyclone Pam: Vanuatu Awaits First Wave of Relief and News from Worst-Hit Islands', *The Guardian*, 15 March 2015, https://www.theguardian.com/world/2015/mar/15/cyclone-pam-death-toll-may-reach-50-in-port-vila-alone-as-full-impact-still-unknown [accessed 14 March 2017].

[17] See Peter Walker and Paul Farrell, 'Cyclone Pam: 24 Confirmed Dead as Vanuatu President Blames Climate Change', *The Guardian*, 16 March 2015, https://www.theguardian.com/world/2015/mar/16/vanuatus-president-blames-climate-change-for-extreme-weather [accessed 14 March 2017]; 'State of Emergency in Tuvalu', Radio New Zealand, 14 March 2015, http://www.radionz.co.nz/international/pacific-news/268612/state-of-emergency-in-tuvalu [accessed 14 March 2017]; 'Cyclone Pam: Vanuatu Islanders Forced to Drink Saltwater', BBC News, 17 March 2015, http://www.bbc.com/news/world-asia-31917913 [accessed 14 March 2017].

[18] UNFCCC, 1992, FCC/INFORMAL/84/Rev.1, art. 1.

[19] Overseas Development Institute and Climate and Development Knowledge Network, 'The IPCC's Fifth Assessment Reports: What in It for Small Island Developing States?', 2014, p. 2, https://cdkn.org/wp-content/uploads/2014/08/IPCC-AR5-Whats-in-it-for-SIDS_WEB.pdf [accessed 14 September 2018].

[20] Calvy Aonima and Shivanal Kumar, 'Could Vanuatu Claim Reparations Under International Law for Damages Sustained from Cyclone "Pam"?', *Journal of South Pacific Law*, issue 1, 2015, pp. A-23–A-40.

This allows us to ask whether the anthropogenic nature of climate change concerns cyclones in general, or cyclone Pam in particular? Indeed there is no doubt that cyclones occured in the Pacific region, as well as in other parts of the world.

The simple assertion that climate change is the direct cause of a given cyclone is only a very unreliable simplification. However, already a little deeper observations allow us to observe natural regularities that significantly made them more likely. Scientists point to three factors that make cyclone-related damage more acute than it was a few decades ago. They include: extremely mild sea surface temperatures, increased water vapor in the atmosphere and rising sea levels.[21]

The impact of these factors was noticeable before the cyclone Pam hit in Vanuatu. The rising of oceanic waters is a phenomenon that has been not questionable for many years and does not require any special evidence. But in the terms of ocean surface temperatures, where the activity of the Pam cyclone just before the impact in Vanuatu became particularly intense, the temperature was higher than the annual average by about two Celsius degrees.[22]

On the one side, there is a relationship between the intensity of the Pam cyclone and the climate change caused by the increasing temperature in surface of the ocean. On the other side, the relationship between sea level rising and the tragic effects of its activity in Vanuatu seems rather obvious. They would not be so intense and harmful if climate change would not be a fact.[23]

Similar conclusions have been drawn, for example, from analysis of the cyclone Ian tragic effects that hit the group of islands belonging to the Tonga Kingdom of Ha'apai on 11 January 2014.[24]

---

[21] See Andrew Friedman, 'Vanuatu's President Makes a Leap in Tying Cyclone Pam to Climate Change', 16 March 2015, Mashable, http://mashable.com/2015/03/16/vanuatu-cyclone-pam-global-warming/#jvZuC9iGsGqi [accessed 17 March 2017].

[22] Ibid.

[23] See Aonima and Kumar, 'Could Vanuatu Claim Reparations Under International Law', p. A-29.

[24] See Fitilagi Ioane Fa'anunu, 'A Breach of Fundamental Human Rights as the Legal Basis for Reparations for Climate Change Damages and Injuries Under International Law: Case Study of Ha'apai Islands (Tonga) Following Cyclone Ian', *Journal of South Pacific Law*, issue 1, 2015, pp. A-41–A-58.

One of the most difficult issues to consider in the scope of international responsibility of states in the context of climate change is the following question: who and on what basis should pay the costs not only to prevent dangerous anthropogenic interference of the climate system, as the United Nations Framework Convention on Climate Change prescribed, but also to remove and repair of the damage resulting from its consequences?

The authors of the Framework Convention were interested in spreading the burden of responsibility to the whole international community. On the one hand, Convention points out that 'the largest share of the former and present global greenhouse gas emissions are in the highly developed countries', but on the other hand it was almost certain that the participation of developing countries 'in global gas emissions will increase due to the need for social and economic development of these countries.'[25]

It is therefore prudent to consider carefully the historical, present and future emissions. Greenhouse gas concentrations in the atmosphere have been increasing since the 18th century and have been caused by emissions from states considered as developed as it is indicated in Annex I to the Framework Convention (e.g. United States, Great Britain, Germany, etc.). These are the past emissions that are responsible for current damage. But nowadays, emissions from developing countries experiencing intense economic growth (e.g. China, India) are more and more affected today. These emissions will contribute to future damage and will also serve as critical points for further climate change[26]

Certain guidelines for potential solutions in this area can be found in art. 9 sec. 1 of the Paris Agreement, which states that: 'Developed country Parties shall provide financial resources to assist developing country Parties with respect to both mitigation and adaptation in continuation of their existing obligations under the Convention.'

These provisions are in principle consistent with art. 4 of Framework Convention, but Margaretha Wewerinke-Singh and Curtis Doebbler

---

[25] UNFCCC, 1992, FCC/INFORMAL/84/Rev.1.

[26] See Roda Verheyen and Peter Roderick, 'Beyond Adaptation: The Legal Duty to Pay Compensation for Climate Change Damage', WWF-UK Climate Change Programme Discussion Paper, November 2008, p. 29, http://assets.wwf.org.uk/downloads/beyond_adaptation_lowres.pdf [accessed 14 September 2018].

reasonable note that this compatibility is not complete because the Paris Agreement does not explicitly include the Convention indication, which states that these sources of funding from developed countries should be 'new and additional'.[27]

Besides difficulties indicating the countries responsible for the damage caused by climate change, many uncertainties raise the issue of legal formula of possible compensation system of damage which will have to clearly define whether only the state will be responsible for climate change, or the weight of the wine to share with private entities operating within their jurisdiction, and perhaps also with international corporations?

In literature, there is a view that countries like Vanuatu, Tonga or the Maldives, which suffer from the consequences of climate change, can claim any other state or even a group of states unless the consequences of this act do not undermine the interests of third countries, which are not parties to such proceedings.[28]

In the current legal status, possible claims could be done on basis of demonstrating violations by other states their obligations under the Framework Convention and the United Nations Convention on the Law of the Sea of 10 December 1982[29] or on basis of failure to comply with the greenhouse gas emission reduction obligations set out in the Kyoto Protocol.

It seems doubtful that the possibility of redress is based on the project of the principles of the liability of states for internationally wrongful acts and on the basis of the project of rules designed in 2001 for liability for cross-border damage caused by dangerous activities.[30]

---

[27] Margaretha Wewerinke-Singh and Curtis Doebbler, 'The Paris Agreement: Some Critical Reflections on Process and Substance', *University of New South Wales Law Journal*, vol. 39, no. 4, 2016, p. 1506.

[28] See Joe-Dee Davis, 'State Responsibility for Global Climate Change: The Case of the Maldives', MALD thesis, The Fletcher School, Tufts University, 2005, pp. 64–65, https://dl.tufts.edu/bookreader/tufts:UA015.012.DO.00078#page/1/mode/2up [accessed 14 September 2018].

[29] See Keely Boom, 'Exposure to Legal Risk for Climate Change Damage Under UNFCCC, Kyoto Protocol and LOSC: A Case Study of Tuvalu and Australia', PhD thesis, Faculty of Law, University of Wollongong, 2012, http://ro.uow.edu.au/theses/3919 [accessed 29 March 2017].

[30] See International Law Commission, 'Draft Articles on Prevention of Transboundary Harm from Hazardous Activities, with Commentaries: Report of the ILC on the Work of Its Fifty-Third Session', *Yearbook of the International Law Commission*, vol. 2, part 2, 2001.

In the first case it is indicated by the content of articles on responsibility of states for internationally wrongful acts designed by the International Law Commission in 2001, which preclude any unlawful.

Among other things, it is about art. 20, according to which, as proposed by the Commission, the consent expressed by the state precludes the un-lawfulness of the act in question with respect to the consenting state, pro-vided that the specific activity remains within the limits of the consent granted. Based on this principle, it could be concluded that the States Parties to the Kyoto Protocol have agreed to the emission levels and in-ternational trade rules set out therein, and consequently also presume their consent to a certain level of damage caused by the effects of climate change, which may arise after all, below the ceiling of the targets set out in the mentioned Protocol.

The danger of such interpretations was too readable for many states, primarily from the South Pacific. Therefore, already signing the Frame-work Convention Fiji, Kiribati, Nauru and Tuvalu made reservation in accordance which this act cannot be interpreted as a renunciation of any rights under investigation responsibility of states for the adverse effects of climate change.[31] Very similar in content objections to the Kyoto Protocol were submitted by Kiribati, Nauru, Niue and the Cook Islands.[32]

Another doubt related to the merits and also the advisability of pursu-ing claims by the countries suffering the consequences of climate change based on the principles of responsibility of states for internationally wrong-ful acts, arises in connection with the designed by the International Law Commission art. 25, in which the notion of 'necessity' is used. It allows the possibility of exceptional cases in which the only means by which the state can preserve its vital interests threatened by the inevitable danger is failing to perform other international obligations or to lesser importance or urgency. Under the conditions strictly defined in art. 25 it is possible to exclude the unlawfulness of the act.

---

[31] UNFCCC, Declaration Status of Ratification of the Convention, http://unfccc.int/essen-tial_background/convention/items/5410.php [accessed 29 March 2017].

[32] UNFCCC, Declarations by Parties – Kyoto Protocol, http://unfccc.int/kyoto_protocol/status_of_ratification/items/5424.php [accessed 29 March 2017].

One of the most characteristic contemporary examples of acts which unlawfulness is excluded on this basis is Japan's conduct in the Okinotorishima case, which consist clear violation of the United Nations Convention on the Law of the Sea.[33]

Okinotorishima is an atoll located about 1,740 kilometres from Tokyo in the Philippine Sea, almost in half of the distance separating Taiwan from the American Guam. There are only three rock fragments above the sea level, but the Japanese, in order to consider it as an island, have made investments within the atoll to strengthen the rocks and safeguard them against erosion caused by typhoons. In addition, they have built a helicopter landing pad and an observatory to monitor the movement of ships in this area. Japan recognises the maintenance of the observatory, and its repairs and maintenance, as necessary to protect its interests.[34]

In fact, maintaining the 'island' at all costs is necessary for Japan to justify its claim to establish an exclusive economic zone of maximum size (up to 200 nautical miles) around Okinotorishima, not just the territorial sea (up to twelve nautical miles).[35]

China is also interested in marine resources in this region. That is why China emphasises that Okinotorishima is not an island but a rock and cannot maintain an exclusive economic zone under the Convention on the Law of the Sea. Okinotorishima's exclusive economic zone would be greater than the land area of Japan.[36]

Despite so many objections to Japan's conduct towards Okinotorishima, there is still no clear basis for the recognition of these acts as unlawful. All the above doubts show how many traps lurk on states that would like

---

[33] See Guifang Xue, 'How Much Can a Rock Get? A Reflection from the Okinotoroshima Rocks', in Myron H. Nordquist et al. (eds.), *The Law of the Sea Convention: US Accession and Globalization*, Leiden and Boston, Martinus Nijhoff, 2012, p. 360.

[34] See Justin McCurry, 'Japan to Spend Millions on Tiny Islands 1,000 Miles South of Tokyo', *The Guardian Weekly*, 3 February 2016, https://www.theguardian.com/world/2016/feb/03/japan-spend-billions-yen-tiny-okinotori-islands-1000-miles-south-of-tokyo [accessed 31 March 2017].

[35] See Yukie Yoshikawa, 'The US-Japan-China Mistrust Spiral and Okinotorishima', *The Asia-Pacific Journal*, vol. 5, issue 10, 2007, p. 2, http://apjjf.org/-Yukie-YOSHIKAWA/2541/article.html [accessed 31 March 2017].

[36] See Dariusz Rafał Bugajski, 'Klimatyczna deterytorializacja państwa na przykładzie Tuvalu', *Stosunki Międzynarodowe*, vol. 41, no. 1–2, 2010, p. 217.

to pursue their claims based on draft art. 20 and art. 25 on the responsibility of states for international misconduct, not only those related to the consequences of climate change.

It seems that the authors of the article on liability for cross-border damage caused by dangerous activities have come up to these problems with much more attention. In a comment published by the Committee on International Law we can see that climate factors are considered as one of the elements that should be taken into account every time in determining whether to take reasonable care in undertaking hazardous activities. In the light of the action plan, which may be considered dangerous, it requires significantly higher standards of security in policy design and much higher levels of state involvement in their enforcement.[37]

The references in the analysed project to the principles of the Stockholm Declaration 1972 and the Rio Declaration of 1992 are significant in the context of international liability of states for damage caused by their dangerous activities and effects of climate change in consequences. Strengthening of these provisions gives hope to many states suffering from the dramatic consequences of climate change for effective attempts to enforce them.

Apart from this, it seems that today the surest basis of accountability in this field remain the United Nations Framework Convention on Climate Change of 9 May 1992 and concerning its Kyoto Protocol of 11 December 1997. Despite of many doubts both to the intentions of their authors and the results of their adoption and implementation, the principle of equal and common but differentiated and adequate accountability is perhaps the most important provision of international law applicable to climate change.[38]

The Framework Convention consists a fairly precisely regulated system of commitments that takes into account the shared but differentiated

---

[37] See International Law Commission, 'Draft Articles'.

[38] See Margreet Wewerinke and Vicente Paolo Yu III, 'Addressing Climate Change Through Sustainable Development and the Promotion of Human Rights', *South Centre Research Papers*, no. 34, South Centre 2010, p. 48, https://www.southcentre.int/wp-content/uploads/2013/05/RP34_Climate-Change-Sustainable-Development-and-Human-Rights_EN.pdf [accessed 14 September 2018].

responsibility for climate change in both developed and developing countries. In this context this system demonstrates the potential for international cooperation on effective mitigation of climate change. It also becomes a tool to investigate potential claims against international tribunals that can resolve the legal obligations of states under international law on climate change. In order to do so, this opportunity should be understood primarily as an incentive for appropriate action to address the damage caused by climate change and to treat it as developed countries that still fail to comply with their obligations under the Framework Convention as a viable business.[39]

As regards the possibility of redress before the courts seem to be a natural step to refer the matter to the International Court of Justice, whose task is to settle in accordance with international law, legal disputes between states. However, unconditional or at least conditional recognition of his jurisdiction would be necessary. Both Tonga and Tuvalu, whose cases have been described in this article, have not yet decided on this step. But this does not stop them from any other way to enforce their claims and investigate possible claims.[40]

Once again many opportunities in this area can be found in the Framework Convention of 9 May 1992, which in the current state of the public international law is still fundamental plane on which countries such as Tonga or Tuvalu would seek to reach agreement with other countries on the acquisition of possible compensation.

In the framework of the Conference of the Parties to the Convention (hereafter: COP), which is the supreme body of the Framework Convention, in Warsaw in 2013 (the 19th session of the Conference of the Parties – COP 19) decision was taken on the Establishment of an International Mechanism of Loss and Damage, which was demanded by small island states especially.[41]

---

[39] Ibid.

[40] See Aonima and Kumar, 'Could Vanuatu Claim Reparations Under International Law', p. A-39.

[41] UNFCCC, Report of the Conference of the Parties on its nineteenth session, held in Warsaw from 11 to 23 November 2013. Addendum. Part two: Action taken by the Conference of the Parties at its nineteenth session, FCCC/CP/2013/10/Add.1, 31 January 2014, pp. 6–8.

The provisions on the Mechanism have been confirmed in art. 8 of the Paris Agreement. It states, *inter alia*, that: 'parties should enhance understanding, action and support, including through the Warsaw International Mechanism, as appropriate, on a cooperative and facilitative basis with respect to loss and damage associated with the adverse effects of climate change.'

This mechanism should fulfill its role within the Framework Convention promoting the implementation of solutions to tackle climate change harms in a comprehensive integrated and coherent manner by financing both adaptation measures and the effects of violent climatic events in developing countries.

At the next Conference of the Parties to the Framework Convention held on 7–18 November 2016 in Marrakech (COP 22), a new five-year programme on the basis of the Warsaw International Loss and Damage Mechanism was launched addressing issues not addressed in the adaptation area like movement of people, migration, mobility and comprehensive risk management.

Critical analysis of the provisions of Warsaw as well as those with the latest Marrakech[42] raises legitimate doubts as to whether not made before our eyes the process of blurring of responsibility for climate change and its consequences.

A rationale for confirming the validity of these doubts may be the decision to award the Presidency of the Twenty-third Conference of the Parties to the Republic of Fiji, small island state in the Pacific, and to point out the German city Bonn as the host of COP 23. Ironically, when the decision was announced Fiji was still fighting with effects of the cyclone Winston which struck this state in February 2016.[43]

---

[42] UNFCCC, Report of the Conference of the Parties on its twenty-second session, held in Marrakech from 7 to 18 November 2016. Addendum. Part two: Action taken by the Conference of the Parties at its twenty-second session, FCCC/CP/2016/10/Add.1, 31 January 2017.

[43] Oliver Holmes, 'Cyclone Winston: Tens of Thousands Homeless in Fiji a Week After Storm', *The Guardian Weekly*, 29 February 2016, https://www.theguardian.com/world/2016/feb/29/cyclone-winston-forces-thousands-fijians-out-of-homes [accessed 6 April 2017]; 'Fiji's Cyclone Winston Death Toll Rises as News Comes in from Remote Areas', *The Guardian*, 23 February 2016, https://www.theguardian.com/world/2016/feb/23/fijis-cyclone-winston-death-toll-rises-as-news-comes-in-from-remote-areas [accessed 6 April 2017].

It is still unclear whether the arrangements for the International Loss and Damage Mechanism under the Framework Convention will be sufficient to provide 'adequate and effective' measures to combat the consequences of climate change. That is why it is so important to rely on the responsibility of states to be an option for local communities affected by climate change and the countries that represent these communities at international level.[44]

Bibliography

Literature

Aonima, Calvy and Shivanal Kumar, 'Could Vanuatu Claim Reparations Under International Law for Damages Sustained from Cyclone "Pam"?', *Journal of South Pacific Law*, issue 1, 2015, pp. A-23–A-40.

Bugajski, Dariusz Rafał, 'Klimatyczna deterytorializacja państwa na przykładzie Tuvalu', *Stosunki Międzynarodowe*, vol. 41, no. 1–2, 2010, pp. 203–213.

Fa'anunu, Fitilagi Ioane, 'A Breach of Fundamental Human Rights as the Legal Basis for Reparations for Climate Change Damages and Injuries Under International Law: Case Study of Ha'apai Islands (Tonga) Following Cyclone Ian', *Journal of South Pacific Law*, issue 1, 2015, pp. A-41–A-58.

Tol, Richard S.J. and Roda Verheyen, 'State Responsibility and Compensation for Climate Change Damages – a Legal and Economic Assessment', *Energy Policy*, vol. 32, issue 9, 2004, pp. 1109–1130.

Verheyen, Roda, *Climate Change Damage and International Law: Prevention Duties and State Responsibility*, Leiden, Martinus Nijhoff, 2005.

Wewerinke-Singh, Margaretha and Curtis Doebbler, 'The Paris Agreement: Some Critical Reflections on Process and Substance', *University of New South Wales Law Journal*, vol. 39, no. 4, 2016, pp. 1486–1517.

Xue, Guifang, 'How Much Can a Rock Get? A Reflection from the Okinotoroshima Rocks', in Myron H. Nordquist et al. (eds.), *The Law of the Sea Convention: US Accession and Globalization*, Leiden and Boston, Martinus Nijhoff, 2012.

---

[44] See Fa'anunu, 'Breach of Fundamental Human Rights', p. A-58.

Documents

Declaration of the United Nations Conference on the Human Environment, Stockholm, 1972, in Report of the United Nations Conference on the Human Environment, UN Doc.A/CONF.48/14/Rev.1.

Draft Articles on Responsibility of States for Internationally Wrongful Acts with Commentaries 2001, text adopted by the International Law Commission at its fifty-third session, in 2001, and submitted to the General Assembly as a part of the Commission's report covering the work of that session (A/56/10).

International Law Commission, 'Draft Articles on Prevention of Transboundary Harm from Hazardous Activities, with Commentaries: Report of the ILC on the Work of Its Fifty-Third Session', *Yearbook of the International Law Commission*, vol. 2, part 2, 2001.

Kyoto Protocol to the United Nations Framework Convention on Climate Change, 1997.

Paris Agreement, *Official Journal of the European Union*, L 282/4 EN, 2015.

Rio Declaration on Environment and Development, 1992, A/CONF.151/26.

United Nations Framework Convention on Climate Change 1992, FCC/INFORMAL/84/Rev.1.

United Nations Framework Convention on Climate Change [UNFCCC], Declarations by Parties – Kyoto Protocol, http://unfccc.int/kyoto_protocol/status_of_ratification/items/5424.php [accessed 29 March 2017].

United Nations Framework Convention on Climate Change [UNFCCC], Declaration Status of Ratification of the Convention, http://unfccc.int/essential_background/convention/items/5410.php [accessed 29 March 2017].

United Nations Framework Convention on Climate Change [UNFCCC], Report of the Conference of the Parties on its nineteenth session, held in Warsaw from 11 to 23 November 2013. Addendum. Part two: Action taken by the Conference of the Parties at its nineteenth session, FCCC/CP/2013/10/Add.1, 31 January 2014, pp. 6–8.

United Nations Framework Convention on Climate Change [UNFCCC], Report of the Conference of the Parties on its twenty-second session, held in Marrakech from 7 to 18 November 2016. Addendum. Part two: Action taken by the Conference of the Parties at its twenty-second session, FCCC/CP/2016/10/Add.1, 31 January 2017.

Websites

Boom, Keely, 'Exposure to Legal Risk for Climate Change Damage Under UNFCCC, Kyoto Protocol and LOSC: A Case Study of Tuvalu and Australia', PhD thesis, Faculty of Law, University of Wollongong, 2012, http://ro.uow.edu.au/theses/3919 [accessed 29 March 2017].

'Cyclone Pam: Vanuatu Islanders Forced to Drink Saltwater', BBC News, 17 March 2015, http://www.bbc.com/news/world-asia-31917913 [accessed 14 March 2017].

Davis, Joe-Dee, 'State Responsibility for Global Climate Change: The Case of the Maldives', MALD thesis, The Fletcher School, Tufts University, 2005, https://dl.tufts.edu/bookreader/tufts:UA015.012.DO.00078#page/1/mode/2up [accessed 14 September 2018].

'Fiji's Cyclone Winston Death Toll Rises as News Comes in from Remote Areas', *The Guardian*, 23 February 2016, https://www.theguardian.com/world/2016/feb/23/fijis-cyclone-winston-death-toll-rises-as-news-comes-in-from-remote-areas [accessed 6 April 2017].

Friedman, Andrew, 'Vanuatu's President Makes a Leap in Tying Cyclone Pam to Climate Change', 16 March 2015, Mashable, http://mashable.com/2015/03/16/vanuatu-cyclone-pam-global-warming/#jvZuC9iGsGqi [accessed 17 March 2017].

Holmes, Oliver, 'Cyclone Winston: Tens of Thousands Homeless in Fiji a Week After Storm', *The Guardian Weekly*, 29 February 2016, https://www.theguardian.com/world/2016/feb/29/cyclone-winston-forces-thousands-fijians-out-of-homes [accessed 6 April 2017].

McCurry, Justin, 'Japan to Spend Millions on Tiny Islands 1,000 Miles South of Tokyo', *The Guardian Weekly*, 3 February 2016, https://www.theguardian.com/world/2016/feb/03/japan-spend-billions-yen-tiny-okinotori-islands-1000-miles-south-of-tokyo [accessed 31 March 2017].

Overseas Development Institute and Climate and Development Knowledge Network, 'The IPCC's Fifth Assessment Reports: What in It for Small Island Developing States?', 2014, https://cdkn.org/wp-content/uploads/2014/08/IPCC-AR5-Whats-in-it-for-SIDS_WEB.pdf [accessed 14 September 2018].

Robertson, Joshua, 'Cyclone Pam: Vanuatu Awaits First Wave of Relief and News from Worst-Hit islands', *The Guardian*, 15 March 2015, https://www.theguardian.com/world/2015/mar/15/cyclone-pam-death-toll-may-reach-50-in-port-vila-alone-as-full-impact-still-unknown [accessed 14 March 2017].

'School of Law', website of the University of the South Pacific, http://www.usp.ac.fj/index.php?id=6193 [accessed 14 March 2017].

'State of Emergency in Tuvalu', Radio New Zealand, 14 March 2015, http://www.radionz.co.nz/international/pacific-news/268612/state-of-emergency-in-tuvalu [accessed 14 March 2017].

Verheyen, Roda and Peter Roderick, 'Beyond Adaptation: The Legal Duty to Pay Compensation for Climate Change Damage', WWF-UK Climate Change Programme discussion paper, November 2008, http://assets.wwf.org.uk/downloads/beyond_adaptation_lowres.pdf [accessed 14 September 2018].

Walker, Peter and Paul Farrell, 'Cyclone Pam: 24 Confirmed Dead as Vanuatu President Blames Climate Change', *The Guardian*, 16 March 2015, https://www.theguardian.com/world/2015/mar/16/vanuatus-president-blames-climate-change-for-extreme-weather [accessed 14 March 2017].

Wewerinke, Margreet and Vicente Paolo Yu III, 'Addressing Climate Change Through Sustainable Development and the Promotion of Human Rights', *South Centre Research Papers*, no. 34, South Centre 2010, https://www.southcentre.int/wp-content/uploads/2013/05/RP34_Climate-Change-Sustainable-Development-and-Human-Rights_EN.pdf [accessed 14 September 2018].

Yoshikawa, Yukie, 'The US-Japan-China Mistrust Spiral and Okinotorishima', *The Asia-Pacific Journal*, vol. 5, issue 10, 2007, http://apjjf.org/-Yukie-YOSHIKAWA/2541/article.html [accessed 31 March 2017].

Dariusz Zdziech

An Overview of the Polish Relation with Vanuatu

Introduction

Last year (2016) the Republic of Poland established official diplomatic relations with Tonga – the last of the independent countries in Australia and Oceania.[1] The Polish Government concluded the first such agreements with the South Pacific countries in the 1970s.[2] At that time did not exist a state bearing the name Vanuatu. Six years after the Republic of Vanuatu announced its independence in 1986 Poland established such relations with Melanesian country of Antipodes. In 2016, thirty years passed from the establishment of bilateral relations between such distant states. The main question remains: what were the contacts between Polish and Vanuatu inhabitants like and what are the perspectives of deepening the relationship between these countries in the next years?

---

[1] See 'Poland Establishes Diplomatic Relations with Kingdom of Tonga', Radio Poland, 31 August 2016, http://www.thenews.pl/1/10/Artykul/268817,Poland-establishes-diplomatic-relations-with-Kingdom-of-Tonga [accesed 29 December 2017].

[2] See Wanda Górnicka-Pawelczyk and Walenty Daszkiewicz, *Stosunki dyplomatyczne Polski 1944–1982 r. Informator*, vol. 4: *Azja, Australia i Oceania*, Warsaw, Wydawnictwa Akcydensowe, 1984, pp. 23, 182 (The Ministry of Foreign Affairs of the Republic of Poland – for internal use).

History

The first contacts between inhabitants of Poland and the Oceania region may be dated back to the 18th century. In the next century, in spite of the partitioning of Poland and its disappearance from the map of Europe, the people from over the Vistula river still went to the Pacific. Poland regained the independence in the 20th century and its inhabitants did not forget about the lands located in the biggest world ocean. At the beginning our relations with Australia or New Zealand were based on relations with London and the general consulates in Sydney[3] and Wellington.[4] The official diplomatic relations with Australia at embassy level began in 1972[5] and with New Zealand in 1973.[6] Poland signed official diplomatic relations with the next countries of the Oceania region: in 1978 with Papua New Guinea and in 1986 with Vanuatu.

The current Vanuatu was inhabited about 3,000 years ago.[7] The first European discoverers of the islands of present day Vanuatu stepped foot on this land not until 17th century (Pedro F. de Quiros – 1606, Terra Australis del Espiritu Santo). Next well-known Europeans were Louis Antoine de Bougainville (1768) who changed the name of these islands to 'the Great Cyclades'[8] and James Cook (1774) who renamed the islands to 'the New Hybrids'.[9] In the 19th century Protestant and Catholic missionaries came,

---

[3] See Krzysztof Szczepanik, Anna Herman-Łukasik, and Barbara Janicka (eds.), *Stosunki dyplomatyczne Polski. Informator*, vol 3: *Azja, Zakaukazie, Australia i Oceania 1918–2009*, Warsaw, Ministerstwo Spraw Zagraniczych, 2010, p. 24.

[4] See Dariusz Zdziech, *Pahiatua – „Mała Polska" małych Polaków* [Pahiatua – Little Poland, Little Poles], Cracow, Societas Vistulana, 2007, p. 67.

[5] See 'Szef MSZ z wizytą w Australii', https://ewpl.com.au/szef-msz-z-wizyta-w-australii/ [accessed 29 December 2017].

[6] See 'Spotkanie ministrów kultury Polski i Nowej Zelandii', http://www.mkidn.gov.pl/pages/posts/spotkanie-ministrow-kultury-polski-i-nowej-zelandii-3598.php [accessed 29 December 2017].

[7] See Stuart Bedford and Matthew Spriggs, 'Northern Vanuatu as a Pacific Crossroads: The Archaeology of Discovery, Interaction, and the Emergence of the "Ethnographic Present"', *Asian Perspectives*, vol. 47, no. 1 (special issue: *Maritime Migration and Colonization in Indo-Pacific Prehistory*), 2008, pp. 95–120.

[8] See Mary Kimbrough, *Louis-Antoine De Bougainville, 1729–1811: A Study in French Naval History and Politics* (Studies in French Civilization, vol. 7), Lewiston, Mellen Press, 1990.

[9] See Nicholas Thomas, *Odkrycia: Podróże kapitana Cooka*, transl. Janusz Szczepański, Poznań, Dom Wydawniczy Rebis, 2007.

as well as entrepreneurs who wanted to make a profit from sandalwood or establishing cotton, coffee, banana and coconut plantations, and since 1860s blackbirding aiming at acquiring cheap labour force for plantations in Australia and Fiji.[10] Newcomers from Great Britain (via Australia) and France perceived these islands as the territory of their home country, however not one of these European powers wanted to give in. Finally, in 1887 both European powers established the Joint Naval Commission to save their citizens on the islands without deeper impact on internal affairs jurisdiction.

In 1906 the British-French Condominium was created from the New Hybrids, which existed with various effects until 1980. How did two European countries administrate the territory situated several thousand kilometres from London or Paris is another question: certainly cons and pros of this state can be found as Janusz Wolniewicz wrote in his book entitled *Vanuatu. Czarny archipelag* ('Vanuatu: A Black Archipelago') published in Warsaw in 1983.[11] Here are some sentences from his publication about the New Hybrids:

> We are in the only in the world so bizarre French and British Condominium. This creation is called by tauters as a pandemonium which means simply confusion, chaos, welter. [...] The New Hybrids has three independent administrations: British, French and condominium and only... two cinemas in the capital. It is also known that the supreme executive body in this country is the Joint Court with the judge appointed by the king of Spain. This post of course vacant [from April 1931 to November 1975 Spain was not a monarchy – D.Z.]. [...] Certainly a newcomer has a right to choose. If they want to be subject to British law – they are welcome to. However, this may entail possible time in prison. The well informed claim that in British prison is poor food and good sleep but at French vice versa. So before making a decision it should be considered... Maybe it is better to be a Frenchman?[12]

---

[10] See Blackbird: 'Finding Family Blong Yumi', http://www.blackbird.vu/home.html [accessed 29 December 2017].

[11] Janusz Wolniewicz, *Vanuatu. Czarny archipelag*, Warszawa, Wydawnictwo Ministerstwa Obrony Narodowej, 1983. Four years later this book was published in Warsaw and entitled: *Czarny archipelag*, without the additional chapter about Vanuatu independence.

[12] Ibid., p. 20. All quotations from non-English sources in this paper translated into English by the author.

In 1967 the population of the British and French Condominium with the centre in Port Vila amounted to only 78,000 inhabitants.[13]

If 1960s mean the golden decade of decolonisation of Africa,[14] the 1970s are the golden period of decolonisation in Australia and Oceania. Fourteen independent states nowadays, members of the United Nations, the half regained the independence in the years 1970–1980.[15] The last of these countries was the New Hybrids that quite late began its road to independence (1974) from the British and French meeting. France was afraid that the independence of Vanuatu would speed up the process of losing its other territories in the Pacific.[16] Despite this it agreed to replace the colonial advisory board by the representatives meeting but only after the Paris conference in 1977. The New Hybrids began the real road to a political independence.[17] The main hero was the Protestant clergyman Walter Hadye Lini, a former English speaking schools on Salomon Island and New Zealand student. He was a co-creator of the New Hybrids National Party that in November 1979 won 62 per cent of the vote in the general elections.[18] At the moment of fighting for independence the population of Vanuatu amounted to over 111,000.[19] The official date of becoming independent by the Melanesian Republic is 30 July 1980.[20] The name Vanuatu

---

[13] Infromation from the website of the Vanuatu National Statistics Office, subject to the Ministry of Finanace and Economic Menagement, Port Vila, Vanuatu: https://vnso.gov.vu/index.php/current-surveys [accessed 29 December 2017].

[14] 'Declaration on the Granting of Independence to Colonial Countries and Peoples', adopted by General Assembly resolution 1514 (XV) of 14 December 1960, http://www.un.org/en/decolonization/declaration.shtml [accessed 29 December 2017]. In the 1960s over thirty African states became independent.

[15] United Nations General Assembly Member States, http://www.un.org/en/member-states/index.html [accessed 29 December 2017].

[16] French territories, such as New Caledonia, Wallis and Futuna islands as well as French Polynesia have not become independent yet.

[17] 'Vanuatu: History', http://thecommonwealth.org/our-member-countries/vanuatu/history [accessed 29 December 2017].

[18] 'Walter Lini', Encyclopaedia Britannica, https://www.britannica.com/biography/the-Rev-Walter-Hayde-Lini [accessed 29 December 2017].

[19] Information from the website Vanuatu National Statistics Office, subject to Ministry of Finance and Economic Management, Port Vila, Vanuatu: https://vnso.gov.vu/index.php/current-surveys [accessed 29 December 2017].

[20] 'Vanuatu – a Brief History', http://www.radionz.co.nz/collections/u/new-flags-flying/nff-vanuatu/about-vanuatu [accessed 29 December 2017].

(our land/state) chosen for the new state consists of two words: *Vanua* – in Austronesian mainly means a land, territory (in the language of New Zealand Maoris it is *Whenua* – country, land, nation, state, ground[21]). The second word *Tu* in Austronesian means the verb stand, establish (in the language of New Zealand Maoris it is the word *Tū* – to stand, take place, set in place, establish, hold, convene, to remain, placed[22]). The first Prime Minister of Vanuatu became Walter Lini who held office until 1991. At that time he supported national liberation movements in New Caledonia, Western Papua as well as he was favourably disposed towards the cooperation with Vietnam, Libya and Cuba creating the framework of Melanesian socialism.[23]

The beginning of contacts between the territories occupied by the Republic of Vanuatu today and the Republic of Poland dates back to 18th century when during the French expedition around the world of Louis Antoine de Bougainville (1768)[24] the prince Charles Henry Nicholas Otto de Nassau-Siegen, a French colonel of German origin, since 1779 living in the Republic of Poland, stepped his foot on the Great Cyclades.[25] Here is the description by Bougainville of landing on the islands that nowadays belong to the Republic of Vanuatu:

23 May 1768 – 'At 1 pm together with the other few people I boarded a dinghy to visit my people who landed in the morning. We found them at work: they were cutting trees and the islanders helped them to carry them to boats. The officer in command of the troop told me that when they approached the coast they were

---

[21] 'Whenua', Maori Dictionary, http://maoridictionary.co.nz/search?&keywords=whenua [accessed 29 December 2017].

[22] 'Tū', Maori Dictionary, https://maoridictionary.co.nz/search?idiom=&phrase=&proverb=&loan=&histLoanWords=&keywords=tu [accessed 29 December 2017].

[23] See Marc Kurt Tabani, 'Walter Lini, la coutume de Vanuatu et le socialisme mélanésien', *Journal de la Société des Océanistes*, no. 111, 2000-2, pp. 173–194, http://www.academia.edu/1860711/Walter_Lini_la_coutume_de_Vanuatu_et_le_Socialisme_M%C3%A9lan%C3%A9-9sien [accessed 29 December 2017].

[24] The Frenchman Louis Antoine de Bougainville gave such name the present day archipelago of the Vanuatu islands in 1768.

[25] See Wacław Słabczyński, *Polscy podróżnicy i odkrywcy*, Warszawa, PWN, 1988, p. 428; Ryszard Badowski, *Odkrywanie świata. Polacy na sześciu kontynentach*, Bielsko-Biała, Pascal, 2009, pp. 111–112.

greeted by the large group of islanders armed with bows and arrows giving them
signs not to land: but when, despite their threats, he ordered to come ashore they
went back by a few steps and as ours went forward they kept going back, did not
allow to approach but their behaviour showed that they were ready to attack at any
moment. The troop stopped and when the prince Nessau alone moved towards
them they no longer went back. The gifts of pieces of red fabric changed their
behaviour.[26]

The next guests on the New Hybrids were two participants of the second James Cook's voyage to the Pacific (1772–1775).[27] Johann Reinhold
Forster[28] and Johann Georg Adam Forster[29], father and son, the authors
of famous trip logs entitled *Voyage Around the World*.[30] They tell about
the encounter with the inhabitants of Molikolo island in July 1774 in the
following words:

We launched two boats that having a captain on the board, my father and me,
dr Sparrman and a number of other people as well as the escorting us troop of
seamen rushed to the island. At a distance of about 30 yards from the shore was
a coral reef. The water behind it was so shallow that we had to leave the boats and
swam across to the beach where the seamen were put in formation not meeting
any resistance. We were greeted by a crowd of at least three hundred natives; all of
them were armed but they were friendly towards us and did not show any hostility
symptoms. A middle-aged man built a little better than the rest and being certainly their chief gave another native the bow and quiver and approached unarmed to
hold our hands as a sign of peace and friendship.[31]

---

[26] Louis Antoine de Bougainville, *Podróż Bougainville'a dookoła świata*, transl. Maria
Szwykowska and Ludwik Szwykowski, Warsaw, Wiedza Powszechna, 1962, p. 154.

[27] During that voyage James Cook named the archipelago of the present day Republic of
Vanuatu as the New Hybrids.

[28] Johann Reinhold Forster – a Polish and German natural history researcher of Scottish
origin, born in Tczew.

[29] Johann Georg Adam Forster – a Polish and German naturalist of Scottish origin, born in
Mokry Dwór. The professor of Natural History in Wilno. He also dealt with ethnology. Taveller
and revolutionary.

[30] Jerzy [Johann Georg Adam] Forster, *Podróż naokoło świata*, transl. Michał Ronikier, Cracow, Libron, 2007.

[31] Ibid., p. 193.

The next decades also documented the stay of people coming from over the Vistula river on the territory of present day Vanuatu. Mainly with the presence of French on this Melanesian archipelago. One of the most distinguished personalities was Adam Joachim Kulczycki[32], the Polish cartographer, meteorologist and astronomer. Since 1844 he worked for the French colonial services in the Pacific, especially on the territory of present day French Polynesia but also in 1850s he created a map of Efate Island, the capital island of present day Vanuatu, on French commission.[33]

In the first half of the 20th century hardly ever Polish traces could be found on the New Hybrids. After the end of the Second World War Leon Laska, a surveyor, emigrated from Europe and settled on the New Hybrids.[34] Over a dozen years later Maciej Bocheński settled there. He was the captain of the ship sailing with goods between the islands of Vanuatu archipelago.[35] His collection of Vanuatu works of art was donated to the Asia and Pacific Museum in Warsaw.[36]

From the hundreds of ships sailing through the then New Hybrids the traces of presence of Ludomir Mączka, Kazimierz Jasica and Jerzy Pisz are preserved. They were sailing on the yacht *Maria* and stopped for a few days on present day Vanuatu.[37]

---

[32] Adam Joachim Kulczycki (1809–1882) – an officer of the November Uprising, decorated with the Gold Cross of Virtuti Militari Medal, emigrated to France, worked as a surveyor and cartographer for the French government in Oceania, mainly in Tahiti and New Caledonia. See also Lech Paszkowski, *Polacy w Australii i Oceanii 1790–1940*, Toruń and Melbourne, Towarzystwo Przyjaciół Archiwum Emigracji: Oficyna Wydawnicza Kucharski, 2008, p. 23.

[33] See Badowski, *Odkrywanie świata*, p. 115.

[34] Leon Laska worked at a post office in Gdynia before the war, he was sent to prisoners' camp during the war and after the war he emigrated to Great Britain and then in 1948 to the New Hybrids. See also Wolniewicz, *Vanuatu*, pp. 16, 175.

[35] Maciej Bocheński – before the war he sailed on *ORP Grom*. During the war he still fought under the Polish flag. After the war he sailed on many ships. He worked in Iraq, Singapore, New Zealand and Tonga, in the 1960s he settled in the New Hybrids where he sailed on the cargo ship *Rocinante* and was known as the captain Maczi. See also ibid., pp. 16–17.

[36] See 'Obszar Pacyfiku', The Asia and Pacific Museum (Warsaw), http://zbiory.muzeumazji. pl/zbiory/?Xkolekcja=8 [accessed 29 December 2017].

[37] Ludomir Mączka – a sailor and geologist; Antoni Jerzy Pisz – a sailor, the author of the book entitled „*Marią*" *przez Pacyfik*, Kazimierz Jasica – a yacht helmsman. See also Antoni Jerzy Pisz, „*Marią*" *przez Pacyfik*, Gdańsk, Wydawnictwo Morskie, 1982, s. 312–322; 'Ludomir Mączka: *Zapiski-notatki z rejsu „Marii*"', http://zeszytyzeglarskie.pl/?p=184 [accessed 29 December 2017].

One of the Polish who documented his stay on the New Hybrids during the period of creation of the new independent Vanuatu Republic was a traveller Janusz Wolniewicz who tells about his memories from the Melanesian archipelago in the aforementioned book entitled *Vanuatu. Czarny archipelag* ('Vanuatu: A Black Archipelago').[38]

The director of the Asia and Pacific Museum in Warsaw Andrzej Wawrzyniak travelling at that time on the Pacific Ocean came to the newly formed state of Vanuatu[39] in order to establish relations with its cultural and science institutions.[40]

Diplomatic relations

An extremely important date in official relations was 15 November 1986. That day the People's Republic of Poland established official diplomatic relations with the Republic of Vanuatu.[41] The relations between the countries were occasional and in the official diplomatic channels often limited to the exchange of wishes for national bank holidays transferred by the representations of both states at the United Nations in New York.[42] Establishment of diplomatic relations between Poland – a state of the socialist block at that time – and the Vanuatu Republic governed by the creator

---

[38] Janusz Wolniewicz (1929–2006) – a writer, reporter and traveller. See also 'Janusz Wolniewicz – obieżyświat', Polskie Radio, https://www.polskieradio.pl/39/156/Artykul/1612627, Janusz-Wolniewicz-obiezyswiat [accessed 29 December 2017].

[39] Andrzej Wawrzyniak – a sailor, diplomat, founder of the Asia and Pacific Museum in Warsaw. See also 'Marynarz', http://polskiepoznawanieswiata.pl/pl/stanowiska_uniq_f5gwB1Xr/ trzy-kontynenty-w-jeden-dzien_uniq_2z6qyyDU/l2321_polskie-poznawanie-azji/l755_bada-cze_uniq_pi45taGO/andrzej-wawrzyniak/sylwetka_uniq_evX21apM/marynarz_uniq_4p5sJw-Pu.html [accessed 29 December 2017].

[40] See Lech Z. Niekrasz (ed.), *Azja i Pacyfik nad Wisłą. 25 lat Muzeum Azji i Pacyfiku w Warszawie. 50 lat działalności Andrzeja Wawrzyniaka*, Warsaw, Muzeum Azji i Pacyfiku, 1998, s. 19.

[41] See 'Nawiązanie stosunków dyplomatycznych z Republiką Vanuatu', Archives of the Ministry of Foreign Affairs of the Republic of Poland, Warsaw, Signature: 23/89, Prot 57, Dep II – 1986, Tajne, Azja, Australia i Oceania, Digital password 0-20, beam no. III; Szczepanik, Herman--Łukasik, and Janicka, *Stosunki dyplomatyczne Polski*, p. 257.

[42] See e.g. 'Depesza gratulacyjna z okazji święta narodowego Republiki Vanuatu od Przewodniczącego Rady Państwa PRL Wojciecha Jaruzelskiego do Prezydenta Republiki Vanuatu A.G. Sokomanu', from 13 July 1988, Archives of the Ministry of Foreign Affairs of the Republic of Poland, Warsaw, Signature: 21/93, Prot.64, Akta Jawne 1988, Digital password no. 110, beam no. XXIII.

of the Melanesian socialism[43] may be considered as a natural course of events. Taking into account that in the 1980s the Prime Minister Walter Lini also established the friendly relationship with Vietnam,[44] China[45] and Cuba.[46] Additionally, it is worth mentioning that a few days before the official relations with Poland were signed, the Republic of Vanuatu had begun the relations with the Soviet Union.[47] In this way the Prime Minister Walter Lini wanted to show the world that Vanuatu, unlike the remaining countries of Oceania, would not opt for the West. In 1983 Vanuatu as the only country of Oceania at that time joined into Non-Aligned Movement trying to treat impacts of the East and West Block equally.[48]

In 1989 Vanuatu had about 142,000 inhabitants. The Prime Minister Walter Lini finished his rule two years later.[49] At the end of the 20th century the contacts between Poland and Vanuatu were occasional and limited to the meetings at the headquarters of the international organisations or visits of the individual tourists from Poland on this Melanesian archipelago.

---

[43] See Walter Lini, *Beyond Pandemonium: From the New Hebrides to Vanuatu*, Wellington, Asia Pacific Books, 1980; Ralph R. Premdas, 'Melanesian Socialism: Vanuatu's Quest for Self-Definition', *The Journal of Commonwealth & Comparative Politics*, vol. 25, issue 2, 2008, pp. 141–160, DOI:10.1080/14662048708447514.

[44] See Michael T. Kaufman, 'Walter Lini, 57, Clergyman Who Led Nation of Vanuatu', *The New York Times*, http://www.nytimes.com/1999/02/23/world/walter-lini-57-clergyman-who-led-nation-of-vanuatu.html [accessed 29 December 2017].

[45] See 'China-Vanuatu Relations', http://vu.china-embassy.org/eng/zwgx/t467290.htm [accessed 29 December 2017].

[46] See Godwin Ligo, 'Fidel Castro and the Vanuatu Conection', *Vanuatu Daily Post*, http://dailypost.vu/news/fidel-castro-and-the-vanuatu-connection/article_8541578a-1110-5e80-a496-427a853183b7.html [accessed 29 December 2017].

[47] See Jonas Cullwick, 'Celebrating 30 Years of Russia-Vanuatu Diplomatic Relations', *Vanuatu Daily Post*, http://dailypost.vu/news/celebrating-years-of-russia-vanuatu-diplomatic-relations/article_a379540f-24e9-522d-981f-dd9541429d80.html [accessed 29 December 2017].

[48] Due to its colonial past Vanuatu had diplomatic relations with the Western block countries: France and Great Britain. See also Howard Van Trease (ed.), *Melanesian Politics: Stael Blong Vanuatu*, Christchurch, Macmillan Brown Centre for Pacific Studies, University of Canterbury, 1995, pp. 62–65; 'Facts About Vanuatu', https://vpmu.gov.vu/index.php/about-vpmu/facts-about-vanuatu [accessed 29 December 2017].

[49] 'Walter Lini [obituary]', *The Economist*, https://www.economist.com/node/355454 [accessed 29 December 2017]: 'Walter Hadye Lini, a voice of the Pacific, died on February 21st, aged 56.'

One of such documented visits was a stay on Vanuatu of a sailor Leszek Kosek[50]. The second important traveller from over the Vistula river was Wojciech Dąbrowski[51] in 1999 who was surprised that Poland as the only Middle-East European country had visa-free entry.[52]

At the turn of the 21th century the population in Vanuatu amounted to over 187,000.[53] In the Polish studies on the Republic of Poland diplomacy in 2005 it can be found that at that time the Republic of Vanuatu was in territorial competence of the Polish Republic embassy in Canberra.[54] Certainly the contacts of Polish inhabitants with Vanuatu were and still are poorly documented. In the 21st century we can find few pieces of information about the stay in Vanuatu of Anna and Michał Semaru[55], Jan M. Fijor[56], Ewelina and Michał Kozok[57], Krzysztof Kryza[58], Maria and Bogusław Nowak[59], Karolina Sypniewska[60], Robert

---

[50] Leszek Kosek – a Polish sailor, traveller. See also 'Leszek w krainie kangurów', http://www.sun-yachts.com/pacyfik/?txt=66 [accessed 29 December 2017].

[51] Wojciech Dąbrowski – a Polish traveller, telecommunications engineer by profession, who visited all the world countries. He made twelve trips around the world and he is plannig the next. See also Filip Frydrykiewicz, 'Kubek – najlepszy przyjaciel w podróży', http://www.rp.pl/artykul/312185-Kubek---najlepszy-przyjaciel-w-podrozy.html [accessed 29 December 2017].

[52] See Wojciech Dąbrowski, 'Pustynie, dżungle i oceany, czyli czwarta podróż dookoła świata, część II: przez Vanuatu, Salomony i Papuę', http://www.kontynenty.net/4rtw2.htm [accessed 29 December 2017].

[53] Information from the website of the Vanuatu National Statistics Office, subject to the Ministry of Finanace and Economic Menagement, Port Vila, Vanuatu, https://vnso.gov.vu/index.php/current-surveys [accessed 29 December 2017].

[54] See Krzysztof Szczepanik, *Dyplomacja Polski, 1918–2005. Struktury organizacyjne*, Warsaw, Askon, 2005, p. 198.

[55] See Ilona Słojewska, 'Vanuatu – ukryty raj', http://www.4wymiar.pl/magiczne-podroze/495--vanuatu-ukryty-raj.html [accessed 29 December 2017].

[56] See Jan M. Fijor, 'Vanuatu, prywatny raj?', https://www.fijor.com/blog/2009/08/24/vanuatu-ziemski-raj/ [accessed 29 December 2017].

[57] See Michał Kozok, 'Melanezja 2011 – Vanuatu', http://kozok.eu/pl/polinezjavanuatu.php [accessed 29 December 2017].

[58] Krzysztof Kryza, *Wyspy koralowe. Podróż po Pacyfiku*, Gdynia, Wydawnictwo Novae Res, 2017, p. 137; Marek Szczepański, 'Kryza na wyspach Oceanii', http://www.benyowsky.com/index.php?index.php&id=preview&news=100075&PHPSESSID=f674730cbce67cea5b25ae612d69623d [accessed 29 December 2017].

[59] Maria and Bogusław Nowak have a tourist company in New Zealand, see Green Lite Travel, http://www.greenlite.travel/index.php/your-travel-manager-pl [accessed: 29 December 2017].

[60] Karolina Sypniewska-Wida – a traveller, see 'Podróże', http://www.karolinasypniewska.pl/podroze/ [accessed 29 December 2017].

Szymański[61], Diana Wosińska and Marcin Dzienniak[62], Magdalena Jurkowska-Bogusz[63], Michał Listkiewicz who trained football referees[64] and Jerzy Grębosz[65] who looked for the last unspoiled places on the earth. The all who were in Vanuatu mention that it is a fast developing country.

In 2009 the population of Vanuatu amounted to almost 235,000.[66] Of course relations of Poland with Vanuatu not only mean visits of Polish people in Melanesia but also stays of inhabitants of the Republic of Vanuatu in Poland. Among a few documented visits it can be mentioned the official delegation of Vanuatu for the Climate Summit COP 14 in Poznań in 2008,[67] in 2010 the visit of the ambassador of Vanuatu in Brussels Roy Mickey Joy and his wife Shirley in Warsaw, Cracow and Oświęcim[68] (a year earlier their son was in Poland on a school trip from one of Belgian schools). The next visits – the participation of Elwin Miller and Henriette Latika in the beach

---

[61] Robert Szymański – a traveller and translator, see 'Sprawozdanie z pierwszej w Polsce konferencji o Vanuatu', http://anzora.org/sprawozdanie-z-pierwszej-w-polsce-konferencji-o-vanuatu/ [accessed 29 December 2017].

[62] More about their trip see 'Kava kava i wypad w głąb dżungli', https://dzienniak.wordpress.com/category/vanuatu/ [accessed 29 December 2017].

[63] See 'Vanuatu', http://www.z2strony.pl/tag/vanuatu/ [accessed 29 December 2017].

[64] See Jerzy Filipiuk, 'Michał Listkiewicz zdążył już zwiedzić ponad 180 krajów', *Dziennik Polski*, http://www.dziennikpolski24.pl/artykul/3438357,michal-listkiewicz-zdazyl-juz-zwiedzic-ponad-180-krajow,id,t.html [accessed 29 December 2017].

[65] Jerzy Grębosz – a physicist, PhD in the Institute of Nuclear Physics of the Polish Academy of Science in Cracow. He has been regularly visiting Vanuatu since 2010, see Jerzy Grębosz, 'Vanuatu Republic, Oceania 2010', http://jacobi.ifj.edu.pl/~grebosz/www_vanuatu_2010/ [accessed 29 December 2017].

[66] Information from the website of the Vanuatu National Statistics Office, subject to the Ministry of Finance and Economic Management, Port Vila, Vanuatu, https://vnso.gov.vu/index.php/current-surveys [accessed 29 December 2017].

[67] See Poznan Climate Change Conference, December 2008, http://unfccc.int/meetings/poznan_dec_2008/meeting/6314.php [accessed 29 December 2017]; Konferencja Narodów Zjednoczonych w sprawie Zmian Klimatu: Poznań 2008, http://www.poznan.pl/mim/trakt/galleries.html?parent=0&lhs=trakt&id=941&co=print&kt_id=0&rhs=trakt&instance=1080 [accessed 29 December 2017].

[68] See [Dariusz Zdziech], 'Wizyta Ambasadora Vanuatu w Krakowie i Oświęcimiu', http://anzora.org/wizyta-ambasadora-vanuatu-w-krakowie-i-oswiecimiu/ [accessed 29 December 2017]; Agata Grabau, 'Rajskie wyspy', *Tygodnik Przegląd*, https://www.tygodnikprzeglad.pl/rajskie-wyspy/ [accessed 29 December 2017].

volleyball tournament in Stare Jabłonki in 2013,[69] in the same year we had
an honour to host the official Vanuatu delegation on the Climate Summit
in Warsaw.[70]

In 2015 Vanuatu with 264,000 inhabitants,[71] was visited by 287,000 inter-
national visitors including 51 per cent from Australia, 15 per cent from New
Zealand and 12 per cent from New Caledonia.[72] In comparison, in 1972
New Hybrids were visited by 13,600 visitors and in 1979 by 30,400 visitors.[73]

Against this background, tourism between Poland and Vanuatu is
marginal and is influenced by a lot of geographical, social and economic
factors. The distance between the countries, ignorance of the region: for
Polish people Melanesia and for the inhabitants of Vanuatu the area of
Middle and Eastern Europe, as well as lack of the close economic relations
resulted in such symbolic data.

The Polish Central Statistical Office do not announce on its official
websites the similar information about the amount of Vanuatu inhabitants
coming to Poland every year.[74]

In case of tourism traffic from Poland to Vanuatu in the years indicated
in the above table it should be assumed that about 50 per cent of tourism
traffic is organised individually by travellers. The rest are people travelling
in organised groups with travel agents.[75]

---

[69] See Edyta Kowalczyk, 'Brazylijka o polskich korzeniach, były baseballista i siatkarki z Vanuatu w Starych Jabłonkach', *Przegląd Sportowy*, https://www.przegladsportowy.pl/siatkowka/
siatkowka-plazowa/ezgotyka-na-mistrzostwach-swiata-w-starych-jablonkach/mqx9mv3 [acces-
sed 29 December 2017].

[70] See 'Vanuatu, Well Represented at Global Climate Forum', http://www.sprep.org/cli-
mate-change/vanuatu-well-represented-at-global-climate-forum [accessed 29 December 2017].

[71] Information according to the data from the website of the World Bank, 'Vanuatu', https://
data.worldbank.org/country/Vanuatu [accessed 29 December 2017].

[72] Data from the website of the Vanuatu National Statistics Office: 'International Arrival 2015',
https://vnso.gov.vu/images/Picturs/Inforgraphs/Iternational_Arrivals.png [accessed 29 December 2017].

[73] *Vanuatu: Twenti Wan Tingting Long Team Blong Independens* [Suva, Fiji], Institute of Pacific Studies, University of the South Pacific, 1980, p. 135.

[74] Due to a minimal number of people from Vanuatu visiting Poland, the Central Statistical
Office do not give the data on the official websites, only upon written request.

[75] For example, the travel agent Prestige Tours from Cracow every year sends on average
twelve persons to Vanuatu from Poland (data from October 2017, thanks to the courtesy of Miss
Iwona Torbicz Prestige Tours & Incentive Sp. z o.o., ul. Lubicz 3, lok. 212, Kraków 31-034, https://
www.egzotyka.tv [accessed 29 December 2017]).

Table 1. Vanuatu – annual visitors from Poland by Residential Country being Poland

Vanuatu – annual visitors from Poland		
No.	Year:	No. of visitors
1	2009	68
2	2010	73
3	2011	46
4	2012	90
5	2013	91
6	2014	80
7	2015*	57
8	2016	89
9	2017**	48
	Total:	642

* The decrease in number of tourists in Vanuatu was probably connected with gigantic damage, the biggest in the history of this country, caused by the cyclone Pam in March 2015.
** Data collected by the Vanuatu National Statistics Office until 28 August 2017.
Source: Information sent to the author by email by Rara Soro, the Vanuatu National Statistics Office, on 29 August 2017. Thanks to the courtesy of Susie Mento Assistant Statistician, the Vanuatu National Statistics Office, PMB 9019.

In the year of 30th anniversary of establishing diplomatic relations between Poland and Vanuatu the population of both countries amounted to proportionally: 38,000,000 (Poland)[76] and 272,000 (Vanuatu).[77] Despite growing development of both countries their mutual relations seem to be less than symbolic. An example can be a lack of any information on the official websites of the Ministry of Foreign Affairs of the Republic of Poland as well as its equivalent in the Republic of Vanuatu about the celebration of the very important anniversary of their mutual diplomatic relations. The only example of memory of Vanuatu in Poland was the scientific conference entitled *Vanuatu – 34 years of independence* organised in Cracow

---

[76] See 'Podstawowe dane', http://stat.gov.pl/podstawowe-dane/ [accessed 29 December 2017].
[77] 'Mini – Census 2016/Infographics', https://vnso.gov.vu/index.php/mini-census-2016#infographics [accessed 29 December 2017].

by the Scientific Association of Australia, New Zealand and Oceania on 5 December 2014.[78]

At present the population in Vanuatu amounted to about 282,000 people.[79] It is worth paying attention for the significant growth of tourism in this island state. In 2015 for 287,000 tourists only 90,000 came by air, remaining 197,000 on boards of passenger ships. In 2016 the number of people coming by air to Vanuatu increased by 6 per cent compared to the previous year.[80] Taking into account a significant growth (year to year), the number of tourists coming from Poland to this Melanesian country of *smiling people*, there is a chance that in the next years, due to more air services, the distance between Vanuatu and Poland will be decreasing and tourist statistics will be substantially improving.[81]

At present, the only subject that convince both countries for bilateral talks is the matter of ban on bringing in a product called *kava kava*.[82] It is a *Piper methysticum* which in a liquid form is commonly used in the culture of Vanuatu inhabitants and neighbouring countries. Polish people visiting Vanuatu sometimes buy powdered *kava kava* as a medicine for neurological problems. It turns out that in Poland, as the only European country, *kava kava* is considered a drug, and bringing it to Poland can lead to imprisonment.[83] Currently Vanuatu Government[84] and the group estab-

---

[78] See Program VII konferencji naukowej Towarzystwa Naukowego Australii, Nowej Zelandii i Oceanii, 'Vanuatu – 34 lata niepodległości' (5 December 2014), http://anzora.org/zaproszenie/ [accessed 29 December 2017].

[79] 'Vanuatu Population Clock', http://countrymeters.info/en/Vanuatu [accessed 29 December 2017].

[80] See 'Trade, Industry and Ni-Vanuatu Business', https://tourism.gov.vu/presentations.php [accessed 29 December 2017].

[81] In 2006 the inhabitants of Vanuatu was named the Happiest People on the Earth, see 'Vanuatu Judged the Happiest Place on the Planet: So What Can We Learn from This?', *Daily Mail*, http://www.dailymail.co.uk/news/article-395422/Vanuatu-judged-happiest-place-planet-So-learn-this.html [accessed 29 December 2017]. It is still on the top of this ranking.

[82] See 'Warning not to Take Kava into Poland', http://www.loopvanuatu.com/vanuatu-news/warning-not-take-kava-poland-71597 [accessed 29 December 2017].

[83] See Len Garae, 'Kava Banned in Poland', *Vanuatu Daily Post*, http://dailypost.vu/news/kava-banned-in-poland/article_845575d3-6dd0-5c03-a1c4-e0720c868a7a.html [accessed 29 December 2017].

[84] See 'Appeals for Vanuatu to Seek Dialogue with Poland on Kava Ban', https://www.radionz.co.nz/international/pacific-news/347184/appeals-for-vanuatu-to-seek-dialogue-with-poland-on-kava-ban [accessed 29 December 2017].

lished in Poland named Campaign for Kava Relegalisation in Poland[85] are trying to persuade the Government in Warsaw to delete the specific from the list of drugs.

There are great possibilities to develop relationships between Poland and Vanuatu starting from development of tourism, through cultural and scientific exchange with one of the most culturally diversified countries in the world,[86] to the import of high quality exotic products.

Conclusions

The above article presents the overview of the relations between the Republic of Poland and the Republic of Vanuatu. It is not a comprehensive publication on the subject, nevertheless clearly shows the weakness of both political and economic mutual contacts between the states. Obviously, the enormous distance between the countries and costs associated with it can be reminded, however in the 21st century world resembling a global village, with well developing economic relations between Poland and Australia as well as New Zealand, it is difficult to defend this argument. Diversification of import and export, frequently mentioned at meetings, as well as inflected by the media in all possible cases does not allow to ignore the subject. Delays in development of knowledge on such distant coutries, both of Poland and Vanuatu, are understandable, nevertheless we should not stay at this place.

Tourism is an economy branch that first begins expansion to increasingly distant regions. Supported by the scientific knowledge and the support of the governments of both countries certainly may significantly revive our mutual relations. Is the vote of Vanuatu for Polish candidacy for a rotating member of the UN Security Council for the years 2018–2020 the end of our possibilities in mutual relations?

---

[85] See Kampania Na Rzecz Relegalizacji Kavy w Polsce, https://www.facebook.com/legalna-kava [accessed 29 December 2017].

[86] Vanuatu is the country of the biggest concentration of languages in the world. See also Nicole Nau et al. (eds.), *Języki w niebezpieczeństwie. Księga wiedzy*, Poznań 2016, p. 12.

Bibliography

Literature

Badowski, Ryszard, *Odkrywanie świata. Polacy na sześciu kontynentach*, Bielsko-
-Biała, Pascal, 2009.

Bedford, Stuart and Matthew Spriggs, 'Northern Vanuatu as a Pacific Crossroads: The
Archaeology of Discovery, Interaction, and the Emergence of the "Ethnographic
Present"', *Asian Perspectives*, vol. 47, no. 1 (special issue: *Maritime Migration and
Colonization in Indo-Pacific Prehistory*), 2008, pp. 95–120.

de Bougainville, Louis Antoine, *Podróż Bougainville'a dookoła świata*, transl. Maria
Szwykowska and Ludwik Szwykowski, Warsaw, Wiedza Powszechna, 1962.

Forster, Jerzy [Johann Georg Adam], *Podróż naokoło świata*, transl. Michał Ronikier,
Cracow, Libron, 2007.

Kimbrough, Mary, *Louis-Antoine De Bougainville, 1729–1811: A Study in French Naval History and Politics* (Studies in French Civilization, vol. 7), Lewiston, Mellen
Press, 1990.

Kryza, Krzysztof, *Wyspy koralowe. Podróż po Pacyfiku*, Gdynia, Wydawnictwo Novae
Res, 2017.

Lini, Walter, *Beyond Pandemonium: From the New Hebrides to Vanuatu*, Wellington,
Asia Pacific Books, 1980.

Nau, Nicole et al. (eds.), *Języki w niebezpieczeństwie. Księga wiedzy*, Poznań 2016.

Niekrasz, Lech Z. (ed.), *Azja i Pacyfik nad Wisłą. 25 lat Muzeum Azji i Pacyfiku
w Warszawie. 50 lat działalności Andrzeja Wawrzyniaka*, Warsaw, Muzeum Azji
i Pacyfiku, 1998.

Paszkowski, Lech, *Polacy w Australii i Oceanii 1790–1940*, Toruń and Melbourne, Towarzystwo Przyjaciół Archiwum Emigracji: Oficyna Wydawnicza Kucharski, 2008.

Pisz, Antoni Jerzy, „*Marią*" *przez Pacyfik*, Gdańsk, Wydawnictwo Morskie, 1982.

Premdas, Ralph R., 'Melanesian Socialism: Vanuatu's Quest for Self-Definition', *The
Journal of Commonwealth & Comparative Politics*, vol. 25, issue 2, 2008, pp. 141–
160. DOI:10.1080/14662048708447514.

Słabczyński, Wacław, *Polscy podróżnicy i odkrywcy*, Warszawa, PWN, 1988.

Szczepanik, Krzysztof, *Dyplomacja Polski, 1918–2005. Struktury organizacyjne*, Warsaw, Askon, 2005.

Szczepanik, Krzysztof, Anna Herman-Łukasik, and Barbara Janicka (eds.), *Stosunki dyplomatyczne Polski. Informator*, vol. 3: *Azja, Zakaukazie, Australia i Oceania 1918–2009*, Warsaw, Ministerstwo Spraw Zagraniczych, 2010.

Thomas, Nicholas, *Odkrycia. Podróże kapitana Cooka*, transl. Janusz Szczepański, Poznań, Dom Wydawniczy Rebis, 2007.

Van Trease, Howard (ed.), *Melanesian Politics: Stael Blong Vanuatu*, Christchurch, Macmillan Brown Centre for Pacific Studies, University of Canterbury, 1995.

Vanuatu: Twenti Wan Tingting Long Team Blong Independens [Suva, Fiji], Institute of Pacific Studies, University of the South Pacific, 1980.

Wolniewicz, Janusz, *Vanuatu. Czarny archipelag*, Warszawa, Wydawnictwo Ministerstwa Obrony Narodowej, 1983.

Zdziech, Dariusz, *Pahiatua – „Mała Polska" małych Polaków* [Pahiatua – Little Poland, Little Poles], Cracow, Societas Vistulana, 2007.

Documents

'Depesza gratulacyjna z okazji święta narodowego Republiki Vanuatu od Przewodniczącego Rady Państwa PRL Wojciecha Jaruzelskiego do Prezydenta Republiki Vanuatu A. G. Sokomanu', from 13 July 1988, Archives of the Ministry of Foreign Affairs of the Republic of Poland, Warsaw, Signature: 21/93, Prot.64, Akta Jawne 1988, Digital password no. 110, beam no. XXIII.

Górnicka-Pawelczyk, Wanda and Walenty Daszkiewicz, *Stosunki dyplomatyczne Polski 1944–1982 r. Informator*, vol. 4, *Azja, Australia i Oceania*, Warsaw, Wydawnictwa Akcydensowe, 1984 (The Ministry of Foreign Affairs of the Republic of Poland – for internal use).

'Nawiązanie stosunków dyplomatycznych z Republiką Vanuatu', Archives of the Ministry of Foreign Affairs of the Republic of Poland, Warsaw, Signature: 23/89, Prot 57, Dep II – 1986, Tajne, Azja, Australia i Oceania, Digital password 0-20, beam no. III.

Websites

'Appeals for Vanuatu to Seek Dialogue with Poland on Kava Ban', https://www.radionz.co.nz/international/pacific-news/347184/appeals-for-vanuatu-to-seek-dialogue-with-poland-on-kava-ban [accessed 29 December 2017].

Blackbird: Finding Family Blong Yumi, http://www.blackbird.vu/home.html [accessed 29 December 2017].

'China-Vanuatu Relations', http://vu.china-embassy.org/eng/zwgx/t467290.htm [accessed 29 December 2017].

Cullwick, Jonas, 'Celebrating 30 Years of Russia-Vanuatu Diplomatic Relations', *Vanuatu Daily Post*, http://dailypost.vu/news/celebrating-years-of-russia-vanuatu-diplomatic-relations/article_a379540f-24e9-522d-981f-dd9541429d80.html [accessed 29 December 2017].

Dąbrowski, Wojciech, 'Pustynie, dżungle i oceany, czyli czwarta podróż dookoła świata, część II: przez Vanuatu, Salomony i Papuę', http://www.kontynenty.net/4rtw2.htm [accessed 29 December 2017].

'Declaration on the Granting of Independence to Colonial Countries and Peoples', adopted by General Assembly resolution 1514 (XV) of 14 December 1960, http://www.un.org/en/decolonization/declaration.shtml [accessed 29 December 2017].

'Facts About Vanuatu', https://vpmu.gov.vu/index.php/about-vpmu/facts-about-vanuatu [accessed 29 December 2017].

Fijor, Jan M., 'Vanuatu, prywatny raj?', https://www.fijor.com/blog/2009/08/24/vanuatu-ziemski-raj/ [accessed 29 December 2017].

Filipiuk, Jerzy, 'Michał Listkiewicz zdążył już zwiedzić ponad 180 krajów', *Dziennik Polski*, http://www.dziennikpolski24.pl/artykul/3438357,michal-listkiewicz-zdazyl-juz-zwiedzic-ponad-180-krajow,id,t.html [accessed 29 December 2017].

Frydrykiewicz, Filip, 'Kubek – najlepszy przyjaciel w podróży', http://www.rp.pl/artykul/312185-Kubek---najlepszy-przyjaciel-w-podrozy.html [accessed 29 December 2017].

Garae, Len, 'Kava Banned in Poland', *Vanuatu Daily Post*, http://dailypost.vu/news/kava-banned-in-poland/article_845575d3-6dd0-5c03-a1c4-e0720c868a7a.html [accessed 29 December 2017].

Grabau, Agata, 'Rajskie wyspy', *Tygodnik Przegląd*, https://www.tygodnikprzeglad.pl/rajskie-wyspy/ [accessed 29 December 2017].

Green Lite Travel, http://www.greenlite.travel/index.php/your-travel-manager-pl [accessed 29 December 2017].

Grębosz, Jerzy, 'Vanuatu Republic, Oceania 2010', http://jacobi.ifj.edu.pl/~grebosz/www_vanuatu_2010/ [accessed 29 December 2017].

'International Arrival 2015', website of the Vanuatu National Statistics Office, https://vnso.gov.vu/images/Picturs/Inforgraphs/Iternational_Arrivals.png [accessed 29 December 2017].

'Janusz Wolniewicz – obieżyświat', Polskie Radio, https://www.polskieradio.pl/39/156/Artykul/1612627,Janusz-Wolniewicz-obiezyswiat [accessed 29 December 2017].

Kampania Na Rzecz Relegalizacji Kavy w Polsce, https://www.facebook.com/legalna-kava [accessed 29 December 2017].

Kaufman, Michael T., 'Walter Lini, 57, Clergyman Who Led Nation of Vanuatu', *The New York Times*, http://www.nytimes.com/1999/02/23/world/walter-lini-57-cler-gyman-who-led-nation-of-vanuatu.html [accessed 29 December 2017].

'Kava kava i wypad w głąb dżungli', https://dzienniak.wordpress.com/category/vanuatu/ [accessed 29 December 2017].

Konferencja Narodów Zjednoczonych w sprawie Zmian Klimatu: Poznań 2008, http://www.poznan.pl/mim/trakt/galleries.html?parent=0&lhs=trakt&id=941&co=print&kt_id=0&rhs=trakt&instance=1080 [accessed 29 December 2017].

Kowalczyk, Edyta, 'Brazylijka o polskich korzeniach, były baseballista i siatkarki z Vanuatu w Starych Jabłonkach', *Przegląd Sportowy*, https://www.przegladsportowy.pl/siatkowka/siatkowka-plazowa/ezgotyka-na-mistrzostwach-swiata-w-starych--jablonkach/mqx9mv3 [accessed 29 December 2017].

Kozok, Michał, 'Melanezja 2011 – Vanuatu', http://kozok.eu/pl/polinezjavanuatu.php [accessed 29 December 2017].

'Leszek w krainie kangurów', http://www.sun-yachts.com/pacyfik/?txt=66 [accessed 29 December 2017].

Ligo, Godwin, 'Fidel Castro and the Vanuatu Conection', *Vanuatu Daily Post*, http://dailypost.vu/news/fidel-castro-and-the-vanuatu-connection/article_8541578a-1110-5e80-a496-427a853183b7.html [accessed 29 December 2017].

'Ludomir Mączka: *Zapiski-notatki z rejsu „Marii"*', http://zeszytyzeglarskie.pl/?p=184 [accessed 29 December 2017].

'Marynarz', http://polskiepoznawanieswiata.pl/pl/stanowiska_uniq_f5gwB1Xr/trzy-kontynenty-w-jeden-dzien_uniq_2z6qyyDU/l2321_polskie-poznawanie-azji/l755_badacze_uniq_pi45taGO/andrzej-wawrzyniak/sylwetka_uniq_evX21apM/marynarz_uniq_4p5sJwPu.html [accessed 29 December 2017].

'Mini – Census 2016/Infographics', https://vnso.gov.vu/index.php/mini-census-2016#infographics [accessed 29 December 2017].

'Obszar Pacyfiku', The Asia and Pacific Museum (Warsaw), http://zbiory.muzeumazji.pl/zbiory/?Xkolekcja=8 [accessed 29 December 2017].

'Podróże', http://www.karolinasypniewska.pl/podroze/ [accessed 29 December 2017].

'Podstawowe dane', http://stat.gov.pl/podstawowe-dane/ [accessed 29 December 2017].

'Poland Establishes Diplomatic Relations with Kingdom of Tonga', Radio Poland, 31 August 2016, http://www.thenews.pl/1/10/Artykul/268817,Poland-establishes-diplomatic-relations-with-Kingdom-of-Tonga [accesed 29 December 2017].

Poznan Climate Change Conference, December 2008, http://unfccc.int/meetings/poznan_dec_2008/meeting/6314.php [accessed 29 December 2017].

Program VII konferencji naukowej Towarzystwa Naukowego Australii, Nowej Zelandii i Oceanii, 'Vanuatu – 34 lata niepodległości' (5 December 2014), http://anzora.org/zaproszenie/ [accessed 29 December 2017].

Słojewska, Ilona, 'Vanuatu – ukryty raj', http://www.4wymiar.pl/magiczne-podroze/495-vanuatu-ukryty-raj.html [accessed 29 December 2017].

'Spotkanie ministrów kultury Polski i Nowej Zelandii', http://www.mkidn.gov.pl/pages/posts/spotkanie-ministrow-kultury-polski-i-nowej-zelandii-3598.php [accessed 29 December 2017].

Sprawozdanie z pierwszej w Polsce konferencji o Vanuatu, http://anzora.org/sprawozdanie-z-pierwszej-w-polsce-konferencji-o-vanuatu/ [accessed 29 December 2017].

Szczepański, Marek, 'Kryza na wyspach Oceanii', http://www.benyowsky.com/index.php?index.php&id=preview&news=100075&PHPSESSID=f674730cbce67cea5b25ae612d69623d [accessed 29 December 2017].

'Szef MSZ z wizytą w Australii', https://ewpl.com.au/szef-msz-z-wizyta-w-australii/ [accessed 29 December 2017].

Tabani, Marc Kurt, 'Walter Lini, la coutume de Vanuatu et le socialisme mélanésien', *Journal de la Société des Océanistes*, no. 111, 2000-2, pp. 173–194, http://www.academia.edu/1860711/Walter_Lini_la_coutume_de_Vanuatu_et_le_Socialisme_M%C3%A9lan%C3%A9sien [accessed 29 December 2017].

'Trade, Industry and Ni-Vanuatu Business', https://tourism.gov.vu/presentations.php [accessed 29 December 2017].

'Tū', Maori Dictionary, https://maoridictionary.co.nz/search?idiom=&phrase=&proverb=&loan=&histLoanWords=&keywords=tu [accessed 29 December 2017].

United Nations General Assembly Member States, http://www.un.org/en/member-states/index.html [accessed 29 December 2017].

'Vanuatu', http://www.z2strony.pl/tag/vanuatu/ [accessed 29 December 2017].

'Vanuatu', World Bank, https://data.worldbank.org/country/Vanuatu [accessed 29 December 2017].

'Vanuatu – a Brief History', http://www.radionz.co.nz/collections/u/new-flags-flying/nff-vanuatu/about-vanuatu [accessed 29 December 2017].

'Vanuatu: History', http://thecommonwealth.org/our-member-countries/vanuatu/history [accessed 29 December 2017].

'Vanuatu Judged the Happiest Place on the Planet: So What Can We Learn from This?', *Daily Mail*, http://www.dailymail.co.uk/news/article-395422/Vanuatu-judged-happiest-place-planet-So-learn-this.html [accessed 29 December 2017].

'Vanuatu Population Clock', http://countrymeters.info/en/Vanuatu [accessed 29 December 2017].

'Vanuatu, Well Represented at Global Climate Forum', http://www.sprep.org/climate-change/vanuatu-well-represented-at-global-climate-forum [accessed 29 December 2017].

'Walter Lini', Encyclopedia Britannica, https://www.britannica.com/biography/the-Rev-Walter-Hayde-Lini [accessed 29 December 2017].

'Walter Lini [obituary]', *The Economist*, https://www.economist.com/node/355454 [accessed 29 December 2017].

'Warning not to Take Kava into Poland', http://www.loopvanuatu.com/vanuatu-news/warning-not-take-kava-poland-71597 [accessed 29 December 2017].

Website of the Vanuatu National Statistics Office, subject to the Ministry of Finanace and Economic Menagement, Port Vila, Vanuatu, https://vnso.gov.vu/index.php/current-surveys [accessed 29 December 2017].

'Whenua', Maori Dictionary, http://maoridictionary.co.nz/search?&keywords=whenua [accessed 29 December 2017].

[Zdziech, Dariusz], 'Wizyta Ambasadora Vanuatu w Krakowie i Oświęcimiu', http://anzora.org/wizyta-ambasadora-vanuatu-w-krakowie-i-oswiecimiu/ [accessed 29 December 2017].

Others

Data from October 2017, thanks to the courtesy of Miss Iwona Torbicz Prestige Tours & Incentive Sp. z o.o., ul. Lubicz 3, lok. 212, Kraków 31-034, https://www.egzotyka.tv [accessed 29 December 2017].

Information sent to the author by email by Rara Soro, the Vanuatu National Statistics Office, on 29 August 2017. Thanks to the courtesy of Susie Mento Assistant Statistician, the Vanuatu National Statistics Office, PMB 9019.

Authors

H.E. Paul Wojciechowski – Ambassador of Australia to the Republic of Poland, Australian Embassy, Nowogrodzka 11, Warsaw, Poland.

H.E. Mary Thurston – Ambassador of New Zealand to the Republic of Poland, New Zealand Embassy, Al. Ujazdowskie 51, Warsaw, Poland.

Assoc. Prof. Zuzanna Jakubowska-Vorbrich – Institute of Iberian and Ibero--American Studies, University of Warsaw, Warsaw, Poland.

Assoc. Prof. Jan Lencznarowicz – Institute of American Studies and Polish Diaspora of the Jagiellonian University in Kraków, Poland.

Assoc. Prof. Mieczysław Sprengel – Faculty of Law and Administration, Adam Mickiewicz University in Poznań, Poland.

Assoc. Prof. Jerzy Grębosz – The Henryk Niewodniczański Institute of Nuclear Physics, Polish Academy of Sciences, Cracow, Poland.

PhD Krzysztof Konstanty Vorbrich – Polish Academy of Sciences, Poznań, Poland.

PhD Cecylia Małgorzata Dziewięcka – 'Atenisi Institute, Nuku'alofa, The Kingdom of Tonga (visiting professor).

PhD Eng. Piotr Grzybowski – Faculty of Chemical and Process Engineering, Warsaw University of Technology, Warsaw, Poland.

PhD Joanna Siekiera – Faculty of Military Studies, War Studies University, Warsaw, Poland.

M.A. Pedro Henrique Melchior Nunes da Horta – Federal University of the Latin-American Integration, Foz do Iguaçu, Brazil.

PhD Justyna Eska-Mikołajewska – University of Bydgoszcz (Bydgoska Szkoła Wyższa), Bydgoszcz, Poland.

PhD Jowita Brudnicka – Institute of Strategy Studies, War Studies University, Warsaw, Poland.

PhD Masum Billah – Department of Law, Jagannath University, Dhaka, Bangladesh (PhD – Victoria University of Wellington, New Zealand).

PhD Adam Jakuszewicz – Institute of Law, Administration and Management, Kazimierz Wielki University, Bydgoszcz, Poland.

PhD Przemysław Osóbka – Institute of Law, Kujawy and Pomorze University in Bydgoszcz, Poland.

PhD Dariusz Zdziech – Institute of the Middle and Far East of the Jagiellonian University in Kraków, Poland.

TECHNICAL EDITOR
Agnieszka Lipińska

PROOFREADIGN
Helena Piecuch

TYPESETTING
Hanna Wiechecka

Jagiellonian University Press
Editorial Offices: Michałowskiego 9/2, 31-126 Kraków
Phone: +48 12 663 23 80, Fax: +48 12 663 23 83